DIARY OF A PEDESTRIAN
IN
CASHMERE AND THIBET

Hanhart, Lith.

LADAK

DIARY OF A PEDESTRIAN IN CASHMERE AND THIBET

BY

CAPTAIN KNIGHT, FORTY-EIGHTH REGIMENT

GYAN

Published by

Gyan Publishing House
5, Ansari Road
Daryaganj, New Delhi-110002
Phone: 011-47034999, 9811692060
E-mail: books@gyanbooks.com

Distribution Network
gyanbooks.com
India, USA, Canada, UK, Australia, France

ISBN : 978-81-212-3319-4 (PB)
First Published, 1863

2nd Impression 2020

Printed at: Gyan Press, Delhi.

Diary of a Pedestrian in Cashmere and Thibet
Author: Captain Knight, Forty-Eighth Regiment

DIARY OF A PEDESTRIAN

IN

CASHMERE AND THIBET.

BY

CAPTAIN KNIGHT, FORTY-EIGHTH REGIMENT.

LONDON:

RICHARD BENTLEY, NEW BURLINGTON STREET.

Publisher in Ordinary to Her Majesty.

1863.

TO THOSE

FOR WHOSE PERUSAL

THE FOLLOWING PAGES WERE ORIGINALLY WRITTEN

THEY ARE AFFECTIONATELY

DEDICATED.

PREFACE.

With the fullest sense of the responsibility incurred by the addition of another volume to the countless numbers already existing, and daily appearing in the world, the following Diary has been committed to the press, trusting that, as it was not written *with intent* to publication, the unpremeditated nature of the offence may be its extenuation, and that as a faithful picture of travel in regions where excursion trains are still unknown, and Travellers' Guides unpublished, the book may not be found altogether devoid of interest or amusement. Its object is simply to bring before the reader's imagination those scenes and incidents of travel which have already been a source of enjoyment to the writer, and to impart, perhaps, by their description, some portion of the gratification which has been derived from their reality. With this view, the original Diary has undergone as little alteration of form or matter as possible, and is laid before the reader as it was sketched and written during the leisure moments of a wandering life, hoping that faithfulness of detail may atone in it for faults and failings in a literary and artistic point of view.

Although the journey it describes was written without the advantages of a previous acquaintance with the writings of those who had already gone over the same ground, subsequent research has added much to the interest of the narrative, and information thus obtained has been added either in the form of Notes or Appendix. Under the latter head, acknowledgment is principally due to an able and interesting essay on the architecture of Cashmere, by Capt. Cunningham, and also to a paper by M. Klaproth, both of whom appear to have treated more fully than any other writers the subjects to which they refer.

As differences will be found to occur in the names of places, &c. between the parts thus added and the remainder of the book, it may be well to explain that in the former only are they spelt according to the usually received method of rendering words of Eastern origin in the Roman character. By this system the letters *ā, e, ī, o,* and *ū,* are given the sounds of the corresponding Italian vowels; *i* and *u* are pronounced as in "hit" and "put;" and the letter *a* is made to represent the short *u* in the word "cut." In this way it is that Cashmere, correctly pronounced *Cushmere,* comes to be written Kashmīr, and Mutun, pronounced as the English word "mutton," * is written Matan, both of which, to the initiated, represent the true sound of the words. Those who have adopted the system, however, have not always employed it throughout, nor given with it the key by which it alone becomes intelligible; and the result has been that in many ways, but principally from the un-English use made of the letter *a*, it has tended quite as much to mislead and confuse, as to direct.

* *Vide* Appendix A.

In the narrative, therefore, wherever custom has not already established a particular form of spelling, the explanation of the sound has been attempted in the manner which seemed least liable to misconception, and, except as regards the letters *a* and *u*, no particular system has been followed. These have been invariably given the sounds they possess in the words "path" and "cut" respectively, a circumflex being placed over the latter to denote the short *u* in the word "put."

Such names, therefore, as Cushmere, Tibbut, Muhummud, Hijra, &c. have been left as custom has ruled them, and will appear in their more well-known costume of Cashmere, Thibet, Mahomet, and Hegira.

The concluding sketch was originally intended to accompany a series of brightly-coloured Cashmerian designs illustrative of the life of "Krishna;" and the reproduction of these, in their integrity, not having been found feasible, the sketch itself may appear *de trop*.

It has, however, been retained on the possibility of the translations which occur in it being of interest to those who may not be acquainted with the style of Eastern religious literature; while the outline it presents of some of the religions of the East, bare and simple as it is, may be acceptable to such as are not inclined to search out and study for themselves the necessarily voluminous and complicated details.

LONDON,
June, 1863.

CONTENTS.

PART VI.

PART VII.

APPENDIX A.

APPENDIX B.

APPENDIX C.

ILLUSTRATIONS.

ERRATUM.

Page 116, line 5, *for* A.D. 1612, *read* A.D. 1619.

DIARY OF A PEDESTRIAN
IN CASHMERE AND THIBET.

"Who has not heard of the Vale of Cashmere,
With its roses the brightest that earth ever gave,
Its temples, and grottoes, and fountains as clear
As the love-lighted eyes that hang over their wave?"

INTRODUCTION.

MORE than a year and a half had been spent in the hottest parts of the plains of India, and another dreaded hot season was rapidly making its approach, when, together with a brother officer, I applied for and obtained six months' leave of absence for the purpose of travelling in Cashmere and the Himalayas, otherwise called by Anglo-Indians "The Hills."

We had been long enough in the country to have discovered that the gorgeous East of our imagination, as shadowed forth in the delectable pages of the "Arabian Nights," had little or no connexion with the East of our experience—the dry and dusty East called India, as it appeared, wasted and dilapidated, in its first convalescence from the fever into which it had been thrown by the Mutiny of 1857-58. We were not long, therefore, in making our arrangements for escaping from Allahabad, with the prospect before us of exchanging the discomforts of another hot season in the plains, for the pleasures of a sojourn in the far-famed valley of Cashmere, and a tramp through the mountains of the Himalayas—the mountains, whose very name breathes of comfort and consolation to the parched up dweller in the plains. The mountains of "the abode of snow!"

Our expeditionary force consisted at starting of but one besides the brother officer above alluded to—the F. of the following pages—and myself. This was my Hindoo bearer, Mr. Rajoo, whose duty it was to make all the necessary arrangements for our transport and general welfare, and upon whose shoulders devolved the entire management of our affairs. He acted to the expedition in the capacity of quartermaster-general, adjutant-general, commissary-general, and paymaster to the forces; and, as he will figure largely in the following pages, under the title of the "Q. M. G.," and comes, moreover, under the head of "a naturally dark subject," a few words devoted to his especial description and illumination may not be out of place.

With the highest admiration for England, and a respect for the Englishman, which extended to the very lining of their pockets, Mr. Rajoo possessed, together with many of the faults of his race, a certain humour, and an amount of energy most unusual among the family of the mild Hindoo. He had, moreover, travelled much with various masters, in what are, in his own country, deemed "far lands;" and having been wounded before Delhi, he had become among the rest of his people an authority, and to the Englishman in India an invaluable medium for their coercion and general management.

To us he proved a most efficient incumbent of the several offices we selected him to fill. His administration no doubt did display an occasional weakness; and his conduct as paymaster to the forces was decidedly open to animadversion; for, in this capacity, he seemed to be under the impression that payments, like charity, began at home, and he also laboured under a constitutional and hereditary infirmity, which prevented him in small matters from discerning any difference between *meum* and *tuum*.

Having been employed collectively, however, it would be unfair to judge of his performances in detail; and from his satisfactory management of the expedition, occasionally under such trying circumstances as a break-down in the land transport, or an utter failure in his tobacco supply, we had every reason to be satisfied with our choice. The latter misfortune was the only one which really interfered at any time with his efficiency, or upset his equanimity, and it unfortunately occurred always at the most inopportune seasons, and at a time when he was undergoing his greatest hardships.

As long as the supply lasted, the mysterious gurglings of his "Hubble Bubble," or cocoa-nut water-pipe, might be heard at almost any hour of the day or night. "Hubble bubble, toil and trouble," was the natural order of his existence; and when in some peculiarly uncivilised region of our wanderings, the compound of dirt, sugar, and tobacco, in which his soul delighted, was not forthcoming, he and his pipe seemed at once to lose their vitality, and to become useless together.

The temporary separation which ensued, being in its way *a mensa et thoro*, was a source of trouble and inconvenience to all concerned, and we had, more than once, cause to regret not having given the tobacco question that forethought and consideration to which it would be well entitled by any one undertaking a similar expedition.

Overlooking these weaknesses, Mr. Rajoo's character was beyond reproach, and for the particular work he had to perform, his combination of efficiency, portability, and rascality, rendered him in every respect "the right man in the right place."

Such was our "head of affairs," and such the small force he had at first to provide for. As we passed out of India, and got further from regions of comparative civilisation, his cares increased: cellar, kitchen, larder, farm-yard, tents, &c. had then to accompany our wandering steps, and the expedition gradually increased in size, until it attained its maximum of nearly forty. From this it again as gradually decreased, and as one by one our retainers disappeared, it dwindled in dimensions until it finally reached its original limited proportions, and then "we three met again," once more upon the plains of India.

All our necessary preparations having been completed, and a sacrifice of three precious weeks having been duly offered to the inexorable genius who presides over public correspondence, we reduced our impedimenta to the smallest possible compass, and with about a hundred pounds to commence life with, all in two shilling pieces, that being the only available coin of the realm in this our second century of British administration, we took our departure by railway for Cawnpore. Here we found ourselves located and hospitably entertained in the house in which our unfortunate fellow-countrywomen were confined on their recapture from the river by the Nana Sahib, one of the few mementos of the mutiny still left standing at Cawnpore.

Next day we laid our dâk for Simla, and about six o'clock in the evening, with the Q.M.G. on the roof, and ourselves and our possessions stowed away in the innumerable holes and corners of the rude wooden construction called a "Dâk garee," or post coach, we took our departure. After a few mishaps with our steed, involving the necessity of getting out to shove behind, we entered upon the Grand Trunk Road, and with a refreshing sense of freedom and relief, soon left Cawnpore in all its native dust and dreariness behind us.

PART I.

THE PLEASURES OF THE PLAINS.

May 21, 1860.—Being fairly under weigh, our first attention was directed towards the machine which was to be, in a great measure, our home for many days to come. Not overburdened with springs, and not much to look at, though decidedly an extraordinary one to go, our conveyance was by no means uncomfortable; and, stretched upon a mattress extending its entire length, F. and I chatted over our plans and projects, and star-gazed, and soon fell asleep, in spite of the ruts on the road and the wild discordant bugling of our ragged coachman, who seemed to consider that, however inferior in other respects, in a matter of music we were not to be outdone, not even by Her Majesty's own royal mail. At first sight, the necessity of trying to clear such lonely roads as we were travelling was not altogether apparent; but a slight acquaintance with the general principles and laws of progression of the national Indian institution called a bullock-cart, or "beil-garee," soon clears up the difficulty. Built entirely of wood, and held together by scraps of ropes and cord, a more hopeless-looking machine cannot exist; and drivers and bullocks alike share in the general woodenness and impassibility of the structure. The animals, too, having probably lost all the better feelings of their nature in such a service, are appealed to entirely through the medium of their tails, and the operation occasionally results in the whole creaking mass being safely deposited in some capacious rut, there to remain until "the Fates"—assuming, perhaps, the appearance of three additional bullocks—arrive to draw it out again. Occasionally, too, the institution comes to a halt for the night, comfortably drawn up in the centre of the line of traffic, with a delightful disregard for aught but the present, and an air of supreme contempt for the most eloquent music of all the ragged coachmen on the Grand Trunk Road.

Every five miles we stopped to change our

horse, and miserable indeed was the raw-boned little animal that made his appearance on every occasion. Still the pace was kept up in spite of appearances, and at seven A.M. we reached "Ghoorsahagunge"—more generally known as *Gooseygunge*—sixty miles from Cawnpore, and 197 from Delhi.

Here we slept in peace until eleven o'clock, and awoke from dreams of Cashmere to the unpleasant realities of a violent dust-storm. The usual "Khus-khus tatties," or screens of fragrant grass, which are kept in a continual state of moisture at door and window, and convert the dust-charged scorching blast into a comparative coolness, were not forthcoming, and our halt was not a pleasant one by any means: still our faces were towards the mountains, and the pleasures of hope enabled us to take our misfortunes with entire philosophy. We started again about five P.M., when the power of the sun was somewhat abated, and encountered the usual difficulties with refractory horses at every change. A start was in no case effected without much management and exertion. A half-naked black generally attaches himself to each wheel; the driver, from a post of vantage, belabours the miserable horse with all his might and main; the Q.M.G. takes a firm hold of the rails on the roof; and all shouting, grunting, and using bad language together, away we go at full gallop, if we are in unusual luck, for about 300 yards. Then comes a dead stop: the same operation commences again, and so on, until the animal is sufficiently far from his last stable to be able to look forward with some confidence to the one ahead, and resigns himself to circumstances accordingly. One peculiarity in this peculiar country we found to be, that in putting our steed-to, the English custom is reversed. The cart is "put-to," not the horse; and the latter being left standing anywhere on the road, the lumbering "garee" is dragged up to his tail, and fastened up with a combination of straps and ropes, marvellous to behold.

May 23.—To-day we arrived at "Etawah," where we found a very comfortable little staging bungalow, but no supplies of either beer or butter procurable. On the road in the early morning there were herds of deer and antelope in sight, but time being precious we left them unmolested.

As yet very little change makes its appearance in the character of the country. Level plains, with patches of trees, mango and palm, as far as the eye can reach, and everywhere dust, dust, dust! The palm-trees, however, with toddy parties scattered about among them, serve to make the scene look cheerful, and, for an eastern one, comparatively lively. In the evening we again took the road, with a hot wind blowing strongly and steadily, and before long we were overtaken by a dust-storm, which completely enveloped us in its murky folds, and interfered with our happiness a good deal. Got through the night much as usual, with the addition of a midnight vocal entertainment, which some hundreds of wolves and jackals treated us to, while the "authorities" were looking to our welfare, by taking off and greasing our wheels. Of travellers we meet but few, generally bullock-train parties, with soldiers, &c., return dâks, and an occasional old Mussulman, or other native, taking advantage of the early morning for his journey, and wrapped and swaddled up as if afraid of being congealed by the coolness of the morning air.

Every day's journey leaves one more and more at a loss to discover the sources of the wealth of this enormous country. The soil, for miles and miles a dead flat, is now barren as a desert, and we meet hardly a sign of active traffic. During the night we certainly did encounter a long train of heavily-laden bullock-waggons; but the merchandize was gunpowder, and its destination was up, instead of down the road.

May 24.—Arrived at "Kurga," where we

found neither bread nor butter forthcoming—nothing but—"plenty fowl, Sahib!" In the evening we again encountered a heavy dust-storm, the worst of the season; the whole night it continued to blow in our teeth; and between the fierce dryness of the wind and the searching particles of dust, which visited us without ceremony, we spent anything but an agreeable night. At three A.M. we reached the "Hingus Nuddee," or river; and changing our solitary horse for two fat bullocks, we crossed its sandy bed, and over a bridge of boats—not so genteelly, perhaps, but much more securely, than we could have otherwise done. There were the remains here of a handsome suspension bridge; but the chains had been cut by the rebel Sepoys, and nothing but the pillars now remained.

May 25.—At four A.M. we crossed the bridge of boats over the Jumna, and found ourselves under the gloomy battlements of the Fort of Delhi.

Entering by the Calcutta Gate, we drove through large suburbs, lighted up with rows of oil lamps, reminding one, in the dim light, a good deal of Cairo. Arriving at the dâk bungalow, we found it such a dirty looking deserted building, and the interior so much of a piece with the exterior, that we mounted again, and set off to try the Hotel, or "Pahunch Ghur," —a name originally intended to convey the meaning "An arriving house," but neatly and appropriately corrupted into the term "Punch Gur," which speaks for itself, and troubles no one much about its derivation. We were rather disappointed with the general appearance of the city: dirt and grandeur were closely combined, and the combination gave the usual impression of shabby genteelness in general, not at first sight prepossessing. After driving through what might have been an Eastern Sebastopol, from the amount of ruin about, we reached a cut-throat-looking archway; and the coachman, here pointing to a dirty board above his head, triumphantly announced the "Punch Gur!" Hot and thirsty, we got out, with visions of rest and cooling sherbets, too soon to be dispelled. Passing through long dirty halls, and up unsavoury steps, we at last reached a sort of court, with beds of sickly flowers, never known to bloom, and from thence issued to a suite of musty hot Moorish-looking rooms, with gold-inlaid dust-covered tables, and a heavily-draped four-post bedstead, the very sight of which, in such a climate, was almost enough to deprive one of sleep for ever. Our speech forsook us, and without waiting to remark whether the lady of the house was an ogress, or possessed of a "rose-coloured body" and face like the full moon, we fairly turned tail, and drove in all haste to our despised dâk bungalow, where, meekly and with softened feelings towards that edifice, we were glad to deposit ourselves on a couple of charpoys, or "four-legs," as the bedstead of India is called, and endeavour to sleep the best way we could. "Delhi," we found, quite kept up its reputation of being the hottest place in India. All idea of sight-seeing was out of the question, and the whole of our energies we were obliged to expend in endeavouring to keep moderately cool.

After enjoying the two first of blessings in a hot climate—viz. a plentiful supply of cold water and a change of raiment, we felt ourselves able to undergo the exertion of meeting the traditional grilled fowl at breakfast, and of inspecting the curiosities from the bazaars. At the first wish on the latter subject, we were invaded by a crowd of bundle-carrying, yellow-turbaned, rascally merchants, who, in half a minute, had the whole of their goods on the floor—rings, brooches, ivory ornaments, and inutilities of all sorts and kinds, all of them exorbitantly dear, and none of any real value.

We left Delhi again at about six P.M., after loitering about the city for a short time, among the teeming bazaars, some parts of which were picturesque and "Eastern" enough. Outside the city walls, the country was ruined and dilapidated in the extreme; demolished houses and wasted gardens telling their tale of the loss of Delhi, and our struggle for its recapture.

May 26.—During the night, we got over seventy-three miles, and reached "Kurnaul" at seven A.M. The bungalow we found unusually comfortable, being a remnant of the old régime, and one of the few which escaped from the hands of the rebels during the mutiny.

The country here begins to improve in appearance—more trees and cultivation on all sides; and the natives appear finer specimens than their more southern relations. The irrigation, too, seems to be carried on with more systematic appliances than further south—the water being raised by the Persian wheel, and bullock-power introduced in aid of manual labour.

May 27.—Arrived at Umballa at three A.M., and found the staging bungalow full. The only available accommodation being a spare charpoy in the verandah, F. took a lease of it, while I revelled in the unaccustomed roominess of the entire carriage, and slept till six, when we got into our lodgings. Although so near the foot of the Himalayas, the weather was so oppressive here that exploring was out of the question; and at six P.M., changing our carriage for palankeens, or dolies, we commenced a tedious and dusty journey to the village of "Kalka," the veritable "foot of the hills," where we were met by a string of deputies from the different "*dry-lodgings*" in the neighbourhood, soliciting custom. The first house we came to was guarded by an unmistakeable English hotel-keeper, of some eighteen stone; and so terrible was the appearance she presented, with her arms akimbo, rejoicing in her mountain air, that in our down-country and dilapidated condition, we felt quite unequal to the exertion of stepping into *her* little parlour; and passing her establishment—something in the small bathingplace-style of architecture—we went on to the next, very much of the same order, and called the "Brahminee Bull." Here, to my dismay however, standing in the selfsame position, weighing the same number of stone, and equally confident in the purity of her air as her neighbour, stood another female "Briton," with the come-into-my-parlour expression of countenance, regarding us as prey. Under the circumstances, exhausted nature gave in; though saved from Scylla, our destiny was Charybdis, and we accordingly surrendered ourselves to a wash, breakfast, and the

Brahminee Bull. During the day, we had a visit from a friend and ex-brother officer, whom we had promised to stay with, at "Kussowlie," on our road up. Kalka was not *hot*, but *grilling*, so that a speedy ascent to the station was soon agreed upon. Not caring to risk a sun-stroke, I resigned myself to the traditional conveyance of the country, a "jhampan," while the other two rode up; but here, for the second time, it was "out of the fryingpan into the fire." Such an infernal machine as my new conveyance turned out never could have existed in the palmiest days of the Inquisition. It was a sort of child's cradle, long enough for a creature of some five or six summers, made like a tray, and hung after the fashion of a miniature four-post bedstead, with goat's-hair curtains. The structure is suspended, something in the fashion of a sedan-chair which has been stunted in its growth, between two poles; between the projections of these again, before and behind, connected by a stout strap, are two shorter bars, each supported, when in travelling order, on the shoulders of two bearers. When the machine is in motion, therefore, there are four men in line between the shafts.

The pace is always rather fast, and down a declivity the torturers go at a run; the result is, that prominent parts of one's body are continually in collision with the seat or sides of the machine, coming down from various altitudes, according to the nature of the ground and the humour of the inquisitors. After getting over about six miles in this graceful and pleasing manner, we reached the first of the fir-trees, and as we rose still higher a delicious breeze came over the hills, as precious to the parched and travel-stained pilgrim from the plains as a drop of water to the thirstiest wanderer in the desert. Kussowlie appeared a picturesque little station, perched at the summit of one of the first of the hilly ranges, and here I found my two companions, burnt and red in the face as if they, too, had had their sufferings on the road, occupied in looking over the goods of a strolling Cashmere merchant; luckily for themselves, however, it was under the protecting superintendence of our hostess. Our friends were living on a miniature estate commanding a magnificent view of the mountain ranges on one side, and, on the other, the plains of the Punjab, the scorching country from which we had just made our escape lying stretched out before us like an enormous map in relief. Towards the mountains were the military stations of "Dugshai" and "Subathoo," and the boys' asylum of "Senore," the latter rather marring the face of nature by the workhouse order of its architecture. "Simla" we could just distinguish, nestled among the blue mountains in the far distance.

Here we spent a couple of days very pleasantly with our hospitable entertainers, and satisfactorily pulled up all arrears of sleep—a luxury none can really appreciate who have not travelled for six days and nights in the different local conveniences I have mentioned.

Before leaving we had an opportunity of seeing how England in the Himalayas makes its morning calls. Walking, which amounts almost to an impossibility in "the plains," seems to be voted *infra dig.* in "the hills," and Mrs. Kussowlie accordingly made her appearance seated in state in a jhampan, and borne on the shoulders of four of her slaves.

These were active, wiry-looking natives, dressed in long green coats, bound with broad, red, tight-fitting pantaloons, and with small turbans of red and green on their heads. Altogether, a more startling-looking apparition to the uninitiated than this Himalayan morning visitor could hardly be imagined, even in a tour through the remotest regions of the earth.

May 29.—About six o'clock in the evening we remounted our instruments of torture and took the road to Simla. For about seven miles the path was down hill, and the bearers being fresh, they huddled us along at a pace calculated to outrage our feelings most considerably, and, at the same time, with no more consideration for our welfare than if we were so many sacks of coal. In spite of the sufferings of the principal performers, the procession was most amusing; and as we jolted, bumped, and bundled along, it was impossible to keep from laughing, although crying, perhaps, would, under the circumstances, have been more appropriate. My machine led the way, four of the inquisition being in the shafts, and four in waiting, running along at the side with pipes, bundles, sticks, &c. Then came F. similarly attended, and finally the Q. M. G., hubble bubble in hand, and attired in a gold embroidered cap, surrounded by a lilac turban: seated in a sort of tray, and reclining at his ease in full enjoyment of his high position, he looked the priest of the procession, and managed to retain his dignity in spite of the rapid and unceremonious way in which he was being whirled along. As the moon went down we had the additional effect of torchlight to the scene, three bearers having the special duty of running along to show the pathway to the rest. This seemed a service of some danger, and our torch-bearers at times verged upon places where a stumble would have apparently extinguished both themselves and their torches for ever. About half way we stopped for about an hour for the bearers to partake of a light entertainment of "ghee and chupatties"—otherwise, rancid butter and cakes of flour and water. This was their only rest and only meal, from the time they left Kussowlie at six P.M. until they reached Simla at eight A.M. The same set of bearers took us the entire distance, about thirty-five miles; and the four men who were not actually in the shafts used to rest themselves by running ahead and up precipitous short cuts, so as to insure a few minutes' pull at the pipe of consolation before their turn arrived again. To us, supposed to be the *otium cum dig.* part of the procession, the road seemed perfectly endless. No sooner were we up one ascent than we were down again on the other side; and when we thought Simla must be in sight round the next turn, it seemed suddenly to become more hid than ever. In one of these ups and downs of life my machine, during a heavy lurch, fairly gave way to its feelings, and with a loud crash the pole broke, and down we both came, much to my temporary satisfaction and relief. A supply of ropes and lashings, however, formed part of the inquisitors' stores, and we were soon under weigh again to fulfil the remainder of our destiny.

The entrance to Simla led us through a fine forest of oaks; firs, cedars, and other large trees; and winding along through these we could, every now and then, discern, towering over the backs of endless ranges of blue and hazy mountains, ridge upon ridge of glittering snow, which cast its icy breath upon us even where we were, helping us to forget the horrors of the night, and giving us a renewal of our lease of existence. Simla itself soon opened on our view, a scattered and picturesque settlement of houses of the most varied patterns perched about over the mountain top, just as an eligible spot presented itself for building purposes. It is situated 8,000 feet above the level of the sea and 7,000 over the average level of "the plains," Umballa, which is near the foot of the range, being 1,000 above the sea-level. From our halting-place we could discern the scene of our night's journey, with Kussowlie looking like a mere speck in the distance, and we felt a proud sort of consciousness of having accomplished a desperate undertaking in very good style. Passive endurance was, under the circumstances, quite as worthy of praise as the more active virtues displayed by those who were the cause of our sufferings. After the first good breakfast I had eaten for three months, we pulled up arrears of sleep till four P.M. and found, on awaking, that our much-expected letters had arrived from the post, and among them the necessary permission from the Punjab Government to travel in Cashmere, and instructions for our guidance while in the territory. From among the routes laid down in the latter we chose No. 1.* The direct line across the mountains from Simla would have entailed additional delay and permission, and as time was precious we decided upon descending again to the plains and making our way through Lahore, not, however, without a severe pang at leaving so soon the terrestrial paradise of which we had got a glimpse. After arranging our movements with the "authorities," we sallied out to see fashionable Simla airing itself, which, as far as dress is concerned, it appeared to do very much in the fashionable watering-place style at home. The jhampans, palkies, dandies,† &c. which took up the entire road, however, loudly proclaimed India, Simla being much too dainty to touch the

* ROADS.—I. There are four authorized routes for European visitors to Cashmere.

First. The principal road from the plains by Bimbhur and Rajâoree. This road over the "Peer Punjal" range is not open until May, and is closed by snow at the beginning of November: it is the old imperial route, and the stages are marked by the remains of serais.

† A hill conveyance something similar to a hammock, suspended from a pole, with straps for the feet and back, and carried by two bearers.

ground with its pretty feet, and too lazy to use its own legs for purposes of out-door locomotion. The station seems a curious combination of many styles and places; the scenery and houses, Swiss; the people Anglo Indians, Affghans, Cashmeeries, &c.; the conveyances, Inquisito-Spanish; and the bazaars, in their native dirt, pure Indian.

May 31.—After making our leave secure, we made up our minds for a plunge into the plains again and a forced march to Lahore, being rather expedited in the determination by hearing that several travellers had been recalled from leave in consequence of there being a scarcity of officers with their regiments.

With a fine moonlight night in our favour we again took the road; and practice slightly assuaging our sufferings, we got on smoothly enough till within a few hours from Hureepore Bungalow, when my machine again broke with a crash, and the nature of the fracture being compound, I walked on and left the executioners to repair the instrument at their leisure.

June 1.—Reached Hureepore at four A.M., and found the place in possession of a crowd of monkeys of all sorts and sizes, taking an early breakfast. Here, chicken and eggs being again written in our destiny, we halted for an hour or two, and at eleven again took the road with our cast-iron bearers, and hurried along in the noon-day sun, up hill and down dale, through Kussowlie, and on and on till we were once more fairly deposited at the feet of "Mrs. Charybdis." A slight dinner here, and at 8.30 P.M. we were again in train, shuffling along through several feet of dust, which the bearers, and torch-carriers, and the rest of our numerous train, kicked up about us, in clouds nearly dense enough to cause suffocation.

June 2.—At 8.30 A.M. we arrived again at Umballa, and with nothing to comfort us in our dusty and worried condition but the reflection that our start from Simla was a magnificent triumph of stern determination over present enjoyment and unwonted luxury, we again resumed

our forced march. At six P.M. we took our departure, in a very magnificent coach, but in an "unpropitious moment," for the horse was unusually averse to an advance of any sort, and when we did get clear of the station his opinions were borne out by a terrific storm of dust, with a thunder, lightning, and rain accompaniment, which effectually put a stop to all further progress. The horse for once had his wish, and was brought to a regular stand. The wind howled about us, and the dusty atmosphere assumed a dull red appearance, such as I had only once before seen at Cawnpore, and the like of which might possibly have prevailed during the last days of Pompeii. After getting through the worst of the storm, we pushed along, and had reached the twentieth mile-stone, when, catching a flavour of burning wood, I looked out and found the wheel at an angle of some 30 degrees, and rubbing against the side preparatory to taking its leave altogether. Here was another effect of starting in an unpropitious moment. The interruption in the great forced march preyed heavily upon our minds, but, on the principle of doing as "Rome does," we took a lesson from the religion of "Islam," and concurring in the views expressed by our attendant blacks, viz. that "whatever is written in a man's destiny that will be accomplished," we ejaculated "Kismut" with the rest, and resignedly adapted ourselves to the writings in our own particular page

of fate. Having sent back to Umballa the news of our distress, a new conveyance in a few hours made its appearance; and hauling it alongside the wreck, we unshipped the stores, reloaded, and eventually reached "Thikanmajura" at eight A.M.

June 3.—Starting at about three o'clock P.M., we found the unpropitious moment still hanging over us: first a violent dust-storm, and then a refractory horse, which bolted completely off the road, and nearly upset us down a steep bank, proved to demonstration that our star was still obscured.

About midnight we reached the river "Sutlej," and exchanged our horse for four fat and humpy bullocks, who managed, with very great labour and difficulty, to drag us through the heavy sands of the river-bed down to the edge of the water. Here we were shipped on board a flat-

bottomed boat, with a high peaked bow; and, after an immensity of hauling and grunting, we were fairly launched into the stream, and poled across to the opposite shore. The water appeared quite shallow, and the coolies were most of the time in the water; but its width, including the sands forming its bed, could not have been less than two miles and a half. It was altogether a wild and dreary-looking scene, as we paddled along—the wild ducks and jackals, &c. keeping up a concert on their own account, and the patient old bullocks ruminating quietly on their prospects at our feet.

On arriving at what appeared to be the opposite bank, we were taken out, and again pulled and hauled through the deep sand, only to be reshipped again on what seemed a respectable river in its own right; and here, getting out of patience with a stream that had no opposite bank, I fell asleep, and left the bullocks to their sorrows and their destiny.

June 4.—Arrived at Jullundur, where we had to share the bungalow with another traveller and a rising family, who kept us alive by howling vigorously all day. The road from this being "Kucha," literally *uncooked*, but here meant to express "unmetalled," we had yet another form of conveyance to make acquaintance with. It was a palkee, rudely strapped upon the body of a worn-out "Dâk garee;" and although a more unpromising-looking locomotive perhaps never was placed upon wheels, the actual reality proved even worse than the appearance foreboded.

Anybody who has happened to have been run

away with in a dust-cart through Fenchurch Street, or some other London pavement, the gas pipes being up at the time, might form some idea of our sensations as we pounded along, at full gallop, over some thirty miles of uneven, *un-cooked* road; but to anybody who has not had this advantage, description would be impossible. About half way, it appeared that it was written in my miserable destiny that the off fore-wheel of my shay was to come off, and off it came accordingly; so that once more I became an involuntary disciple of Islam, and went to sleep among the ruins, with rather a feeling of gratitude for the respite than otherwise. On awaking, I found myself again under way; and effecting a junction with my companion, we had a light supper off half a water-melon; and, after crossing the River Beas by a bridge of boats, and being lugged through another waste of sand by bullocks, we once again reached a "cooked" road, and arrived at "Umritsur" at six A.M.

June 5.—Found the heat so great here that we were unable to stir out.

As a consolation, we received a visit from four "Sikh Padres," who rushed in and squatted themselves down without ceremony, previously placing a small ball of candied sugar on the table as a votive and suggestive offering. The spokesman, a lively little rascal, with a black beard tied up under his red turban, immediately opened fire, by hurling at us all the names of all the officers he had ever met or read of. The volley was in this style: First, the number of the regiment, then Brown Sahib, Jones Sahib, Robinson Sahib, Smith Sahib, Tomkins Sahib, Green Sahib, and so on, regiment after regiment and name after name, his brother Padres occasionally chiming in in corroboration of their friend's veracity and in admiration of his vast stock of military information. After much trouble, we got rid of the pack, at the price of one rupee, which was cheap for the amount of relief afforded by their departure.

June 6.—Reached Lahore at ten P.M. and had a night in bed, for the third time only since leaving Cawnpore. The Q. M. G. being at once set to work to make the necessary arrangements for our final start for Cashmere, we paid a hurried visit to the Tomb of Runjeet Sing and the Fort and City of Lahore. These were worth seeing, but they abounded in sights and perfumes, which rendered the operation rather a trying one, considering the very high temperature of the weather.

June 7.—Drove out in a dilapidated buggy,

and with an incorrigible horse, to Mean Meer, the cantonments of Lahore. The place looked burnt up and glaring like its fellows, and a fierce hot wind swept over it, which made us glad enough to turn our backs on it and hurry home again as fast as our obstinate animal would take us. The Q. M. G., we found, had collected our staff of servants together, and was otherwise pushing on our preparations as fast as the dignity and importance of the undertaking would admit.

The staff consisted of khidmutgar, bawurchie, bhistie, dhobie, and mihtar; or, in plain English, butler, cook, water-carrier, washerman, and sweeper.

Of these, the washing department only brought with it its insignia and badge of office. This was an enormous smoothing-iron, highly ornamented with brass, decorated with Gothic apertures, and made to contain an amount of charcoal that would have kept an entire family warm in the coldest depths of winter. Being of great weight, we rather objected to such an addition to our stores—the more so as our linen was not likely to require much *getting-up*. The *dhobie*, however, declared himself unable to get on without it, and it accordingly had to be engaged with its master.

June 8.—To-day Rajoo is still hard at work laying in stores from the bazaars and arranging means of transport for them; the weather hot beyond measure; and as neither our food nor quarters are very good, we begin to forget our lessons of resignation, more especially as the mosquitoes begin to form a very aggravating item in our destiny.

June 9.—About four P.M. the Q. M. G. came in triumphantly with about sixteen tall baskets covered with leather, which he called "khiltas;" and having ranged them about the room like the oil-jars of "Ali Baba," he proceeded to cram them with potatoes, tea, clothes, brandy, and the whole stock of our earthly goods, in a marvellous and miscellaneous manner, very trying to contemplate, and suggestive of their entire separation from us and our heirs for ever.

Coolies not being procurable in sufficient numbers to carry away all our stores together, F. and I agreed to start in the morning, leaving the head of affairs with the rearguard to follow at his leisure. Got away at last in two "palkees," with four "banghy wallahs," or baggage-bearers, carrying our immediate possessions, guns, &c. Spent the night wretchedly enough, the roads being of the worst, and covered nearly a foot deep everywhere with fine dust, which our bearers very soon stirred up into an impenetrable cloud, enveloping us in its folds to the verge of suffocation.

The sensation is strange enough, travelling in this way along a lonely road at dead of night, closely shut up in an oblong box, and surrounded by some twenty or more dusky savages, who could quietly tap one on the head at any time, and appropriate the bag of rupees—inseparable from Indian travelling—without the slightest difficulty. That they do not do so is probably from the knowledge they possess that with the bag of rupees there is generally to be found a revolver, and that an English traveller is of so generous a disposition that he seldom parts from his money without giving a little lead in with the silver.

June 10.—After a dusty jolt of forty miles, we reached "Gugerwalla" at eight A.M., and felt the change from Lahore most refreshing. The village seemed a quiet little settlement, very little visited by Englishmen, and the inhabitants, probably on that account, appeared of a different stamp from those we had hitherto met. The women, in particular, were more gaily dressed, and not so frightened at a white face as more south. The rearguard not having come up at six P.M. we started off without it. Crossed the Chenab during the night. The fords, by torchlight, were most picturesque, and rather exciting, in consequence of the water at times taking it into its head to see what was inside the "palkee." The Chenab makes the fourth out of the "five waters" from which the "Punjab" takes its name. The Jhelum only remains—the ancient Hydaspes of Alexandrian notoriety.

June 11.—Reached "Goojerat" at five A.M. and enjoyed a few hours of quiet sleep in a very comfortable bungalow. The "khiltas" not making their appearance, we halt here for the night. In the evening we explored the city—a straggling rabbit-burrow settlement, inclosed by a mud wall, and boasting the narrowest streets I had ever seen. In an open space we came upon a marvellously-ornamented "mundir," or Hindoo temple, painted in the most florid style, with effigies of dark gentlemen in coloured pants riding on peacocks, antelopes, and other beasts of burden common in the country. It seemed the centre of attraction to a numerous concourse of strangers from the north; among others, a bevy of young ladies with loose trousers and fair complexions, evidently "Cashmeeries," who seemed to regard the "heathen temple" as one of the wonders of the world. In the middle of the night the rearguard came in with the supplies, and we at once turned it into an advanced-guard, and packed it off to make preparations for our arrival at "Bimber."

June 12.—Spent a very hot day at Goojerat, and amused ourselves by inspecting the gold-inlaid work for which the place is famous. At 5·30 P.M. we started for our last night's journey in British territory; and thus terminated, for the present, our experiences of all the hot and dusty "pleasure of the Plains."

PART II.

CASHMERE.

June 13.—About two A.M. we passed out of India into the territory of His Highness the Maharajah of Cashmere, and halted at Bimber. The accommodation here turned out to be most indifferent, although in our route the edifice for travellers was called a "Baraduree," which sounded grandly. It means a summer-house with twelve doors; but beyond the facilities it afforded of rapid egress, we found it to possess but few advantages.

Putting a couple of charpoys outside, we managed a few hours' sleep *al fresco*, in spite of the flies and mosquitoes innumerable, who lost no time in taking possession of their new property.

On being able to discern the face of the country, we found ourselves at the foot of a range of hills of no great height, but still veritable hills; and although the sun was nearly as hot as in the plains, we felt that we were emancipated from India, and that all our real travelling troubles were over. In the evening we inspected the Maharajah's troops, consisting of eight curiously-dressed and mysteriously-accoutred sepoys under a serjeant. These same troops had rather astonished us in the morning by filing up in stage style in front of our two charpoys just as we awoke, and delivering a "Present arms" with great unction as we sat up in a half-sleepy and dishevelled condition, rubbing our eyes, and not exactly in the style of costume in which such a salute is usually received. We now found the "army" in the domestic employment of cooking their victuals, so that we were unable to have much of a review. However, we looked at their arms and accoutrements; ammunition they had none; and saw them perform the "manual and platoon." Their arms had been matchlocks, but had been converted, these stirring times, into flintlocks! In addition to these, which were about as long as a respectable spear, they had each a sword and shield, together with a belt and powder-horn, all clumsy in the extreme.

In loading, we found an improvement on the English fashion, for, after putting the imaginary charge in with the hand, they *blew* playfully down the muzzle to obviate the difficulty of the powder sticking to the sides. After presenting the troops with "bukhshish," we strolled through the village and met the "thanadar," or head man, coming out to meet us, arrayed in glorious apparel and very tight inexpressibles, and mounted on a caparisoned steed. Dismounting, he advanced towards us salaaming, and holding out a piece of money in the palm of his hand; and not exactly knowing the etiquette of the proceeding, we touched it and left it where we found it, which appeared to be a relief to his mind, for he immediately put it in his pocket again.

His chief conversation was on the subject of the Maharajah and the delights of Cashmere, and anxiety as to our having got all supplies, &c. which we required, as he had been appointed expressly for the purpose of looking after the comfort of the English visitors. What with our friend and his train, and the detachment of "*the army*" which had accompanied us, our retinue began to assume the appearance of a procession; and it was with great difficulty that we induced them all to leave us, which they did at last after we had expressed our full satisfaction at the courtesy displayed by the Maharajah's very intelligent selection of a "thanadar."

June 14.—Broke up our camp about three A.M. and started our possessions at four o'clock, after some difficulty in prevailing upon the coolies to walk off with their loads. On mustering our forces, we found that they numbered thirty-seven, including ourselves. Of these twenty-four were coolies, carrying our possessions—beer, brandy, potatoes, &c.; our servants were six more; then there were four ponies, entailing a native each to look after them; and, last of all, one of the redoubtable "army" as a guard, who paraded in the light marching order of a sword, shield, bag of melons, and an umbrella. F. and I travelled on "yaboos," or native ponies—unlikely to look at, but wonderful to go. Mine was more like a hatchet than anything else, and yet the places he went over and the rate he travelled up smooth faces of rock was marvellous to behold.

About eight o'clock we found ourselves once more among the pine-trees; and, although the sun was very powerful, we had enough of the freshness of the mountain air to take away the remembrance of the dusty plains from our minds. No rain having fallen as yet, the springs and rivers were all nearly dry; but we saw several rocky beds, which gave good promise of fly-fishing, should they receive a further supply of water.

About nine A.M. we reached our halting-place, "Serai Saidabad," a ruined old place, with a mud tenement overlooking, at some elevation, the banks of a river.

Here we were again received with a salute, by a detachment of warriors drawn up in full dress —viz. red and yellow turbans, and blue trousers with a red stripe.

After undergoing a refreshing bath of a skin of water, taken in our drawing-room, we got our artist to work at breakfast, and shortly after found, with considerable satisfaction, that we were in for the first of the rains. This welcome fact first proclaimed itself by the reverberation of distant thunder from among the mountains to the north; then an ominous black cloud gradually spread itself over us, and, with a storm of dust, down came the rain in torrents, making the air, in a few minutes, cool and delicious as possible, and entirely altering the sultry temperature which had previously prevailed. The thirsty ground soaked up the moisture as if it had never tasted rain, and the trees came out as if re-touched by Nature's brush; while as for F. and myself, we turned the unwonted coolness to the best account we could, by setting ourselves to work to pull up all arrears of sleep forthwith.

June 15.—Started at four A.M., with our numerous train, and found the road all the pleasanter for the rain of the previous evening, and all things looking green and fresh after the storm. Our path led us up a rocky valley, with its accompanying dashing stream, in the bed of which we could see traces of what the brawler had been in his wilder days, in huge and polished boulders and water-worn rocks, which had been hurled about in all directions. We afterwards went straight up a precipitous mountain, wooded with pine, which was no light work for the coolies, heavily laden as they were. No sooner, however, were we on the top of this than down we went on the other side; and how the ponies managed their ups-and-downs of life was best known to themselves; certainly, nothing but a cat or a Cashmere pony could have got over the ground. About nine A.M. we reached "Nowshera," under another salute, where we found an indifferent-looking "Baraduree," completely suffocated among the trees of a garden called the "Bauli Bagh," or "Reservoir Garden," from a deep stone well in the centre of it. Here we got on indifferently well, the weather being close after the rain, and the place thickly inhabited by crowds of sparrows, all with large families, who made an incessant uproar all day long; besides an army of occupation of small game, which interfered sadly with our sleeping arrangements at night. In the evening we made the acquaintance of a loquacious and free-and-easy gardener, entirely innocent of clothes, who came and seated himself between F. and myself, as we were perched upon a rock enjoying the prospect. According to his account, the Maharajah's tenants pay about seven rupees, or fourteen shillings, per annum for some five acres of land. In the middle of the night we came in for another storm of thunder and lightning, which took a good many liberties with our house, but cooled the air; and only for the mosquitoes, and other holders of the property, whose excessive attentions were rather embarrassing, we would have got on very well. As it was, however, I hardly closed an eye all night, and spent the greater part of it in meandering about the Bauli Bagh, *vestito da notte*—in which operation I rejoice to think that, like the Russians at the burning of Moscow, I at least put the enemy to very considerable inconvenience, even at the expense of my own comfort.

June 16.—About half-past four A.M. we got under weigh again, heartily delighted to leave the sparrows and their allies in undisputed possession of their property.

The "kotwal," and other authorities, who had been extremely civil in providing supplies, coolies, &c., according to the Maharajah's order, took very good care not to let us depart without a due sense of the fact, for they bothered us for "bukhshish" just as keenly as the lowest muleteer; and when I gave the kotwal twelve annas, or one shilling and sixpence, as all the change I had, he assured me that the khidmutgar had more, and ran back to prove it by bringing me two rupees. I gave the scoundrel one, and regretted it for three miles, for he had robbed the coolies in the morning, either on his own or his master's account, of one anna, or three-halfpence each, out of their hardly-earned wages. To-day we find ourselves once more among the rocks and pines, and as we progressed nothing could exceed the beauty of the views which opened upon us right and left. A mountain stream attended our steps the whole way, sometimes smoothly and placidly, sometimes dancing about like a mad thing, and teasing the sturdy old battered rocks and stones which long ago had settled down in life along its path, and which, from the amount of polish they displayed, must themselves have been finely knocked about the world in their day. Rounding a turn of the river, where it ran deeply under its rocky bank, we came suddenly upon the ghastly figure of a man carefully suspended in chains from a prominent tree. His feet had been torn off by the wolves and jackals, but the upper part of the body remained together, and there he swung to and fro in the breeze, a ghastly warning to all evildoers, and a not very pleasing monument of the justice of the country. He was a sepoy of the Maharajah's army, who had drowned his comrade in the stream below the place where he thus had expiated his crime. Not far from this spot we discovered traces of another marauder, in the shape of a fresh footprint of a tiger or a leopard, just as he had prowled shortly before along the very path we were pursuing.

From this we gradually got into a region of fruit-trees, interspersed with pines; and sometimes we came upon a group of scented palms, which looked strangely enough in such unusual company. Through clustering pomegranates, figs, plums, peach-trees, wild, but bearing fruit, we journeyed on and on; and, as new beauties arose around us, we could not help indulging in castles in the air, and forming visions of earthly paradises, where, with the addition only of such importations as are inseparable from all ideas of paradise, either in Cashmere or elsewhere, one might live in uninterrupted enjoyment of existence, and, at least, bury in oblivion all remembrance of such regions as the "Plains of India."

About ten A.M., after a continuous series of ups-and-downs of varied scenery, we arrived at "Chungas," a picturesque old serai, perched upon a hill over the river. It was marked off in our route as having no accommodation, but, located among the mouldering remnants of grandeur of an old temple in the centre of the serai, we managed to make ourselves very comfortable, and thought our "accommodation" a most decided improvement upon our late fashionable but rather overcrowded halting-place. From the serai we can see, for the first time, the snowy range of the Himalayas, trending northwards, towards the Peer Punjal Pass, through which our route leads into the Valley of Cashmere.

June 17.—Another ride through hill and dale to "Rajaori," or "Rampore," a most picturesque-looking town, built in every possible style of architecture, and flanked at one extremity by a ruined castle. Our halting-place was in an ancient serai, with a dilapidated garden, containing the remains of some rather handsome fountains. It was situated on a rock, several hundred feet above the river which separated us from the town; and, from our elevated position, we had a fine view of the whole place, and got an insight into the manners and customs of the inhabitants, without their being at all aware of our proximity.

The women and children appeared to be dressed quite in the Tartar style: the women with little red square-cornered fez caps, with a long strip of cloth thrown gracefully over them, and either pyjamas of blue stuff with a red stripe, or a long loose toga of greyish cloth, reaching nearly to the feet. The little girls were quite of the bullet-headed Tartar pattern, of Crimean recollection, but wore rather less decoration. The Crimean young ladies generally had a three-cornered charm suspended round their necks, while the youthful fashion of Rajaori, scorning all artificial adornment, selected nature only as their mantua-maker, and wore their dresses strictly according to her book of patterns. After enjoying a delightfully cool night in our elevated bedroom, we started for "Thanna."

Our path led through a gradually ascending valley, cultivated, for the rice crop, in terraces, and irrigated by a complicated net-work of channels, cut off from the mountain streams, and branching off in every direction to the different elevations. The ground was so saturated in these terraces that ploughing was carried on by means of a large scraper, like a fender, which was dragged along by bullocks, the ploughman standing up in the machine as it floundered and wallowed about, and guiding it through the sea of mud.

June 18.—Reached Thanna at nine A.M. and came to a halt in a shady spot outside the village. There was an old serai about half a mile off, but it was full of merchants and their belongings, and savoured so strongly of fleas and dirt, that we gave it up as impracticable.

This was the first instance of our finding no shelter; and, as ill luck would have it, our tents took the opportunity of pitching themselves on the road, a number of coolies broke down, and one abandoned our property and took himself off altogether. Under these interesting circumstances, we were obliged to spend the day completely *al fresco*, and to wait patiently for breakfast until the fashionable hour of half-past two P.M. The inhabitants took our misfortunes very philosophically, and stopped to stare at us to their heart's content as they went by for water, wondering, no doubt, at that restless nature of the crazy Englishman, which drives him out of his own country for the sole purpose, apparently, of being uncomfortable in other people's. Our position, although at the foot of the grander range of mountains, we found very hot, and a good deal of ingenuity was required in order to find continued shelter from the scorching rays of the sun. The natives here seemed to suffer to a great extent from goitre, and one of our coolies in particular had three enormous swellings on his neck, horrible to look at. During the night, Rajoo came in with the missing baggage, except two khiltas, for which no carriage could be procured, and which he was in consequence obliged to abandon on the road until assistance could be sent to them.

June 19.—Started at daybreak from our unsatisfactory quarters, and enjoyed some of the finest scenery we had yet encountered. The road ascended pretty sharply into what might be called the *real* mountains, and finding our spirits rise with the ground, we abandoned our ponies and resolved to perform the remainder of our wanderings on foot. As we reached the summit of our first ascent, and our range of view enlarged, mountain upon mountain rose before us, richly clothed with forest trees; while, overtopping all, peeped up the glistening summits of the snowy range, making everything around seem cool and pleasant, in spite of the hot sun's rays, which still poured down upon us. Our road from this, descending, lay among the nooks and dells of the shady side of the mountain; and the wild rose and the heliotrope perfumed the air at every step as we walked along in full enjoyment of the morning breeze. Our sepoy guide of to-day was not of the educated branch of the army. He was the stupidest specimen of his race I had ever met; and as his language was such a jargon as to be nearly unintelligible, we failed signally in obtaining much information from him.

Among other questions, I made inquiries as to woodcock, the cover being just suited to them, and after a great deal of difficulty in explaining the bird to him, he declared that he knew the kind of creature perfectly, and that there were plenty of them. By way of convincing us, however, of his sporting knowledge, he added that they were in the habit of living entirely on fruit; and he was sadly put out when F. and I both burst into laughter at the idea of an old woodcock with his bill stuck into a juicy pear, or perhaps enjoying a pomegranate for breakfast. Shortly after, we came suddenly upon quite a new feature in the scene—a strange innovation of liveliness in the midst of solitude.

At a bend in the road, what should appear almost over our heads but a troop of about a hundred monkeys, crashing through the firs and chestnuts, and bounding in eager haste from tree to tree, in their desire to escape from a party of natives coming from the opposite direction. They were large brown monkeys, of the kind called lungoors, standing, some of them, three feet high, and having tails considerably longer than themselves. Their faces were jet black, fringed with light grey whiskers, which gave them a most comical appearance; and as they jumped along from tree to tree, sometimes thirty and forty feet through the air, with their small families following as best they could, they made the whole forest resound with the crashing of the branches, and amused us not a little by their aërial line of march.

After crossing a dashing mountain-torrent by a rude bridge of trees thrown across it, we arrived at the village of Burrumgulla. Here our guide wanted us to halt in a mud-built native serai, but, with the recollection of past experience fresh upon us, we declined, preferring to choose our own ground and pitch our first encampment. The ground we selected was almost at the foot of a noble waterfall, formed by a huge cleft in a mass of rugged rock. The water, dashing headlong down, was hidden in the recess of rock below, but the spray, as it rose up like vapour and again fell around us, plainly told the history of its birth and education. Even had we not seen the snowy peaks before us from the mountain top, there was no mistaking, from its icy breath, the nursery in which its infant form had been cradled. Just at our feet was one of the frail and picturesque-looking pine bridges spanning the torrent; while just below it another mountain river came tumbling down, and, joining with its dashing friend, they both rolled on in life together. As soon as our traps arrived, F. and I had a souse in the quietest pool we could find, and anything so cold I never felt; it was almost as if one was turned into stone, and stopping in it more than a second was out of the question. After breakfast and a *siesta*, we sallied out to try and explore the head of the cataract above us. After rather a perilous ascent over loose moss and mould, and clutching at roots of shrubs and trees, we were brought to a stand by a huge mass of perpendicular rock, which effectually barred us from the spot through which the water took its final leap. The upper course of the torrent, however, amply repaid us for our labour, for it ran through the most lovely dell I ever saw; and as it bounded down from rock to rock, and roared and splashed along, it seemed to know what there was before it, and to be rejoicing at the prospect of its mighty jump. Torrent as it seemed, it was evidently nothing to what it could swell to when in a rage, for here and there, far out of its present reach, and scattered all about, were torn and tattered corpses of forest trees, which had evidently been sucked up and carried along until some rock, more abrupt than its neighbours, had brought them to a stand and left them, bleached and rotting, in the summer's sun. At night we found ourselves glad to exchange our usual covering of a single sheet for a heavy complement of blankets, and found our encampment not the least too warm. The authorities here were particularly civil and obliging, and supplied us with the best of butter, eggs, and milk. The latter was particularly good, and, not having often tasted cow's milk in the Plains, we did it ample justice here.

June 20.—Found it rather hard to turn out this morning, in consequence of the great change in the temperature, but got under weigh very well considering. Our path led us up the main torrent towards the snow, and in the first three miles we crossed about twenty pine-tree bridges thrown across the stream, some of them consisting of a single tree, and all in the rudest style of manufacture. Near one of these, under an immense mass of rock, we passed our first snow. It looked, however, so strange and unexpected, that we both took it for a block of stone; and being thatched, as it were, with leaves and small sticks, &c., and discoloured on all sides, it certainly bore no outward resemblance to what it really was.

After an almost perpendicular ascent up natural flights of steps, we reached our next stage, Poshana—a little mud-built, flat-roofed settlement on the mountain-side. Here we engaged a couple of "shikàrees," or native sportsmen, and made preparations for a *détour* into the snows of the Peer Punjal in search of game.

June 21.—Having made a division of our property, and sent the Q. M. G. with an advanced guard two stages on to Heerpore, F. and I started at daybreak for a five-days' shooting expedition in the mountains.

We took with us a khidmutgar and bhistie—both capital servants, but unfortunately not accustomed to cold, much less to snow. Besides these, we had ten coolies to carry our baggage, consisting of two small tents, bedding, guns, and cooking utensils, &c.; and our two shikàrees with their two assistants. The two former were named Khandàri Khan and Baz Khan,—both bare-legged, lightly clothed, sharp-eyed, hardy-looking mountaineers, and well acquainted with the haunts of game, and passes through the snow.

For the first time we had now to put on grass shoes or sandals; and though they felt strange at first, we soon found that they were absolutely necessary for the work we had before us. Our shoemaker charged us six annas, or ninepence, for eight pairs, and that was thirty per cent. over the proper price. However, as one good day's work runs through a new pair, they are all the better for being rather cheap. Along the road in all directions one comes across cast-off remains of shoes, where the wearer has thrown off his worn-out ones and refitted from his travelling stock; and in this way the needy proprietor of a very indifferent pair of shoes may, perchance, make a favourable exchange with the cast-off pair of a more affluent pedestrian; but, to judge from the specimens we saw, he must be very needy indeed in order to benefit by the transaction. On leaving Poshana, we immediately wound up the precipitous side of a mountain above us, and soon found that, from the rarification of the air, and the want of practice, we felt the necessity of calling a halt very frequently, for the purpose, of course, of admiring the scenery and expatiating upon the beauties of nature. About two miles on the way we came to a slip in the mountain-side, and just as we scrambled, with some difficulty, across this, our foremost shikàree suddenly dropped down like a stone, and motioning us to follow his example, he stealthily pointed us out four little animals, which he called "markore," grazing at the bottom of a ravine. Putting our sights to about 250 yards, we fired both together, with the best intentions, but indifferent results; for they all scampered off apparently untouched, and we again resumed our march.

Our encamping ground we found situated among a shady grove of fir-trees, with a mountain-torrent running beneath, bridged over, as far as we could see, with dingy-looking fields of snow and ice. Here, in the middle of June, with snow at our feet, above us, and around us, we pitched our tent, and had breakfast, and laid our plans for a search for game to-morrow. Though the wind blew cold and chilly off the snows, we soon found that the midday sun still asserted his supremacy, and our faces and hands soon bore witness to the fierceness of the trial of strength between the two. Our camp, although so high up, was not more than six miles from Poshana, and from thence we drew all our supplies, such as milk, eggs, and fowls, &c., the coolies' and shikàrees' subsistence being deducted from their pay. Our own living was not expensive: fowls, threepence each for large, three-halfpence small; milk, three-halfpence per quart, and eggs, twelve for the like amount, or one anna. For the rest, we lived upon chupatties, or unleavened cakes of flour—very good hot, but "gutta-percha" cold—potatoes from Lahore, and, in the liquid line, tea and brandy. At night we slept upon the ground—pretty hard it was while one was awake to feel it—and not having any lamp, we turned in shortly after dark, while in the morning we were up and dressed before the nightingales had cleared their voices. These latter abounded all about us, and formed a most agreeable addition to our establishment.

June 22.—Left our camp before sunrise, and crossing a large field of snow over the main torrent, we clambered up the precipitous side of our opposite mountain. The snow at first felt piercingly cold as it penetrated our snow-shoes, but before we reached the top, we had little to complain of in the way of chilliness. Our sharp-sighted guides soon detected game on the rocks above us, and off we went on a stalk, over rocks and chasms of snow—now running, now crawling along, more like serpents than respectable Christians, and all in a style that would have astonished nobody more than ourselves, could we have regarded the performance in the cool light of reason, and not influenced by the excitement of chasing horned cattle of such rare and curious proportions.

The markore, however, were quite as interested in the sport as we were, and after an arduous and protracted stalk, they finally gave us the slip, and we called a halt at the summit of a hill for breakfast and a rest during the heat of the day. The former we enjoyed as we deserved, but for the latter I can't say much: occasionally a cold blast from off the snow would run right through us, while the sun bore down upon our heads with scorching power, making havoc with whatever part of us it found exposed to its rays, and blistering our hands and legs. The guides helped us out by building up a most ricketty-looking shanty with sticks and pieces of their garments and our own, and under this apology for shelter, with our feet almost in the snow, we passed the day, until it was cool enough again to look for game. In the evening we came suddenly upon a kustura, a sort of half goat, half sheep, with long teeth like a wolf. He was, however, in such thick cover, that we were unable to get a shot at him.

Our camp, we found, moved, according to

order, some three miles higher up, to facilitate the shooting on that side: it was still, however, among the firs and nightingales.

June 23.—Up again before sunrise, and off to the tops of the mountains in search of game. The pull-up took us about an hour and a half, and on reaching the summit, we found ourselves above the pass of the Peer Punjal, the rocky and snow-covered ranges of mountain around us gradually trending off on all sides, and losing themselves in pine-covered slopes, till they finally blended with the blue outlines of the ranges of hills we had crossed on our route from Bimber. While taking a sharp look around us for a herd of some twenty animals which we had seen the day previously, we suddenly found ourselves close to a party of five markore, but they scampered off so fast over rock and snow-drift, that they gave us no opportunity of getting a shot.

Following them up, we came, while clinging to an overhanging ledge of rock, upon one solitary gentleman standing about 150 yards below. We both fired together, but the pace we had come, and the ground we had crossed, had unsteadied our aim, and though my second bullet parted the wool on his back, it was not written that our first markore was to fall so easily.

After this we tracked the first herd for a long distance over the snow, until they scampered down an almost perpendicular face of snow and ice, and here we gave them up, halting on a spur of the mountain for a repast of chicken, eggs, chupatties, and cold tea. During our morning's work we had come across some most break-neck places, and had one or two narrow escapes, which, at the time, one was hardly conscious of. The snow was wedged into the ravines like sheets of ice, and being most precipitous, and continuing to the very foot of the mountains, terminating in the numerous torrents which they fed, a single false step in crossing would have sent one rolling down, without a chance of stopping, to be dashed to pieces at the bottom. In this way, a couple of years before, two coolies and a shikàree had been killed, while shooting with an officer. F. and I generally crossed these places in the footsteps of the guides, or in holes cut by them for our feet with a hatchet; but the men themselves passed them with a dash, which only long practice and complete confidence could have imitated. During our halt we suffered a good deal from the sun, although the snow was only six inches off. In spite of the shade which our guides constructed for us out of mysterious portions of their dress, both our wrists and ankles were completely swollen and blistered before evening, while our faces and noses in particular began to assume the appearance so generally suggestive of Port wine and good living.

Our descent to the camp was a good march in itself, and we arrived there about five P.M. hot and tired, but quite ready for our mountain fare. On our road, we luckily discovered a quantity of young rhubarb, growing in nature's kitchen-garden, and pouncing on it, we devoted it to the celebration of our Sunday dinner.* We also saw a number of minaur, or jungle-fowl, something of the pheasant tribe; but they were so wild that nothing but slugs would secure them, and they entirely declined the honour of an invitation to our Sunday entertainment.

June 24.—We were not at all sorry to remember this morning, as the sun rose, that it was a day of rest, for after our last few days of work we were fully able to enjoy it. Amused ourselves exploring all about us, and picking wild flowers in memory of our camp. The commonest were wild pansy and forget-me-not, and the rhododendron grew in quantities. In the afternoon we made a muster of our standing provi-

* M. Jacquemont, in his "Letters from Kashmir and Thibet," carried away no doubt by the ardour of Botanical research, mentions having made a similar discovery, in the following glowing terms: —"The mountains here produce rhubarb; celestial happiness!"

sions, having only brought four days' supply, and seeing little chance of getting back for ten. The result was, that tea was reported low, potatoes on their last legs, and brandy in a declining state. Under these melancholy circumstances, we agreed to stop another day for shooting, and then march over the snows for Aliabad and Heerpore, to join our main body at the latter place. A road by Cheta Panee was declared impracticable for coolies, in consequence of the hardness of the snow; so we gave it up.

June 25.—All over the mountains again this morning before daybreak, and up to breakfast-time without seeing game. However, one of our sharp-sighted guides then detected markore, grazing at a long distance up the mountains; even through the glasses they were mere specks, and, to our unpractised eyes, very like the tufts and stones around them; but in all faith that our guides were right, off we started in pursuit. The first step was to lose all our morning's toil by plunging for a mile or so down a steep descent. After that being accomplished, up we went again, up and up an apparently interminable bank of snow, at an angle of about sixty degrees, and slippery as glass. At the summit, exhausted and completely out of breath, we did at last arrive, and from this our friends of the morning were expected to be within shot. Not a sign of a living creature appeared, however, to enliven the solitude around us, and we began to think that our guides were a little *too* clear-sighted this time, when what should suddenly come upon us but a solitary old markore, slowly and leisurely rounding a rugged point of rock below. We were all squatted in a bunch upon a space about as large as a good-sized towel; but, hidden as we thought ourselves, I could discern that our friend had evidently caught a glimpse of something which displeased him in his morning cogitations. Still, on he came, and just as he crossed a small field of snow, F. opened fire at him across the ravine: the ball struck just below his body, and, as he plunged forward, I followed with both barrels. On he went, however, and before another shot could be fired he was coolly looking down upon us from a terrace of inaccessible rocks, completely out of range. Nothing remained but to descend again, and this we accomplished very much more speedily, though perhaps not quite in such a graceful style as we had ascended. The shikàrees merely sat down on the inclined plane, and with a hatchet or a stick firmly pressed under the arm as a lever to regulate the pace, or a rudder to steer clear of rocks as occasion might require, down they went at a tremendous pace, until the slope was not sufficient to propel them further.

Our own wardrobe being limited in dimensions we declined adopting this mode of locomotion, and slipping and sliding along, soon accomplished the descent, in a less business-like but equally satisfactory manner. While taking the direction of our camp, we espied seven more animals, perched apparently upon a smooth face of rock; and after a short council of war off we started on a fresh stalk, down another descent, over more fields of snow, and up a place where a cat would have found walking difficult.

While accomplishing this latter movement, our guides detected two huge red bears, an enormous distance off, enjoying themselves in the evening air, and feeding and scratching themselves alternately, as they sauntered about in the breeze. Abandoning our present stalk, which was not promising, down we went again, and crossing about a mile and a half of broken ground, snow, rocks, &c., we reached a wood close to the whereabouts of our new game. F. and I, separating, had made the place by different routes, and just as I had caught sight of one enormous monster, F. and the shikàree appeared, just on the point of walking into his jaws. Having, by great exertion, prevented this catastrophe, we massed our forces, and taking off our hats, just as if we were stalking an unpopular landed proprietor in Tipperary, we crept up to within sixty yards of the unsuspicious monster, and fired both together. With a howl and a grunt, the huge mass doubled himself up, and rolled into the cover badly wounded. Being too dangerous a looking customer to follow directly, we reloaded and made a circuit above him; and after a short search, discovered him with his paws firmly clasped round a young tree. By way of finishing him, I gave him the contents of my rifle behind the ear, and we then rolled him down a ravine on to the snow beneath, where, a heavy storm of rain, hail, and thunder coming on, we left him alone in his glory. Putting our best legs foremost, we made for our camp, amid a pelting shower of hail like bullets and an incessant play of lightning around us, as we pushed our way along the frozen torrent. About five P.M. tired and drenched, we reached the camp, when we discovered that our tents, though extremely handy for mountain work, were not intended to keep out much rain, and that all our rugs, and other comforts, were almost in as moist a state as ourselves. During the entire night it continued to hail, rain, thunder, and lighten; and with the exception of the exact spots we were each lying on, there was not a dry place in the tent to take refuge in.

June 26.—After an exceedingly moist night, we made the most of a little sunshine by turning out all our property, and hanging it around us on stones and bushes to dry. After we had distinguished ourselves in this way, for a couple of hours, down came the rain again; and after stowing our half-dried goods, we assembled under a tree, and held a council of war as to our future movements. The rain had swelled the mountain torrents considerably, and the hail, lying on the old snow, had made it slippery as glass, so that we were obliged to give up the mountain pass we had agreed upon, and decided on a retreat to "Poshana," our present ground being fairly untenable. Sending off our tents and traps, and half-drowned servants, who were completely out of their element, we remained behind under the pines till the rain a little abated, and having secured the bear-skin for curing, we started off with our rear-guard for Poshana. The road was so slippery, that even with grass-shoes we could hardly keep from falling; and the snow we found as hard as ice, and proportionately difficult to cross. The consequence was, that in passing a steep incline with the guide, he slipped, and I followed his example, and down we both went like an engine and tender, the guide fishing about with his legs for obstacles, and I above him, endeavouring to use my pole as an anchor to bring us to.

Luckily, we both reached *terra firma* safely, after a perilous run, though at the same side we started from, and a long distance from our point of previous departure. On at length reaching the opposite side, we found a disconsolate coolie bemoaning himself and reckoning his bones, having also fallen down the snow, while a little further on we came upon the bhistie lamenting over a similar disaster. The latter functionary had also lost a valuable pot of virgin honey, which had only come up from Poshana the day before, and which we had not had time to see the inside of even, ere it was thus lost to us for ever, and made over as a poetical reparation to the bears of the country for the ruthless murder we had committed on one of their number. Found the hut at Poshana empty, and were glad to get into its shelter again. The rain seeming quite set in, we determined to discharge our shikàrees, and after paying them three rupees each for their week's work, we sent them away perfectly happy, with a few copper caps and a good character apiece.

June 27.—Left Poshana at five A.M., and

made for the Peer Punjal pass. A sharp struggle brought us to the summit, where we found a polygon tower erected, apparently as a landmark and also a resting-place for travellers to recover themselves after their exertions.* At the Cashmere side of the pass I had expected to see something of the far-famed valley, but nothing met the eye but a wild waste of land, bounded on all sides by snow, while a few straggling coolies toiled up towards us with some itinerant Englishman's baggage like our own.

This turned out to belong to a party returning to Sealkote, and we were rather elated by seeing among their possessions several enormous antlers, which promised well for sport at the other side of the valley. They turned out, however, to have been bought, and, as their owners informed us, there was no chance of meeting such game until October or November. About two miles down the pass we reached the old serai of Aliabad, and found the only habitable part of it in possession of a clergyman and a young Bengal artilleryman bound for the shooting-grounds we had just left. With much difficulty we obtained a few eggs, and a little milk with which we washed down the chupatties we had

* The Pass of the Peer Punjal is 13,000 feet above the level of the sea; the highest peak of the range being 15,000.

brought with us; but the coolies were so long getting over the path, that no signs of breakfast made their appearance until about two o'clock. At mid-day it came on to rain heavily, and we took up our quarters in a miserable den, with a flooring of damp rubbish and a finely carved stone window not very much in keeping with the rest of the establishment. Here we spent the day drearily enough, the prospect being confined to a green pool of water in the middle of the serai, around which the Pariah dogs contended with the crows for the dainties of offal scattered about. As soon as it was dark, we were glad enough to spread our waterproof sheets on the ground, and sleep as well as the thousands of tenants already in possession would allow us.

June 28.—Up at sunrise, and packed off our things down the mountain for Heerpore, where the main body of our possessions were concentrated.

Shortly after their departure it began to rain an Irish and Scotch combined mist, and after warming our toes and blinding our eyes over a wood fire for about three hours, in hopes of its clearing, we donned grass-shoes and, putting our best legs foremost, accomplished about thirteen miles of a most slippery path without a halt, except for the occasional purpose of adjusting our dilapidated shoes.

After the first five or six miles the path entered a beautifully-wooded valley, and at one spot, where two torrents joined their foaming waters at the foot of a picturesque old ivy-grown serai, the landscape was almost perfection. Passing this, we entered a thickly-shaded wood, studded with roses and jessamine, and peopled with wood-pigeons and nightingales, who favoured us with a morning concert as we passed. Crossing a wooden bridge over the torrent, we reached a fine grass country, and here the presence of a herd of cows told us we were near our destination. At Heerpore we found Mr. Rajoo located with all our belongings in a little wooden sort of squatter's cabin, where we were glad to take shelter out of the dripping rain. It reminded one strongly of Captain Cuttle's habitation and a ship's cabin together, and made one feel inclined to go on deck occasionally. It was on the whole, however, very comfortable, and seemed, after our late indifferent quarters, to be a perfect palace. After breakfast, we made inquiries as to our worldly affairs, and found that all were thriving with the exception of the potatoes, which had been taken worse on the road, and were already decimated by sickness. We added a sheep to our stock, for which we paid three shillings, and laid in a welcome supply of butter. The khidmutgar and bhistie, we found, had retailed the history of their many sorrows to the other servants, and, having expatiated most fully on the horrors they had endured among the snows and thunderstorms of the mountains, were promising themselves a speedy end to all their woes among the peace and plenty of the promised land of Cashmere.

June 29.—After some trouble in procuring coolies, we started at eleven in a shower of rain, and found ourselves gradually passing into the valley, and exchanging rocks and firs for groves of walnut; and moss and fern for the more civilized strawberry and the wild carnation. The strawberries, though small, had a delicious flavour, and we whiled away the time by gathering them as we passed. About two o'clock we reached the village of Shupayon, and here began to perceive a considerable change in the style of architecture from what we had been accustomed to; the flat mudden roof giving place to the sharply-pitched wooden one, thatched with straw, or coarsely *tiled* with wood.

Our halting-place we found, for the first time, to possess a staircase and upper story. A little square habitation it was, with a verandah all round it, and built entirely of wood. From this,

as the clouds lifted from the mountain-tops around, a most lovely view opened out before us.

Wherever the eye rested toward the mountains, the snow-capped peaks raised themselves up into the clear blue sky; while at our feet lay the far-famed valley, reaching towards the north, to the very base of the mountain range, and rising gradually and by a gentle slope to our halting-place, and so back to the pass from which we had just descended.

As the sun appeared to have come out again permanently, we took the opportunity of getting our tents and other property which had suffered from the wet out for a general airing.

June 30.—Marched about nine miles through fertile slopes of rice-fields, shaded by walnuts and sycamores, and found our halting-place situated in a serai, shrouded in mulberry and cherry trees, and with a charming little rivulet running through it, discoursing sweet music night and day. Our habitation was a baraduree, or summer-house, of wood, and having an upper room with trellised windows, where we spent the day very pleasantly. At dinner we had the first instalment of the land of promise, in the shape of a roly-poly pudding of fresh cherries, a thing to date from in our hitherto puddingless circumstances.

July 1.—Started at daybreak for our last march into the capital. The first appearance of the low part of the valley was rather disappointing, for there was nothing striking in the view; still, the country was extremely fertile, and its tameness was redeemed by the glorious mountain range, which bounded the valley in every direction, with its pure unsullied fringe of snow. Our path was occasionally studded with the most superb sycamores and lime-trees; and as we approached the town we entered a long avenue of poplars, planted as closely together as possible, and completely hiding all the buildings until close upon them. Passing through the grand parade-ground, we found a bustling throng of about four hundred Cashmeeries, with heavy packs beside them, waiting for an escort to take out supplies to the Maharajah's army, now on active service at a place called Girgit, in the mountains. The said army seemed to be fighting with nobody knew who, about nobody knew what; but report says that his Highness, having a number of troops wanting arrears of pay, sends them out periodically to contend with the hill tribes, by way of settlement in full of all demands.

Having engaged a boat's crew at Ramoon, we were, on arriving at the River Jhelum, which runs through the city, immediately inducted to the manners and customs of the place; and being safely deposited in a long flat-bottomed boat, with a mat roof and a prow about twelve feet out of the water, we were paddled across by our six new servants, and landed among a number of bungalows on the right bank, which were erected by the Maharajah for the reception of his English visitors. These are entirely of wood, of the rudest construction, and are built along the very edge of the river, which is here about a hundred yards broad.

We were received on landing by the Baboo and Moonshee, the native authorities retained by the

Maharajah for the convenience of his visitors; and learning from them that there were no bungalows vacant, we pitched our little camp under a shady grove of trees close by; and thus, in the capital of the land of poetry and promise, the far-famed paradise of the Hindoo, we brought our wanderings to an end for the present, and gave ourselves and our retainers a rest from all the toils and troubles of the road.

PART III.

A HALT IN THE VALLEY.

BEING fairly settled in our quarters, we were not long in putting our new staff of dependants into requisition; and, taking to our boat, sallied forth to get a general view of the city of Sirinugger.* Finding, however, a review of the army going on, we stopped at the parade-ground to witness the interesting ceremony. The troops we found drawn up in lines, forming the sides of a large square, and dressed in what his Highness Rumbeer Singh believes confidently to be the *English costume.* As far as one could see, however, the sole foundation for this belief lay in the fact of their

* Supposed to designate "The City of the Sun;" Sûrya meaning in Sanscrit "the Sun," and Nugger "a City."

all wearing trousers! These were certainly the only articles of their equipment that could in any way be called English in style; and they bore, after all, but a slender resemblance to the corresponding habiliments of the true Briton.

The head-dress, generally speaking, was a turban. One regiment, however, had actually perpetrated a parody on the English shako—a feat which I had always hitherto considered absolutely impossible.

The cavalry were mounted upon tattoos, or native ponies, and wore white trousers, with tight straps, which rendered them for the time being the most miserable of their race.

A few of them had imitations of Lancer caps, some had boots, some slippers, some spurs, others none; some had wondrous straps of tape and cord, others wore their trousers up to their knees; but one and all were entirely uniform in looking completely ill at ease and out of their element in their borrowed would-be-English plumage. Just as we had finished taking a general view of the army, the Maharajah appeared upon the stage, dressed in a green-and-gold embroidered gown and turban and tight silk pantaloons, mounted on a grey caparisoned Arab steed. After riding round the lines with his retinue, he came up, and we were presented in due form; and after asking us if we had come from Allahabad, and expressing his opinion that it was a long way off, in which we entirely concurred with him, he shook hands in English style; and, taking his seat in a chair which was placed for him, we collected ourselves around, and, similarly seated, prepared to inspect the marching past of his highness's redoubtables. Before this began, however, the Maharajah's little son made his appearance, dressed in all respects like his papa, with miniature sword and embroidered raiment; and to him we were also introduced in form. During the marching past, I congratulated myself upon being several seats distant from his highness's chair, for the effect was so absurd that it was almost impossible to preserve that dignity and composure which the occasion demanded.

The marching was in slow time, and the step being fully thirty-six inches the fat little dumpy officers nearly upset themselves in their efforts to keep time, and at the same time prevent their slippers from deserting on the line of march; while, in bringing their swords to the salute, they did it with a swing which was suggestive of their throwing away their arms altogether. Besides artillery, five regiments of infantry and two of cavalry marched past—in all, little over 2,000 men—colours flying and bands playing

"Home, sweet home!" After this the *irregulars* began to appear; and although the first part of the army might have almost deserved the name, these put them completely in the shade. One colonel had a pair of enormous English gold epaulettes and a turban; another a black embroidered suit, with white tape straps, and slippers; and as for the men, there were no two of them dressed alike, while in the way of arms, each pleased his own particular fancy also. A long gun over the shoulder was the most popular weapon; but each had, in addition, a perfect armoury fastened in his girdle: pistols with stocks like guns, daggers and even blunderbusses made their appearance; and the general effect, as the crowd galloped independently past, dressed in their many-coloured turbans and flowing apparel, was most picturesque. As soon as the last of the flags and banners and prancing horses had gone past, the Maharajah set us the example of rising, and mounting his grey steed, cantered off in state, surrounded by the crowd of dusky parasites, arrayed in gold and jewels, who formed his court.

His Highness appeared to be about thirty-eight years old, and was as handsome a specimen of a native as I had ever seen. He wore a short jet-black beard, and mustachios turned up from the corners of his mouth, and reaching, in two long twists, nearly to his eyes. He appeared absent and thoughtful, which, considering the low state of his exchequer, was perhaps not to be wondered at.* His English visitors spend a good deal of money every summer in his kingdom; and for this reason alone, he is anxious enough to cultivate their acquaintance, and gives naches, or native dances, and champaigne dinners periodically to amuse them. He presents, also, an offering to each traveller that arrives, and we in due course received two sheep, two fowls, and about fourteen little earthen dishes containing rice, butter, spices, eggs, flour, fruit, honey, sugar, tea, &c., all of which were laid at the door of our tent, with great pomp and ceremony, by a host of attendants.

After the review, we took boat again and

* Cashmere seems to have been regarded for many ages merely as a source of wealth to its absentee lords or present governors, and to have suffered more than ever, since falling under the dominion of Hindoo rulers.

Of the first of this dynasty, who subdued and took possession of the valley in the year 1819, Vigne remarks, in his Travels, "Runjeet Singh assuredly well knew that the greater the prosperity of Kashmír, the stronger would be the inducement to invasion by the East India Company. 'Après moi le déluge' has been his motto, and its ruin has been accelerated not less by his rapacity than by his political jealousy, which suggested to him at any cost the merciless removal of its wealth and the reckless havoc he has made in its resources."

paddled down the stream to look at the town, and a quainter and more picturesque-looking old place it would be hard to conceive. The houses are built entirely of wood, of five and six stories, and overhanging the river, and are as close as possible to each other, except where here and there interspersed with trees. Communication is kept up between the banks by means of wooden rustic bridges, built on enormous piles of timber, laid in entire trees, crossing each other at equal distances. Not a single straight line is to be seen in any direction—the houses being dilapidated and generally out of the perpendicular; and everywhere the river view is bounded by the snow-capped ranges of mountain, which, towards the north, appear to rise almost from the very water's edge.

July 2.—Taking the Q. M. G. as a guide, we sallied out immediately after breakfast to explore the land part of this Eastern Venice. Entering at the city gate, on the left bank of the river, near the Maharajah's palace, we walked past a row of trumpery pop-guns, on green and red carriages, and so through the most filthy and odoriferous bazaar I ever met with, till we reached the residence of Saifula Baba, the great shawl merchant of Sirinugger. Here we found a noted shawl fancier inspecting the stock, and were inducted to the mysteries of the different fabrics. Some that we saw were of beautiful workmanship, but dangerous to an uninitiated purchaser. They ranged from 300 to 1,000 rupees generally, but could be ordered to an almost unlimited extent of price. After inspecting a quantity of Pushmeena and other local manufactures, Mr. Saifula Baba handed us tea and sweetmeats, after the fashion of his country; and we adjourned to the abode of a worker in papier maché, where we underwent a second edition of tea and sweetmeats, and inspected a number of curiosities. The chief and only beauty of the work was in the strangeness of the design; and some of the shawl patterns, reproduced on boxes, &c., were pretty in their way, but as manufacturers of papier maché simply, the Cashmeeries were a long way behind the age.

On reaching home, we found that the Maharajah had sent his salaam, together with the information that he was going to give a nach and dinner, to which we were invited.

July 3.—After continuing our explorations of Sirinugger, we repaired, about seven o'clock, to the Maharajah's palace, where we were received by a guard of honour of sixty men and four officers, the latter in gold embroidered dresses,

W.H.K. Del. Hanhart lith.

VIEW IN SIRINUGGER.

and hung all over with ear-rings and finery of divers sorts and kinds.

Ascending the stairs, we were met by the *Deewan*, or prime minister, who conducted us into an open sort of terrace over the river, where we found the Maharajah with the few English officers already arrived seated on either side of him, and the nach-girls, about twenty in number, squatted in a semicircle opposite them. Standing behind his Highness were colonels of regiments and native dignitaries of all sorts, dressed in cloth of gold and jewels, and in every variety and hue of turban and appointments. A number of these were Sikhs; and magnificent-looking men they were, with their flowing dress and fiercely-twisted whiskers and mustachios. The nach-girls, too — a motley group — were attired in all the hues of the rainbow, and with the white-robed musicians behind them, awaited in patience the signal to commence. In singular contrast to this glittering throng, which formed the court, were the guests whom the Maharajah, on this occasion, delighted to honour. The British officer appeared generally in the national but uncourtly costume of a shooting-jacket! and though some few had donned their uniform, and one rejoiced in the traditional swallow-tail of unmistakeable civilization, neither the one nor the other contrasted favourably in point of grace with the Cashmerian rank and fashion.

After shaking hands with his Highness, who prides himself upon his English way of accomplishing that ceremony, and does it by slipping into one's hand what might be taken for a dying flat fish, we took our seats, and the dancing began shortly afterwards. Though on a more magnificent scale than anything I had seen of the kind before, the programme was flat and insipid enough. The ladies came out two and two, and went through a monotonous die-away movement, acting, dancing, and singing all at the same time, and showing off their red-stained palms and the soles of their feet to the best advantage. Some of the women were very pretty, but very properly they modified their charms by dressing in the most unbecoming manner possible. Their head-dress was a little cloth of gold and silver cap hung all round with pendent ornaments, and these were becoming enough, but the remainder of the dress was much more trying. A short body of shot silk was separated by a natural border from a gauze skirt, which hung down perfectly straight and innocent of fulness, and allowed a pair of white pyjamas to appear beneath. These were fastened tightly round the ancles, which were encircled by little bunches of the tinkling bells, which the ladies make such use of in the dance. Round the shoulders comes a filmy scarf of various colours, which also plays a prominent part in all their movements, and answers in its way to the fan of more accomplished Western belles.

After each couple had gone through the whole of their performances, they used to squat themselves down suddenly in the most ungraceful style imaginable, and were then relieved by another pair of artistes from the group.

One lady, in addition to the dance, favoured us with "the Marseillaise" with the French words, being occasionally prompted by the head of the orchestra, who nearly worked himself into a frenzy while accompanying the dancers with both vocal and instrumental music at the same time. The Maharajah himself was plainly dressed in white robes, with a pair of pale-green striped silk pantaloons fitting his legs like stockings from the knee down, and terminating in a pair of English socks, of which he seemed immensely proud. His turban was of the palest shade of green, and (in strong contrast to the rest of his court) without any ornament whatever. The little heir to the throne—a nice little blackamoor of about eight years of age—was, like his father, perched upon a chair, and arrayed in a green and gold turban, pants, and socks, with the addition of a velvet gold-embroidered coat, while round his neck were three or four valuable necklaces, one of pear-shaped emeralds of great size and beauty. After a few dances the doors of the banqueting-room were thrown open, and his Highness led the way into dinner with the commissioner. On entering, we found a capital dinner laid out English fashion, and with a formidable army of black bottles ranged along the table. The Maharajah, however, had disappeared, and we were left to feed without a host. The grandees, meanwhile, remained outside, and still enjoyed the dances, ranging themselves upon their haunches in front of the rows of chairs which not one among them would have dared to trust himself in for either love or money. Considering that our entertainer was a Hindoo, and that his dinner-giving appliances were limited, each person having to bring his own knife, fork, spoon, and chair, we fared very well, and after having drunk his health, again assembled in the court, where we found Rumbeer Singh still occupied with the wearisome nach, and reattired in a gorgeous dress of green velvet and gold. After a short stay he got up, and we all followed his example, glad enough to bring the entertainment to an end, and betake ourselves to our boats. At the stairs there was a desperate encounter with innumerable boatmen, each boat having six, eight, or ten sailors, and all being equally anxious to uphold the credit of their craft by being the first to land their masters safe at home. We were fortunate enough to reach our own at once, and, with a shouting crew, away we dashed up the river, leaving the others struggling, fighting, and flourishing their paddles in the air, in a way which was more suggestive of an insurrection scene in Masaniello than the departure of guests from a peaceable gentleman's own hall door on the night of an evening party.

On the stairs there was an extraordinary assemblage of slippers, which seemed to hold the same relative position that hats and cloaks do in more enlightened communities—that is, the good ones were taken by the owners of the bad, and the proprietors of the bad ones were fain to make the best of the exchange. Next morning our khidmutgar came up with a most doleful countenance and presented to our notice a pair of certainly most ill-favoured slippers, which a fellow true-believer had *inadvertently* substituted for a pair of later date. The lost ones had, in fact, only recently been received from the bootmaker; and the blow was difficult to bear with resignation, even by the saintliest follower of Islam—a reputation which our retainer came short of by a very long way indeed.

July 4.—Having an accumulation of letters to answer, we devoted the day to writing—merely enjoying a little *otium cum dig.*—in the evening, reclining in our boat while serenaded by the crew of boatmen.

July 5.—Walked up, before daybreak, to the Tukht e Sûleeman, or Solomon's throne, "the mountainous Portal," which Moore speaks of in *Lalla Rookh*, and which forms the most striking landmark in the valley.*

From the summit there was a curious view of the multitudinous wooden houses and the sinuous windings of the river, which could alone be obtained from such a bird's-eye point of inspection. An old temple at the top was in the hands of the Hindoo faction, being dedicated to the goddess Mahadewee, and in charge of it I found two of the dirtiest fukeers, or religious mendi-

* The Tukt-i-Suliman, an old Hindoo temple, the throne of Solomon the magnificent, the prophet, the mighty magician, whom all pious Mussulmans believe to have been carried through the air on a throne supported by Dives or Afrites, whom the Almighty had made subservient to His will.—VIGNE. The summit stands 1,000 feet above the level of the plain, and the date of its erection is believed to be 220 B.C. *Vide* Appendix A.

SOLOMON'S THRONE

cants, I ever had the pleasure of meeting. One was lying asleep, with his feet in a heap of dust and ashes, and the other was listlessly sitting, without moving a muscle, warming himself in the morning sun. Both were almost naked, and had their bodies and faces smeared with ashes and their hair long and matted. They appeared to have arrived at a state of almost entire abstraction, and neither of them even raised his eyes or seemed to be in the slightest degree aware of my presence, although I took a sketch of one of them, and stared at both, very much as I would have done at some new arrival of animals in the Zoological Gardens.

In the evening we went again to Saifula Baba's and visited the workrooms, where we were much astonished by the quickness with which the people worked the intricate shawl patterns with a simple needle, and no copy to guide them.

The first stages of the work are not very promising, but the finished result, when pressed and rolled and duly exhibited by that true believer Saifula Baba, in his snowy gown and turban, was certainly in every way worthy of its reputation.

Returning home, we visited a garden where any of the English visitors who die in the valley are buried—the Maharajah presenting a Cashmere shawl, in some instances, to wrap the body.

in. There were about eight or ten monuments built of plaster, with small square slabs for inscriptions. One of these was turned topsy-turvey, which was not to be wondered at, for a native almost always holds English characters upside-down when either trying to decipher them himself or when holding them to be read by others.

July 6.—In the early morning I ascended to the throne of Solomon, in order to get a sketch of the Fort of Hurree Purbut, and in the afternoon we repaired to the lake behind the town, where there was a grand Mela or fair, on the water, to which the Maharajah and all his court went in state. The lake is beautifully situated at the foot of the mountains, and was covered so densely in many parts with weed and water-plants that it bore quite the appearance of a floating garden; and as the innumerable boats paddled about, with their bright and sunny cargoes, talking and laughing and enjoying themselves to their heart's content, the scene began to identify itself in some measure with Moore's description of the "Sunny lake of cool Cashmere," and its "Plane-tree isle reflected clear," although the poet's eyes had never rested on either lake or isle. Putting poetry on one side, however, for the present, we made our way to the extremity of the lake, in order to pay a

HURREE PURBUT.

visit to his Highness's gaol, where we were received by a very civil gaoler, equipped with a massive sword and dilapidated shield. We found 110 prisoners in the place, employed generally in converting dhan into chawul, or, in other words, clearing the rice-crop. There was also a mill for mustard oil, and the most primitive machine for boring fire-arms ever invented, both worked by water-power. The prison dress was uniform in the extreme: it consisted simply of a suit of heavy leg-irons and nothing more!

After seeing the fair, we paddled across through a perfect water-meadow to the Shalimar gardens, where we found the Rajah and his suite just taking their departure. The vista on entering the gardens was extremely pretty: four waterfalls appear at the same moment, sending a clear sheet of crystal water over a broad stone slab, and gradually receding from sight in the wooded distance. A broad canal runs right through the gardens, bridged at intervals by summer-houses and crossed by carved and quaintly-fashioned stepping-stones. At the extremity there is a magnificent baradurree of black marble, which looks as if it had been many centuries in existence, and had originally figured in some very different situation. The pillars were entire to a length of seven feet, and were highly polished from the people leaning against them. Around this, in reservoirs of water, were about two hundred fountains, all spouting away together, and on one side a sheet of the most perfectly still water I ever saw. It appeared exactly like a large looking-glass, and it was impossible to discern where the artificial bank which inclosed it either began or terminated.

In these gardens it was that Selim, or Jehangeer the son of Akbar, used to spend so many of his days with the far-famed Noor Jehan in the beginning of the seventeenth century, and here was the scene of their reconciliation, as related by Feramorz to Lalla Rookh ere he revealed himself to her as her future lord, the king of Bucharia. From these founts and streams it was that the fair Persian sought to entice her lord, with "Fly to the desert, fly with me!"

> "When breathing, as she did, a tone
> To earthly lutes and lips unknown;
> With every chord fresh from the touch
> Of Music's spirit,—t'was too much!"

"The light of the universe" overcomes even the "conqueror of the world." Thinking it, after all, wiser to kiss and be friends than be sulky, he surrenders at discretion:—

> "And, happier now for all their sighs,
> As on his arm her head reposes,
> She whispers him with laughing eyes,
> 'Remember, love, the Feast of Roses!'"

Leaving the favourite haunts of the "magnificent son of Akbar," we crossed the lake again to see the Maharajah inspect a party of about 2,000 soldiers, who were departing for the war at Girgit. Nothing in the way of supplies being procurable near the scene of action, the greater part of the review was taken up by the marching past of a horde of Cashmeree and mountain porters, heavily laden with the sinews of war. According to report, the pay of the army here is about five shillings per mensem, with a ration of two pounds of rice per diem.

In the evening, the number of boats congregated on the lake was marvellous. All were perfectly crammed with Cashmerian pleasure-seekers; but the turbaned faithful, in spite of the pressure, in no way lost their dignity, but with pipes and coffee enjoyed themselves in apparently entire unconsciousness of there being a soul on the lake beside themselves. The most wonderful sight, however, was the immense crowd of many-coloured turbans congregated on shore, witnessing the departure of the Cashmerian Guards; and as they thronged the green slopes in thousands, they gave one quite the idea of a mass of very violent-coloured flowers blooming together in a garden. On our way home we had great jostling, and even fighting, in order to maintain our position among the crowds of boats, the result of which was that our crew managed to break two paddles in upholding the dignity and respectability of their masters. The Maharajah himself, however, gave us the go-by in great style, in a long quaint boat, propelled by thirty-six boatmen, and built with a broad seat towards the bows, in shape like the overgrown body of a gig in indifferent circumstances, on which his Highness reclined. By his side was the little prince, in glorious apparel, while half a dozen of his court, arrayed in spotless white, appeared like so many snow-drifts lying at his feet.

July 7.—Made our arrangements to-day for a trip by water to the Wûler Lake, and spent the afternoon in inspecting the jeweller's and other shops in the city. The native workmen appear to engrave cleverly both on stone and metal, and some of their performances would bear comparison with any European workmanship of a similar kind. They also work in filagree silver, charging about sixpence in every two shillings' worth of silver for their labour.

About nine P.M. we took to our boats; F. and I occupying one together, in which we stowed bedding, dressing-things, &c. while the cooking apparatus and servants occupied the other. Passed the night very comfortably, and found the situation most conducive to sleep, as we glided gently along with the stream.

July 8.—Awoke to find an innumerable swarm of mosquitoes buzzing about our habitation, and apparently endeavouring to carry it off bodily. Letting down, however, the muslin curtains, which the foreknowledge of the faithful Q. M. G. had provided us with, we succeeded in puzzling the enemy for the time being. About eight o'clock, the fleet came to an anchor at a luxuriant little island at the entrance of the great lake; to all appearance, however, it might have been situated in a meadow, for we had to force our way to it through a perfect plain of green water-plants, whose slimy verdure covered the face of the lake for miles around. It was wooded by mulberry trees, very prettily entwined with wild vines, and in the midst were the remains of an old Musjid, in which we discovered a slab of black marble, covered with a beautifully carved inscription in Arabic, and appearing as if it had not always held the ignoble position which it now occupied. Scattered about the island, also, were many scraps of columns and carved stones, which gave evidence of having belonged to some ancient temple or palace. While thus surveying our island, we were pestered to death by swarms of prodigious mosquitoes, for which the Wûler Lake is justly celebrated, and during breakfast the eating was quite as much on their side as ours; so that we were glad to weigh anchor, and with our curtains tightly tucked in around us, we floated away, in lazy enjoyment of climate and scenery, towards the centre of the lake. As we cleared the margin of the water-plants, we found ourselves on a glassy surface, extending away towards the west as far as the eye could see, and bordered on all sides by gorgeous mountains and ranges of snow. Around the edges of the lake a sunny mirage was playing tricks with the cattle and the objects on the banks, and as we glided lazily on with the stream, and the splashing paddles, and even the foiled mosquitoes, made music about us, we began to enter more into the spirit of our situation, and to appreciate the peculiar beauties of the "sunny lake of cool Cashmere," with the *dolce far niente* existence which of right belongs to it. About one o'clock we reached Sompoor, at the Baramoula extremity of the lake, and as it came on to blow a little, it was not too soon: our boats were totally unadapted for anything rougher than a mill-pond, and in the ripple excited by the small puffs of wind, I had the misfortune to ship what was, under the circumstances, a heavy sea, and so sacrificed the prospects of a dry lodging for the night. Sompoor we found a picturesque but dirty village, with promise of good fishing in the river below it. We unfortunately had no tackle, but the boatmen succeeded in catching five or six good fish with a hook baited with a mulberry only: a very favourite article of consumption, apparently, among the Cashmerian little fishes.

Dropping down the river, we dined on the bank among the mulberry trees, and I afterwards essayed to take a sketch of the village; such a firm and determined body of mosquitoes, however, immediately fell upon me, that, after a short but unsuccessful combat, I was fairly put to flight, and Sompoor remained undrawn. We passed the night above the town, ready for an early start in the morning.

July 9.—Left our moorings before sunrise, and halted about eight A.M. at a little island stacked with elephant-grass, where, after as good a swim as the tangled weeds would permit, we breakfasted pleasantly under the trees.

From this point we adopted a new mode of progression, the boatmen towing us from the bank; and the motion was a great improvement on the paddling system, except that it had a tendency to set one to sleep altogether. Reached Sirinugger, and our camp again, at four P.M.

July 10.—Paid Saifula Baba, the shawl merchant, a visit to-day, in order to get a bill of exchange on Umritsur cashed. Found him just going out to Mosque, in his snow-white robe and turban, cleanly-shaved pate, and golden slippers. Not having any money, he promised us a hundred rupees of the Maharajah's coinage to go on with. These nominal rupees are each value 10 annas, or 1*s.* 3*d.*, the most chipped and mutilated objects imaginable. On one face of the coin are the letters I. H. S. stamped, a strange enough device for a heathen or any other mint to have adopted. While floating about the Eastern Venice, we discovered a number of finely-cut old blocks of stone in the built-up wall which bounded the river; and on inspecting the place, we came upon an ancient Mussulman cemetery and ruined Musjid, in which there were some very antique-looking carvings, which apparently had commenced life elsewhere than on Mussulman ground. The graveyard, however, was itself extremely old, although many of the turbaned and lettered tombstones of the faithful were in perfect preservation. All began with the "La Ulah ila Ullah," or "B'ism Ullah,"* with which everything connected with a Mussulman does commence, either in life or death.

All through the city one can trace the remains of some much more ancient structure in the huge blocks of carved stone which are scattered about among their more plebeian brethren, and serve to form with them, in humble forgetfulness of past grandeur, the foundations of the lofty rattletrap but picturesque wooden structures which line both sides of the river and form the city of Cashmere in the year of grace 1860.

Some of these houses, as one looks into the narrow lanes leading to the river and sees them in profile, are apparently in the last stage of dissolution, leaning out of the perpendicular and overtopping their lower stories and foundations in a way that would put even the leaning tower of Pisa to shame. One six-storied house, of long experience in this crooked world, had made the most wonderful efforts to redeem his character and to recover his equilibrium by leaning the contrary way aloft from what he did below. Poor fellow! he had been but badly conducted in his youth, and was nobly endeavouring to

* "There is no God but God;" "In the name of God."

correct his ways in a mossy and dilapidated old age. The tracery of much of the wood-work carvings, and particularly of the windows, varies greatly, and in some places is so minute that it requires close inspection to find out the design.

Of these the Zenana windows of the Maharajah's palace are about the finest specimens; but as there is no way of approaching them closely, it is impossible to make out their details.

July 11.—Started this evening by water for Islamabad, the ancient capital of Cashmere.

We made a slight change in our arrangements, rather for the better, by hiring a large boat for ourselves and handing our own over to the servants and culinary department in general.

July 12.—Found ourselves not very far on our road on awakening this morning, the night having been very dark, the current strong against us, and the sailors lazy.

Another cause of delay also, if these were insufficient, was, that the proprietor of the boat dropped his turban overboard, with two rupees in the folds of it, and the old lady his spouse had stopped the fleet for at least an hour to cry over the misfortune. Before breakfast we had a swim, and found ourselves only just able to make way against the stream. Breakfasted on the river bank, under the trees, and surrounded by rocky snow-capped mountains. Reading, scribbling, and eating apricots brought us to about an hour before sunset, when F. and I landed and went ahead to pick out a spot for a dining-room for ourselves. In the search, we passed through orchards and gardens innumerable, and finally decided upon a grove of magnificent sycamores on the river bank, where we laid out our table just as the sun went down. Within view was a picturesque old wooden bridge, on the mossy tree-formed piles of which the bushes were growing, as if quite at home, and hanging gracefully over the flowing river.

July 13.—Found ourselves at sunrise at the end of our boat journey, bathed in the river, and started for Islamabad, about half a kos off.

On the bank we found three other travellers encamped, and leaving them fast asleep, we

pushed ahead and took possession of the baraduree. This we found a charming little place in a garden, full of ponds of sacred fish, with old carved stones scattered about, belonging to the Hindoo mythology. Through one corner of an upper tank a stream of crystal water flowed in from the mountain which rose perpendicularly behind it—the water welling up from below in a constant and abundant stream. Round this corner were some most grotesque stones; and here the sacred fish were assembled in such shoals as to jostle each other almost out of the water; but whether they were attracted by the fresh supply of water or the sacred images, covered as they were with votive offerings of milk and rice, flowers, &c., the fish or the Brahmins alone can tell.

Tradition states that an infidel Christian officer once killed three of these fish, and having eaten one of them, died shortly after. Putting their sanctity out of the question, however, the little creatures are so tame and so numerous that few people would be inclined either to kill or to eat them. While feeding them with bread, I could have caught any number with my hand; and holding a piece of tough crust under water, it was amusing to feel them tugging and hauling at it, making occasional snaps at one's fingers in their efforts. They were generally about half a pound in weight.

Our baradurree was built of wood, in the usual

style, with latticed windows of various designs, and having one room overhanging the stream which ran through the centre of the house from the sacred tanks. Directly below the place we occupied was a little waterfall, which conversed pleasantly day and night; and by taking up a loose plank in the floor we could see as well as hear it. Learning that there were some ruins in the neighbourhood, supposed to have existed from before the birth of our Saviour, we started in the afternoon for a place called Bowūn, or more popularly Mutton, about two and a half kos off.

The sun to-day we found very hot in this same valley of coolness, its rays coming down on the backs of our heads in a very searching and inquisitive manner. Along the entire path there were running streams in every direction: and what with these and the magnificent sycamores and walnut-trees which shaded us as we walked, our opinions of the beauty of the country got a considerable rise. The path from the Peer Punjal Pass by which we entered appears to be the worst point of view from which to see the valley. From either the Peshawur or Murree roads the effect is much finer; and from the north-east, from which direction it is perhaps seldomer seen than any other, it looks greener and more beautiful than from either of the other points.

At Mutton we found our three lazy friends of the morning, encamped under the trees reading green railway-novels, and evidently very much puzzled how to kill time. Beyond a tank teeming with sacred fishes, there appeared nothing whatever to be seen here. Taking warning from this, we thought it not worth while proceeding to Bamazoo, where we were told there were caves; but, treating the fishes to a small coin's worth of Indian maize, we retraced our steps and diverged about a kos off the Islamabad road to Pandau. Here we were rewarded by coming suddenly upon a magnificent old Cyclopeian ruin of grey stone, bearing, from a little distance, the appearance rather of an ancient Christian Church—such as may be seen occasionally in Ireland—than of a heathen place of worship. On entering, we found a number of ancient carvings on the massive stone walls, but they were much worn, and the designs to us were unintelligible. Some of them were like the Hindoo divinities, while others were more like Christian devices, such as cherubims, &c. Altogether, it puzzled us completely as to its origin; but there was no doubt whatever as to its having existed from an extremely ancient date; and from its general style, as well as the absence of any similitude to any other place of heathen worship we have met, we set it down in our own minds as most probably a temple to the Sun.* Most of the figures, as far as their worn state would allow one to judge, appeared to be female; and there was an entire absence of any symbol at all resembling a cross. Many of the huge pillars had been eaten away as if they were of wood, by the combined effects of wind and weather; but hands had also been at work, as pieces of the decorations and figures appeared scattered about in every direction.

Passing through the town of Islamabad on our return, we went into some of the houses to see the people at work at the loom-made shawls. Very hard-working and intricate business it seemed to be, and very hard and *Manchestery* the production looked to my eye, far inferior to the hand-made shawl, though not generally considered so.

I tried to negotiate a shawl with the overseer, but he assured me that the pieces were all made separately, and were sent in to the merchant at

* This was written without being aware that the native name of Mutton is a corruption of Martund, by which name the temple is also designated.

The meaning of Martund being in Sanscrit "the Sun," additional grounds have thus been furnished for determining the origin of the ruin. Vide Appendix A.

W. H. K. Del.

Hanhart, lith.

MARTUND.

Sirinugger to be put together, and that he in fact had nothing whatever to do with the sale of them.

In the evening we dined at a fashionably late hour, and were lulled to sleep by the simple music of our domesticated waterfall.

July 14.—Started at daybreak for Atchabull, three and a half kos off towards the north-east. The baraduree we found situated in the middle of a large reservoir, in a beautiful but half-ruined garden; and here, the commissariat being unusually late in arriving, we took the edge off our appetites with a quantity of small apricots, red plums, cherries, &c.

While exploring the gardens, we found, among other remains of grandeur, a Humaam, or hot-bath room, which was in very good preservation, and had probably in its day been honoured by the fair presence of Noor Jehan, with whom Atchabull was a favourite resort, and who has been, at one time or another, over all these gardens, during her lord's visit to the valley.

About thirty yards from the house, at the base of an almost perpendicular hill, were the great sources of interest which the place possesses—viz., a number of springs of ice-cold water, bubbling up to a height of two or three feet above the surrounding water level, and forming three separate rivers: one in the centre which expanded round our house, and one on either side. Around were fruit-trees of all sorts and kinds, and from every quarter came the gurgling sound of rushing water mingled with the singing of innumerable birds. Here sweetly indeed do the "founts of the valley fall;" and their number and beauty, as well as the purity of the clear and crystal streams which they pour over the length and breadth of the land, it is which forms one of its chief and pleasantest features, and has, no doubt, mainly contributed to its reputation as a terrestrial paradise. To the abundance of these streams the inhabitants are indebted for the crops of waving rice which spread their delicately-green carpetting over the entire valley; the purity of the waters give to the silks the brightness of their dyes and to their shawls their fame; and from its virtues also the love-lighted eyes are supposed to derive their far-famed lustre. No wonder, therefore, that to the Hindoo at least, "Cashmere is all holy land." From his sun-burnt plains and his home by the muddy banks of his sacred Ganges, he can form but a small conception of these cooling streams and shady pleasures. Should he happen to read the glowing descriptions of Lalla Rookh, and be perhaps led to reflect that—

"If woman can make the worst wilderness dear,
What a heaven she must make of Cashmere!"

He no doubt ejaculates "Wa, wa!" in admiration of the poetry of the West, and thinks complacently of the partner of his joys as all his fancy painted her. His highest flights of imagination, however, probably fail to transplant him very far beyond the actual wilderness which bounds his mortal vision, while

Pudmawutee and Oonmadinee, as here depicted by his own artistic skill, present, in all their loveliness of form and feature, his best conceptions

of ideal worth and beauty. No wonder, therefore, that the reality of

> "Those roses, the brightest that earth ever gave,
> Those grottoes and gardens and fountains so clear!"

and above all of—

> "Those love-lighted eyes that hang over their wave,"*

should shed its influence largely on his imagination, and that, in contrast to his own dry and

* On this subject a good deal of difference of opinion seems to exist, and from Moore's descriptions of the furniture of his terrestrial paradise, which have added so much to the fame of the valley,

dusty native plains, Cashmere should well be called the Hindoo's Paradise.

July 15.—Marched at dawn for Vernagh, a distance of eight kos, rather over a Sabbath-day's journey. Here we had to wait a considerable time for our breakfast, the cook being an indifferent pedestrian and the day a very hot one. The baradurree was curiously built, close to an octagon tank, the water from which ran at a great pace through an arch in the middle of the house.* The tank was supplied with water in

it appears probable that his "muse," thinking it useless to search abroad for materials which existed in abundance at home, supplied him with what he supposed to be Eastern celestial creations, entirely from his native shores. Vigne, however, says, "I do not think that the beauty of the Kashmirian women has been overrated. They are, of course, wholly deficient in the graces and fascinations derivable from cultivation and accomplishment; but for mere uneducated eyes, I know of none that surpass those of Kashmir." On the other hand, M. Jacquemont, who found "celestial happiness" in a plant of rhubarb, is unable to discover any beauty whatever in the Cashmerian ladies, and has no patience with his neighbour's little flights of fancy in depicting their perfections. "Moore," he writes, in his "Letters from India," "is a perfumer, and a liar to boot. Know that I have never seen anywhere such hideous witches as in Cashmere. The female race is remarkably ugly." Instead of adding to such conflicting evidence, I have endeavoured to subpœna a credible witness to speak for herself; and the right of private judgment being thus reserved to the reader, Gûlabie will no doubt be charitably dealt with, and will find her proper position somewhere within the limits of a "hideous witch" and a "celestial being."

* This place is mentioned in the "Tûzûk Jehangeery," or "Pre-

great volume, but from no apparent source, and was filled with fine fish, all sacred, and as fat as butter, from the plentiful support they receive from the devout among the Hindoos, not to mention the unbelieving travellers, who also supply them for amusement. The tank itself, the natives informed us, was bottomless, and it really appeared to be so; for from the windows of the baradurree, some fifty feet over the water, we could see the sides stretching back as they de-

cepts of Jehangeer," in a way which shows that the Conqueror of the World had not included himself among his victories.

The name appears on a Persian inscription as Wurnagh, but is called by the natives Vernagh, and is mentioned by Jehangeer in his journal as Tirnagh :—

"The source of the river Bhet (Jhelum)* lies in a fountain in Cashmeer, named Tirnagh, which, in the language of Hindostan, signifies a snake—probably some large snake had been seen there. During the lifetime of my father (Akbar) I went twice to this fountain, which is about twenty kos from the city of Cashmere. Its form is octagonal, and the sides of it are about twenty yards in length.

"I accompanied my father to this spot during the season of flowers. In some places the beds of saffron-flowers extend to a kos. Their appearance is best at a distance, and when they are plucked they emit a strong smell. My attendants were all seized with a headache, and though I was myself at the time intoxicated with liquor, I felt also my head affected I inquired of the brutal Cashmeerians who were employed in plucking them, what was their condition, and they replied that they never had a headache in their lifetime."

---

* The Jhelum is called in Cashmere, Behat—a contraction of the Sanscrit *Vedasta*, which the Greeks slightly altered to Hydaspes.

scended, and losing themselves in the clear water, which looked, from the intensity of its blue, both deep and treacherous to an unlimited extent. The water, too, was so intensely, icily cold, that an attempt to swim across it would have been a dangerous undertaking, and neither F. nor I could summon courage to jump in. We, however, bathed in the stream which ran out of the

inexhaustible reservoir, and its effect we found very similar to that of hot water, so that a little of it went a very long way with us. As for the fish, they swarmed in such numbers that they jostled each other fairly out of the water in a dense living mass, while striving for grains of rice and bread.

This also was a favourite resort of Jehangeer

and Noor Jehan; and I found an inscription in the Persian character which, in a sentence according to Eastern custom, fixed the date of the erection of the building attached to the tank as A. H. 1029, or about A. D. 1612. The inscription runs thus:—

"The king of seven climes, the spreader of justice, Abdool, Mûzuffer, Noor-ûl-deen* Jehangeer Badshah, son of Akbar, conqueror of kings, on the day of the 11th year of his reign paid a visit to this fountain of favour, and by his order this building has been completed. By means of Jehangeer Shah, son of Akbar Shah, this building has raised its head to the heavens."

"The 'Inventor of Wisdom' has fixed its date in this line, viz:—'Aqsirabad o Chushma Wurnak.'"

The fountain or reservoir, and the canal, &c. seem to have been the work of Shah Jehan, Noor

* The title of Noor-ûl-deen is also mentioned by Jehangeer in his Journal from Lahore to Cabul, and its origin is thus accounted for in his own words:—

"Now that I had become a king, it occurred to me that I ought to change my name, which was liable to be confounded with that of the Cæsars of Rome.

"The Secret Inspirer of thoughts suggested to me that, as the business of kings is the conquest of the world, I ought to assume the name of Jehangeer, or Conqueror of the World; and that as my accession to the throne had taken place about sunrise, I ought therefore to take the title of Noor-ûl-deen, or the Light of Religion. I had heard during the time of my youth from several learned Hindoos, that after the expiration of the reign of Akbar, the throne would be filled by a king named Noor-ûl-deen. This circumstance made an impression on me, and I therefore assumed the name and title of Noor-ûl-Deen Jehangeer Badshah."

Jehan's son, or were probably remodelled in his reign. The inscription referring to them runs also in the Persian character on a slab of copper :—

"Hyan, by order of Shah Jehan, King, thanks be to God, built this fountain and canal. From these have the country of Cashmere become renowned, and the fountains are as the fountains of Paradise."

"The poet Survashi Ghaib has written the date in this sentence, viz :—'From the waters of Paradise have these fountains flowed.'"

July 16.—On the road again at daybreak, with the intention of going to a place called Kûkû-nath, where there were more springs, and which, from information obtained from the sepoy who accompanied us, was on our road to Islamabad. However, like most information relative to either direction or to distance in this country, it turned out to be wrong, and we accordingly altered our course and made for our old quarters. Break-fasted under a huge walnut-tree, at a village about six kos off, and reached Islamabad about one P. M., after a very hot tramp of ten kos, through groves of sycamore and walnuts, and hundreds and hundreds of acres of rice-fields, immerged in water, and tenanted by whole armies of croaking frogs. The people were principally employed in weeding their rice-crops, standing up to their knees in mud and water, and grubbing about, with their heads in a position admirably adapted to give anybody but a native, apoplexy in such a hot sun.

July 17.—In the middle of the night we were awoke by a tremendous uproar in our wooden habitation, as if some one was crashing about the boards and panels with a big stick; immediately afterwards something jumped upon my bed, and with a whisk and a rush, clattered through the room to F.'s side, over the table, and back again to my quarter. Half asleep and half awake, I hit out energetically, without encountering anything of our uninvited guest; and the faithful Rajoo coming in with a light, I found F. brandishing a stick valiantly in the air, everything knocked about the room; an earthenware vessel of milk spilt upon the floor, a tumbler broken, and a plate of biscuits on the table with marks of teeth in them. This latter discovery was quite a relief to my mind, for the visitation had a most diabolic savour about it, and we were just beginning to fancy that there was a slight smell of sulphur. However, the milk and the biscuits being such innocent food, we were enabled to fancy that the intruder might have been no worse than a wild cat, which had frightened itself by breaking our tumbler, and had eventually jumped through the window and made its escape. This interpretation, however satisfactory to ourselves, was apparently not so to the Q. M. G., and to his dying day he will probably remain rather doubtful of the kind of company we kept that night.

At sunrise I paid another visit to the ruins of Pandau, or Martund, and sketched it from the north-east; a view which took in the only columns of any perfection that remained standing.

Islamabad being, as its name implies, the "abode of Mahomedanism," I had set the kotwal to work to procure me a good copy of the Koran. On returning, however, I found that he had collected together a bundle of the common editions printed in the Arabic alone, without interlineations. He assured me, however, that they were rare and valuable specimens; and I was amused by the old gentleman reading out a passage in a sonorous voice, following each word with his finger, and astonishing the bystanders by the display of his erudition; but at the same time holding the precious volume upside down, and thus failing in impressing at least one of his audience. In the evening we started again for Sirinugger.

July 18.—Found ourselves, according to sailing directions, at anchor this morning, or in other words, tied to an upright stick, at Wentipore, on the left bank of the river, where there were some old ruins to be seen.

The architecture we found very similar to the Pandau temple. One column, however, was left standing, which was more perfect than any we had seen before.

The ruins consisted of a large quadrangle, with cloisters all round, and the remains of a temple in the centre; both these were completely decayed, but the enormous stones piled together in grand confusion showed that the buildings had been of considerable extent.* The corner stones here alone pointed out the position of the cloisters, which at Pandau had been in very fair preservation.

About fifty yards from the entrance there were three columns of different form, sunk in the ground, their capitals just reaching a little below the surface, and connected by trefoil arches, all in pretty good preservation.

A few hundred yards down the river we found another large ruin, but in a more dilapidated state than either of the others. In both, the

* These ruins appear to be in the greatest dilapidation of any in the valley. The date of their erection is believed to be A.D. 852.

designs carved in the huge stones were something similar in pattern—viz. a female figure, with what appeared to be a long strip of

drapery passing round either arm and descending to the ancles. It was impossible to decipher the exact device, but the breast and head, in most instances, were plainly distinguishable.

About three kos from Sirinugger, we stopped at another very extensive site of Cyclopeian ruins, at a place called Pandreton. Here we found the most perfect building of any we had met; and for a considerable distance around were traces of what must have been, in ages past, a city of some extent.

Among other interesting remains, there was the base of a colossal figure standing in the midst of a field of cut corn. Only from the knees down remained, but this block alone was over seven feet high; the toes were mutilated a good deal, but the legs were in wonderful preservation. There was also, about half a mile off, an enormous base of a column, resting on its side, at the summit of a little eminence, where a considerable amount of mechanical power must have been required to place it. Its diameter was about six feet; and at some distance we found the remainder of the column, split into three pieces. It was about twelve feet long, the lower part a polygon, the upper round, and the top a cone, similar in form to the stones dedicated to Mahadeö in the temples of the Hindoos. The building, which alone remained in at all a perfect state, was situated in a sort of pond or tank of slimy

W. H. K. Delt — Hanhart lith.

PANDRETON.

green, and was quite inaccessible without a boat.* Sending on the cooking apparatus and servants, I remained with the smaller boat; and with a rug and a supply of biscuits, set to work to sketch the ruins. The operation, however, was not performed without very great difficulty. Innumerable mosquitoes made the spot their home, and at critical moments they persisted in settling themselves in the most uncomfortable positions. The ants, too, took a fancy to my paint-box, and even endeavoured to carry off some of the colours; so that between the two I was soon fairly put to flight, and obliged to evacuate the territory.

On consulting my Hindoo authority, Rajoo, on the subject of Cyclopeian ruins, he tells me that they were built, not by man but by "the gods," in the Sut Jûg, or golden age, an epoch which existed no less than 2,165,000 years ago, or thereabouts!

This view of the matter increases the interest of the ruins immensely, besides being very complimentary to the style of building practised by "THE GODS" in that age.

The Hindoo ages are four, and we are believed to be at present in the last of the four, of which 5,000 years have been already accomplished.

* See Appendix A.

The names and duration are as follows, viz:--Sut Jûg, 1,728,000 years; Treth Jûg, 1,296,000 years; Dûapûr Jûg, 864,000 years; and Kul Jûg, 432,000 years. This makes the present age of the world to be about 3,893,000 years!

About five P. M. I reached Sirinugger, and found the advanced guard in possession of one of the bungalows. Spent the night in a succession of skirmishes with innumerable fleas, who appeared to have been out of society for a considerable time previous to our arrival. Up to this moment I fancied that I knew something of the natural history of the race, having studied them and fought with them and slept with them in their happiest hunting grounds. Greek fleas, Albanian fleas, Tartar fleas, Russian fleas, I had combated on their own soil, but never before was I put to such utter confusion. All night long the enemy poured in upon me, and several times during the action was I forced to leave the field and recruit my shattered forces outside in the moonlight. As day dawned, however, I fell upon the foe at a certain advantage, and managed at last to get a few hours of sleep.

July 19.—Made an expedition to the small lake to see a building which we were informed was built by the Puree, or fairies—the Peri of poetical licence.

After a sharp struggle up a steep hill, under a hot sun, we reached the building; but, to all appearance, the fairies had less to do with the edifice than a race of very indifferent engineers. It was evidently the remains of a hill fort, built of stones and mortar, and with nothing wonderful in its construction whatever. It was tenanted by buffaloes and a few natives; and having seen specimens of both before, we took our departure again rather in a bad humour with both the fairies and their partisans.

In the plain below we found the remains of Cyclopeian ruins in an enormous block of stone, part of a column.

July 22.—Started this evening in the direction of the water-lake in further search of ancient ruins.

July 23.—Found ourselves at daybreak among the mosquitoes in a little stream about two kos from Patrun. After breakfasting, we started for the vicinity of the ruins. As usual, in the villages we passed through, we found traces of cut stone doing duty as washing-stones, or corners of walls, &c; and at Patrun we found rather a fine old ruined temple, something similar in style to those towards Islamabad.* It was surrounded at some distance by trees, which had

* Vide Appendix A.

tended apparently to preserve the building, for the stone carvings were clearer and less decayed by time than any others we had seen. Being caught here in a heavy rain, we had a scamper

for our boats, and after a wet journey, reached Sirinugger about eight P. M.

July 26.—Finding ourselves rather tired of Sirinugger, and with no other books than Hindostanee to beguile the time, we resolved upon an expedition across the mountains into the regions of Little Thibet. Began preparations by hiring twelve coolies, at thirteen shillings each per mensem, and a mate or head man to look after them. Increased our stock of ducks to twelve, and otherwise added to our necessary stores, and completed the arrangements for a move.

To-day a number of arrivals and departures took place, and the whole settlement was in a state of excitement and confusion. Boatmen swarmed about in rival application for employment, while all the rascals in the place seemed to have assembled together for the occasion: those who had bills, wanting to get them paid; and those who were either lucky or unfortunate enough to have none, wanting to open them as soon as possible with the new comers. What with these and pistol practice and rifle shooting from upper casements across the river, in order to expend spare ammunition, the European quarter was a very Babel all day long, and we were not sorry to escape the turmoil and get under weigh to new scenes as soon as possible.

About dusk we embarked in two large boats with Rajoo, the cook, and the bhistie, the other servants remaining behind, much to their delight, to take charge of spare baggage, &c. left in the bungalow. One of the Maharajah's army also accompanied us, a rough-and-ready-looking sepoy irregular, whose duty it was to ferret out supplies and coolies, &c. during our march, and at the same time, perhaps, to keep a watch over our own movements and desperate designs. Passed the night under gauze fortifications, the disappointed mosquitoes buzzing about outside in myriads, and striving hard to take a fond farewell of their much-loved foreign guests.

By strange sounds from the direction of my companion's quarters, as if of smacking of hands, &c., I was led to infer that they had partially succeeded in bidding him good-bye. I, however, luckily escaped without receiving even as much as a deputation from the enemy, and slept in happy unconsciousness of their vicinity.

PART IV.

LITTLE THIBET.

July 27.—About six o'clock this morning we found ourselves at anchor under the mountains at the northern extremity of the lake, and at the mouth of a dashing river of ice-cold water, into which we lost no time in plunging. On mustering our forces after breakfast, we found that our possessions required fourteen coolies for their transport. Our own immediate effects took four, viz. bedding two, 'guns one, and clothes, &c. one; the kitchen required four more; tent one, charpoys one, servants' reserve supply of food one, brandy one, plank for table and tent poles one, and last though not least, the twelve ducks took up the services of the fourteenth all to themselves. The rest of our train consisted of the faithful Rajoo, who came entirely at his own request to see a new country, the two servants, the sepoy, and the coolie's mate, who was to act as guide, carry small matters, and make himself generally useful. After a most affectionate parting with our boatmen, Messrs. Suttarah, Ramzan, Guffard, and Co., we started on our new travels at about ten A.M. under a broiling sun. After several halts under shady chestnuts, groves of mulberry, &c., and passing by a gentle ascent through a lovely country, we came to our first encamping ground, at Kungur, and pitched our tent under a chestnut grove, considerably hot and tired by our first march, after all the ease and comparative idleness we had of late been enjoying in the valley. Here we saw the first of the system of extortion which goes on among the government authorities and the people; for after the paymaster to the forces had settled with the seven coolies who were not in our permanent employ, not being able to take all as we had originally intended, they assembled round us, and complained most dolefully of the smallness of their pay. The sepoy, who appeared a most pugnacious customer, cuffed some of them, and made desperate flourishes at others with a big stick, and seemed altogether so anxious to prevent, as he said, the "cherishers of the poor," from being inconvenienced by the "scum of the earth," that we suspected something wrong, and on inquiring, ascertained, that out of the amount due to the seven, viz. one rupee five annas, or about two shillings and eightpence, the organ of government had actually stopped eight annas, or one shilling. The mistake we soon rectified, much to the delight of the "scum of the earth,"—who had certainly earned their three annas, or fourpence halfpenny per man, by carrying our impedimenta eight kos under a hot sun,—and equally to the disgust of "the organ" who handed over the difference with a very bad grace indeed, and was rather out of tune for the rest of the day. Our hearts being expanded by this administration of justice, we proceeded to a further act of charity, and emancipated our twelve ducks from their basket, into a temporary pond constructed for them by the bhistie, where they dabbled about to their hearts' content, and soon forgot the sorrows of the road in a repast of meal and rice.

July 28.—Marched at six A.M., and after proceeding about a kos found that we were in for a regular wetting. Our path lay through a beautifully wooded ravine with precipitous mountain peaks appearing ahead in every direction: these, however, were soon shrouded in impenetrable mist, which gradually gathered in about us, and proceeded to inspect us in a most searching and uncomfortable way.

The road however, though beautiful, was by no means a good one, and it was in many places difficult work to keep one's feet in the wet slush, over wooden bridges, or along the side of a dashing torrent which kept us company, and which seemed to be labouring just now under an unusual degree of temporary excitement, in consequence of having had too much to drink. We had arranged to breakfast on the road, but the rain made us push on, and on reaching the vicinity of our halting-place, we stopped to inspect the condition of our garments, and to satisfy ourselves as to our future prospects in the matter of dry changes of raiment. On opening our small reserve, of which the mate had charge, I found that sad havoc had been made in the precious articles we had been so hopefully depending upon for comfort and consolation at the end of our soaking march. The last efforts of our generally rather useless dhobie had been brought to bear upon our present equipment. The massive brass smoothing-iron and its owner had alike done their best to start us creditably in life with the only clean linen we were likely to behold for many weeks, and now nothing remained of the first instalment of these spotless results, but a wringing mass of wet and dirty linen. The sun, however, coming out opportunely to our assistance, we made the best of our misfortune by spreading out our small wardrobe to the greatest advantage in its rays. Our guide, who by the way appeared to know nothing whatever about the path, proceeded to unroll his turban, and divesting himself of his other garments, took to waving his entire drapery to and fro in the breeze, with a view to getting rid of the superfluous moisture. Leaving him to this little amusement, in which he looked like a forlorn and shipwrecked mariner making signals of distress, I repaired to a torrent close by, and after a satisfactory bathe in the cold snow water, and very nearly losing the whole of my personal property in the rushing stream, donned the few dry articles I was possessed of, and proceeded to pick out our camping ground. We fixed it among the scattered cottages of the little village of Gûndisursing, and while waiting for the main body, stayed our appetites with the few apricots we managed to discover on the already rather closely picked trees.

Got breakfast at two P.M. just as the rain began to come down upon us again. The supplies procurable here were flour, milk, fowls, and eggs; butter, however, was not forthcoming.

July 29.—Marched early after enjoying a drier night than I had anticipated from the look of the evening and the fine-drawn condition of our tent.

Our road continued up a beautifully wooded and watered valley, and reaching a gorge in the mountains, about five kos from our start, we halted at a log hut a little way beyond a wooden settlement dignified by the name of Gûgenigiera.

Here we had a bathe in the rushing snow torrent, a curious combination of pain and pleasure, but the latter considerably predominating, particularly when it was all over.

After breakfast we sent the coolies on again, intending to halt three kos off; however, on reaching the ground, they unanimously requested to be allowed to go on to the village of Soonamurg, the halting-place shown on our route. It was altogether considerably over a Sabbath-day's journey, being nine kos of a bad mountain-path; but as no supplies whatever were procurable short of it, we held on our course. After leaving our halt, the path led us close to the torrent's edge, and the gorge narrowing very much, we were completely towered over in our march by gigantic peaks of rock, blocks of which had come down from their high estate at some remote period of their existence, and now occupied equally prominent though humbler positions in the torrent's bed below. Occasionally they presented themselves in our actual path, and at one place we found that our course was blocked completely, the inaccessible mountain side descending precipitously to the torrent, and leaving us no option but to take to the water, roaring and boiling as it was. Our guide went first with great deliberation and groping his way with a stick, and after an ineffectual attempt to scale the rock above, F. and I also unwillingly followed his example. The water was piercingly cold as it swept against us, and the pain was so great that we were glad to blunder over as quickly as possible, without taking very much trouble about picking our steps. After passing this in safety we came suddenly upon a band of hill-men with their loads, from Thibet; they were the first natives we had encountered, and wild and weird-looking savages they appeared as they congregated about us, gibbering to each other in their astonishment at our sudden appearance. With them, was a strange-looking bullock, with long black mane and tail, and hind quarters like a horse, which they apparently used for carrying their merchandize. To-day we passed the first snow since leaving the valley, although in the distance there was plenty of it to be seen.

Nothing could exceed the beauty of the view as we approached our intended halting-place. Having crossed the torrent by a wooden bridge, the mountains we had been winding through showed out in all their grandeur, while above us, inaccesible peaks, with sharp and fanciful projections, nestled their mighty heads among the fleecy clouds, which hung about after the recent rains. In advance again, other mountain ranges rose behind each other, clothed on their southern faces with delicate grass up to the point where the snow lay lightly on their rocky top-knots and hid itself among the clouds. From the bridge, a rustic structure of entire pine-trees, we passed through an upper valley carpeted with the brightest soft green pasturage, until we reached the usual little cluster of dilapidated wooden tenements which constitute a village in these mountains. This was Soonamurg, and crossing another bridge, formed of two single giant pines, we came to a halt and pitched our camp close to a huge bank of snow on the river's brink. What with our halt, and the badness of the path, we did not arrive until five P.M., and as the sun set, the spray from our snowy neighbour began to wrap its chilling influence about us, and we were glad enough to invest ourselves in some thick cashmere wraps of native manufacture, which we had hitherto considered merely as standbyes in case of extraordinary cold on mountain tops.

According to general report, however, we only reach *the foot of the mountains* to-morrow. This sounds well, considering that we have been ascending steadily for three days, and have left huge avalanches of snow beneath us, not to mention the mountains which we traversed on the Peer Punjal side before even entering the Valley of Cashmere at all.

At Soonamurg, where we had been warned that there were no supplies, we found large herds of sheep and goats. The people, however, were not at all inclined to sell them, and we had some trouble in getting hold of a couple of fine fat sheep from them, for which we paid, what was here considered a high price, viz. two rupees, or four shillings each. We also enlisted the temporary services of two hairy, horny goats, which are to accompany us for the next three marches as portable dairies, no supplies being procurable on the road. Butter and milk are both forthcoming here in abundance, and occasionally rice is to be got. Penetrated with the freshness of the mountain air and the freedom of our vagabond life, we came unanimously to the conclusion that we had made a wise exchange from the *far niente dolces* of Sirinugger, and passed a vote of general confidence in the expedition.

July 30.—The wind this morning blew bitterly cold over the snow and into our tent, rendering the operation of turning out rather more unpopular than usual.

Got off, however, about six, and had a fine bracing march over a grassy valley among the mountains. After about four kos, the sun began again to assert his supremacy, and, in conjunction with the cold of the morning, rather took liberties with our faces and hands. About half-way we came upon the merry ring of axes among the trees, and found a party of natives constructing a log-house for the benefit of travellers towards Ladak. Pitched our camp in a wild spot at the foot of the mountains, bathed in the snow water, and had a sheep killed for breakfast.

One of the live stock died this morning: an unfortunate hen had been sat upon by the ducks, and the result was asphyxia, and consignment to the torrent.

July 31.—Finished up the month by a difficult march of four and twenty miles, encamping at Pandras about eight P.M. and no longer at the *foot* of the mountains. Immediately on leaving our halting-place we commenced the ascent of a steep glacier, and for upwards of four miles our path lay entirely over the snow: so dense and accumulated was it, that even when the sun came out and burned fiercely into our faces and hands, there was no impression whatever made on its icy surface.

The glacier was surrounded on all sides by peaks of perpetual snow, while parts of it were of such ancient date that, ingrained as it was with bits of stick and stones &c., it bore quite the appearance of rock. The path was in some places so indistinct, that on one occasion I found myself far ahead of the rest of the party, and approximating to the clouds instead of to the direction of Ladak. About five kos on our journey we halted to let the kitchen come up, and had our breakfast on the snow in the company of a select party of marmots. The little creatures appeared to live in great peace and seclusion here, for they let us up, in their ignorance of fire-arms, to within thirty yards of them before scuttling into their habitations. They were all dressed in blackish brown suits of long thick fur, and considering that they live in snow for at least eight months out of twelve, they appeared not the least too warmly clothed. As we went by they used to come out and sit up on their hind legs, with their fore paws hanging helplessly over their paunches, while, with a shrill discordant cry, they bid us good-morning and then hurried back to their houses again. Not having our rifles handy they escaped scot free, otherwise we might have borrowed a coat from one of them as a reminiscence of the country. After another kos or two we began to get clear of the glacier; but occasionally we came upon enormous masses of snow jammed up on either side of the torrent, the action of the water having worn away the centre. The path gradually led us through rocky passes, over torrents spanned by snow among the magnificent mountain range; and although the march was rather long for a hill country, we found no fault with it until about the last three kos, when it was getting late in the day, and although fast becoming hungry, we saw no immediate prospect of getting anything to eat.

The last few kos we find invariably longer than their fellows; one kos by *description*, at this stage of the proceedings, being generally equal to two in reality. Asking a native, how far we are from a halting-place, is invariably answered in one of two ways: either *thoree door*, not very far, or *nuzdeek*, close. *Thoree door* means generally about four miles, while *nuzdeek* may be translated five at least. A kos too, which ought to be from one and a half to two miles, means here anything between one mile and seven. Delaying as much as possible, to let our servants up, we reached Pandras at last, and found all the inhabitants turned out to see our arrival; they were dressed in long woollen coats and sheepskins, and looked something between Russians and Tartars, with a strong flavour of the Esquimaux, as depicted by Polar voyagers. As the sun went down it became bitterly cold, and we found the natives even, shuddering under the influences of the snowy wind, which, setting in from the mountains, appeared to blow from all points of the compass at one and the same time. What the village of Pandras must be in mid-winter it is hard to imagine, so covered with snow as the mountains around it are even in August, and so bleak and so barren the valley in which it is situated.

In spite of the cold, we astonished the entire swaddled population by taking off our clothes, and bathing in a little crystal stream close by: two operations, in all probability, which they themselves had never perpetrated within the memory of the oldest inhabitant. This feat accomplished, we were much astonished by the arrival of a *rara avis*, in the shape of a British traveller, from the direction of Ladak. He turned out to be an officer of the Government survey, now being carried on in the mountains, and we took the opportunity of deriving from him all the information we could, relative to the prospect before us. He strongly recommended us to go to the monastery of Hemis, beyond Ladak, and also to the Lakes, but the latter would appear to be beyond the limits of our time. The only natives we had met during our unusually long march to-day, were four hairy-looking savages from the interior, from whom, after much difficulty, I succeeded in purchasing an aboriginal tobacco-pouch, flint, and steel, all combined in one, paying for the same about three times its actual and local value, viz. two rupees. They were dressed in long woollen coats, with thick bands of stuff rolled round their waists; and all four had bunches of yellow flowers stuck in their caps, and pipes, knives, tobacco-pouches, &c. hung round their girdles. Their shoes were of the Esquimaux pattern, the soles sheepskin, coming up all round the front of the foot, where they were joined by woollen continuations—shoes, socks, and leggings, being thus conveniently amalgamated into one article of apparel.

August 1.—On the road a little later than usual, all hands being tired after yesterday's exertions. The path to-day lay among huge boulders of rock, which had come down as specimens from the mountains above, and after a short march of five kos, we reached Dras, a little assemblage of flat-roofed houses, with a mud fort about half a mile from it, in the valley. This was built with four bastions and a ditch scarped with paving-stones, which surrounded it on all sides except one, where it was naturally defended by the torrent. On the road we passed a curious bridge, built entirely of rope manufactured from twigs of trees. The cables thus formed were swung across the torrent, from piles of loose stones, in a most scientific way, though not one calculated to inspire confidence in any traveller with weak nerves who might have to trust himself to its support. It appeared, nevertheless, a most serviceable structure, and was decidedly picturesque. At Dras we were able to get all supplies except fowls.

August 2.—Having a long and up-hill march before us, we were up and dressed by moonlight. Outside the village, we came upon two curious old stones, standing about six feet high, upright, and carved in the way we had already seen at the ruins of Pandau and elsewhere. These stones were of irregular form, and carved on three sides, and the designs, though much worn, were distinctly traceable. They represented, apparently, a male and female figure, standing about five feet high, and surrounded by three smaller figures each. Like all the other sculptured figures we had seen, they were innocent of clothes, with the exception of the rope, or very scant drapery, which ran across their ancles and up either side to the shoulders.

Leaving these, we passed through a wild and rugged valley among the mountains, cultivated in patches, and watered by numerous little sparkling crystal streams. At short intervals, there were little settlements of mud huts, built, Tartar fashion, one on top of another, and peopled by a few miserable-looking natives, who appeared, in their woollen rags, to be cold, even in the middle of this summer's day. The few travellers we met during our march were flat-nosed, heavy-looking creatures, with Chinese skull-caps and pig-tails, and were employed in conveying salt to Cashmere, packed in bags of woven hair, and laden on cows and asses as weird and strange-looking as their owners. About five kos off, we called a halt for breakfast, and reached Tusgam about four P. M.

Here we found a few *Arbor Vitæ*, and other shrubs, in bad health, the first of the tree species we had encountered since ascending the glacier.

August 3.—Struck our camp at sunrise, and crossing the torrent, which still accompanied us, descended the pass by a slight decline. During the day we passed through numerous gorges, studded with giant masses of rock, and bounded on all sides by rugged and inhospitable mountains. We only saw one village, and that some way off the road—Kurroo, the guide called it. Breakfasted under an overhanging rock on the mountain side, just where our path was hemmed in by the torrent, and were disturbed during our repast by several volleys of stones which rattled down over us from above. They were set free by the melting of some large masses of snow, which, being covered with sticks and dirt, we had not noticed when we chose our breakfast parlour so close to their uncomfortable proximity. To-day we met more salt-carrying parties—uncouth-looking savages in pig-tails, speaking a language that not one of our party could understand. We also encountered an original-looking gold-washing association of five, who were wending their way towards the snow with their wooden implements. They were all also weighted with bags of grain, to keep them alive during their search. Their labour consists in sifting the fine sand which comes down in the snow-torrents, charged with minute particles of gold; and the proceeds, from the appearance of "the trade," would not seem to be very great. They say it amounts only to a few annas a day, but would probably not allow to the full amount for fear of being taxed.

At our breakfast-halt we saw the most primitive specimen of a smoking apparatus probably ever invented. It consisted of a dab of mud stuck in a hole of a tree, about five feet from the ground. Two small sticks, inserted in this from above and below and then withdrawn, had evidently served to form the smoke passage; while the bowl as evidently had been fashioned by the simple impression of a Thibetian thumb, the whole forming, for the use of needy travellers, as permanent and satisfactory a public pipe as could well have been devised. It had just been in requisition before we passed, for a small quantity of newly-burned tobacco lay in the bowl; and a fresh patch of clay on the mouthpiece had probably been added, either in the way of general repairs or by some extra-fastidious traveller, who preferred having a private mouthpiece of his own. After rather a severe march through rocky mountain gorges, we reached Chungun, a little oasis of about five acres of standing barley, with three or four flat-roofed houses dotted about it in the usual Tartar style of architecture. It also boasted four poplar-trees, standing in a stiff and reserved little row, evidently in proud consciousness of their family importance among such rugged, treeless, iron mountains.

It was altogether a refreshing little spot for a halt, after the savage scenery we had marched through; and pitching our camp in it, we were not long in introducing ourselves to the little brawling stream of clear cold water to which it owed its existence.

August 4.—Started this morning in a mountain mist. Just outside the village we passed the scene of the fall of an avalanche, which gave one some faint idea of the enormous forces occasionally at work among these mountains. It had taken a small village in its path, and over the place where it had stood we now took our way, among a perfect chaos of masses of rock, and uptorn earth, trees, &c. The whole ground was torn and rent, as by the eruption of volcanoes or the explosion of enormous magazines of powder. Passing this, our path continued to descend the gorge until about two kos from Chungun, when another torrent came down to join its forces to the one we were accompanying; and leaving our old companion to roar its way down to join the Indus, we proceeded up the valley in the society of our new friend. Passing a series of little villages nestled among the rugged rocks, we crossed the stream by a tree-bridge and causeway, to the Fort of Kurgil, where, after a long consultation, we breakfasted. The differences of opinion between the guide and the rest of the natives as to the distance of a village ahead, where milk and supplies were forthcoming, were so wide, some saying three kos, others six, &c., that we finally determined upon getting some breakfast before deciding the true distance for ourselves. The village Hundas was another most perfect little oasis. It was only about five or six acres in extent, under the frowning mountain, and was terraced and planted in the neatest and most economical way imaginable. The fields were beautifully clean, and were quaintly adorned in many instances by huge blocks of rock from the mountain above, bigger considerably than the whole of the houses of the village put together. Leaving Kurgil, we made a sharp ascent, and crossed a plateau bounded by some extremely curious formations of rock and sandstone.

The mountains appeared to have been reared on end and cut with a knife, as if for the especial benefit of geologists in general, although the hues of their many-coloured strata were calculated to attract even the most ungeological mind by their brightness. Descending from this plateau, we came to a pass dotted with three or four little villages, wooded with poplars, and adorned with a few shrubs of different kinds. Here every available inch of ground which the grudging rocks bestowed was cultivated, although all around, the mud-built native huts were broken down and deserted, in such numbers as to give the idea of an Irish settlement whose inhabitants had transplanted themselves to America. At the last of these little villages, called Pushkoom, we pitched our camp, the retainers taking a fancy to the place from the promise it gave of abundant supplies.

August 5.—Made our first day's halt, and enjoyed it considerably—not the least of its advantages being the immunity it gave us from being torn out of bed at grey hours in the morning. The rest of the force also appreciated the day of rest, and made themselves comfortable after their fashion under our grove of trees.

In the afternoon I ascended the mountain opposite to reconnoitre and inspect the curious formation of strata, which formed the principal feature of the place.

The ascent I found at first to be over a soft crumbling small stone, resembling ashes, but of various colours, and in distinctly-marked strata. These were generally of pinkish red and grey, and from them in large masses, rose enormous blocks of concrete, in all manner of forms and shapes, some like towers and fortifications, and others standing out boldly by themselves, worn by the weather into holes and ridges. After a considerably difficult ascent, from the crumbling nature of the stones, I reached the summit of the mountain, and climbing a concrete monster which capped it, had a magnificent survey of the mountain ranges and country around. In every direction the eye rested on snowy summits, and the wind from them fell coolly and refreshingly after the toil of ascent under a hot sun.

Returning through the village, I found the natives hard at work collecting their crops of wheat and barley, and stowing them away, generally upon the flat tops of their houses. They seemed altogether a peaceful, primitive race; but, although their ground appears in first-rate order, they themselves are uncultivated and dirty in the extreme. The ladies, I am sorry to say, are even rather worse in this matter than the gentlemen. The female costume consists generally of robes of sheep and goat skins thrown across the shoulders; while a long tail of twisted worsted plaits, looking like a collection of old-fashioned bell-ropes, forms the chief decoration. This is attached to the back hair, and hangs down quite to the heels, where it terminates in a large tuft, with tassels and divers balls of worsted attached to it. On a hill overhanging the village were the remains of a mud fort, which had been pulled down by Gûlab Singh in one of his excursions to Thibet, with a view to bringing the inhabitants to a proper sense of their position, and enforcing the payment of his tribute.

The number of battered and deserted huts about the village is accounted for by the erratic habits of the people, which induce them never to stay long in one set of houses, but to flit from one side of the valley and from one settlement to another as the fancy strikes them. That the large increase of the flea population among such a race, however, may have something to do with their restlessness, seems more than probable.

Except when impressed for government employ, they seldom leave the vicinity of their villages, and one old gentleman told me he had never been even as far as a place called Lotzûm, which is only two kos off! The religion seems to be a mixture of Buddhism and Mahomedanism —the latter on the decrease as we get farther into the country.

The dress assimilates to the Chinese—pig-tails and little skull-caps being the order of the day. We obtained here good supplies of cow's milk, butter, &c., and among other things, some peas. These enabled us to celebrate our Sunday's dinner by a "duck and green peas," and never since the first invention of ducks could a similar luxury have been so thoroughly appreciated.

August 6.—Started early again, and marched five kos, through the little half-deserted settlement of Lotzûm to the village of Shergol, where we halted for breakfast. Here we found our-

selves fairly among the Buddhists, and saw an entirely new description of monuments connected with religion, from anything we had yet encountered. The most striking objects were a series of tomb-like buildings, without entrances, and adorned on all sides by the most hideous effigies, rudely executed in coloured mud.*

Some of these were men, depicted in bright red on a yellow ground, with horrible staring countenances; others women, adorned with numberless necklaces and other ornaments; besides these, there were peacocks, griffins with human arms, deer, &c., and all in the most flaring colours and the very rudest designs.

In the perpendicular face of a rock beyond was a very curious monastery, or abode of the Lamas. It was built completely *in* the rock, and was reached by a natural cavity on the face of the stone.

Jutting out from the upper part, balconies had been erected overhanging the precipice, and these were decorated with red copings, spotted

* These monuments would appear to be of the kind designated Chod-tens and Dung-tens, which have been thus described:—"In the monuments which are dedicated to the celestial Buddha, the invisible being who pervades all space, no deposit was made; but the Divine Spirit, who was light, was supposed to occupy the interim. Such are the numerous Chod-tens in Tibet dedicated to the celestial Buddha, in contradistinction to the Dung-tens, which are built in honour of the mortal Buddhas, and which ought to contain some portion of their relics, real or supposed. The first means an offering to the Deity, the latter a bone or relic receptacle. In the Sanscrit these are termed Chaitya and Dagoba."—CUNNINGHAM.

with white. From the fact of only one of our party knowing the language, it was difficult to ascertain from the natives the history of this curious abode, but they gave us to understand that it was the home of their Lamas, or spiritual preceptors. Here we met another of the race of wandering Englishmen, who was wending his way back to the valley. He was returning from a shooting tour, was all alone, and appeared to have had very hard work indeed of it, if his face and hands and generally dilapidated appearance might be taken as a criterion. Not being quite in such light marching order ourselves, we were able to ask him to breakfast, and from his ready acceptance and the entire justice he did to our offer, I don't think he could have had anything to eat for a week.

He appeared to be a thorough sportsman, and had bagged several head of large game, which he showed us. They were principally a kind of wild sheep with enormous heads and horns, each of his trophies being almost a coolie load in itself. Leaving Shergol, we entered a curious valley with rocks of concrete standing out like towers and fortifications, and on the summits of these again, airy-looking habitations with red streaks adorning them, and entered, as that at Shergol, by holes in the face of the rock. These were, or had been, the abodes of the Lamas; numbers of them now however, as well as the mud settlements at their feet, appeared in ruins, and gave no sign of habitation, beyond having about them a number of little flags stuck on long poles, which fluttered about in the breeze. According to the account

of our interpreter, which had to pass from Thibetian into Hindostanee before it could clothe itself in English, the cause of this dilapidation was the state of wealth and ambition at which the Lamas had arrived, and the consequent interposition of Gûlab Singh to take down their pride and ease them of a little of their wealth, both of which he accomplished in the style to which he was so partial, by slaughtering some hundreds of them and reducing their airy habitations to ruins.

At a place called Moulwee we came to a curious block of massive rock standing close beside the path, with one of the red-topped

houses built into its side. Above this was a colossal figure with four arms, rudely cut on the face of the rock, and above all was perched an implement, something after the fashion of a Mrs. Gamp's umbrella of large proportions, together with sundry sticks and rags, which seem to be the common style of religious decoration in these parts.

The figure was about eighteen feet high, the lower extremities being hidden behind the building at the base of the rock. It resembled in some measure the sculptures occasionally seen among Hindoo temples, but no one appeared to know anything whatever of its origin or history.

Close to this there were an immense number of stones collected together, bearing inscriptions in two different characters, one of which resembled slightly the Devanagree or Sanscrit. Seeing such a profusion about, I appropriated one which happened to be conveniently small, and carried it off in my pocket.

The sun being intensely powerful, we called a halt at a village named Waka, perched among the rocks, where we found a rattletrap of a baradurree, which saved us the trouble of pitching our tents. Opposite to us was a curiously worn mass of concrete mountain, which might easily have been mistaken for artificial lines of fortification, had not the scale been so large as to preclude the possibility of any but giants or fairies having been the engineers. At the head of the valley there was a fine snow-covered mountain, which helped to keep us cool in an otherwise excessively hot position. The cook having been rather overcome by his exertions to-day, we got our dinner at the fashionable hour of nine P.M.

August 7.—Starting from Waka at cock-crow, we marched up a steep ascent, through a bleak-looking range of hills, to Khurboo, where we bivouacked under a tree and got breakfast about noon.

Afterwards, I examined more minutely the inscription on the stones, which, as we advanced into the country, appeared to increase considerably in number. They consisted in almost every case of the same word, containing five letters in one character and six in the other, though occasionally there were additional letters, and sometimes, though very rarely, a stone with a different inscription altogether. After a good deal of difficulty I succeeded in unearthing a Lama from the village to help me in my researches, and a strange-looking dignitary of the Church he turned out to be when he did make his appearance. He was a bloated and fat old gentleman, dressed in a yellowish red garment of no particular shape, and looked altogether more like a moving bundle of red rags than anything else, human or divine.

Finding that nothing was required of him more expensive than information, he appeared delighted to show off his learning, and by means of the sepoy, who was the only one of our party acquainted with both Thibetan and Hindoostanee, I ascertained that the words carved upon the stones were "Ûm mani panee," and meant,

as far as I could make out, "the Supreme Being." As the old gentleman repeated the mystic syllables, he bobbed and scraped towards a strange-looking monument close by, in an abject, deprecatory way, as if in extreme awe of its presence.*

On inquiring the origin of this new structure, which was built of stones and plaster, and decorated with red ochre, all we could get out of him was a fresh string of "Ûm mani panees," and a further series of moppings and mowings, accompanied by a sagacious expression of his fat countenance, indicative of the most entire satisfaction at the clearness of his explanations, and a sense of his own importance as a Lama and an expositor of the doctrines of Bûddh.

He also explained the only other inscription which I had seen; and according to the interpre-

* This appears to have been one of the Dagobas or bone-holders, which are erected either over the corse of a Lama or the ashes of some person of consequence. "The tribute of respect is paid in Tibet to the manes of the dead in various ways. It is the custom to preserve entire the mortal remains of the sovereign Lamas only. As soon as life has left the body of a Lama, it is placed upright, sitting in an attitude of devotion, his legs being folded before him, with the instep resting on each thigh, and the sides of the feet turned upwards. The right hand is rested with its back upon the thigh, with the thumb bent across the palm. The left arm is bent and held close to the body, the hand being open and the thumb touching the point of the shoulder. This is the attitude of abstracted meditation.

"The bodies of inferior Lamas are usually burnt, and their ashes preserved with the greatest care, and the monuments in which they are contained are ever after looked upon as sacred, and visited with religious awe."—TURNER.

tation of the sepoy, it ran thus :—"As God can do so none other can."*

Not another piece of information could I elicit relative to the religion beyond the continual "Ûm mani panee, Ûm mani panee!" which our friend seemed never tired of mumbling; and although the sepoy was, I believe, considerably more adapted for the extraction of reluctant supplies of food for our kitchen than for eliciting such information on the subject of theology as I was in search of, the real cause of failure was more to be attributed to the extreme ignorance of the particular pillar of the Church that we had got hold of, than to any little literary failings of the interpreter. Such were the quantities of the inscribed stones about this place, that in one long wall I estimated there must have been upwards of 3,000, and this in a country where inhabitants of any sort are few and far between, and where none appear who seem at all capable of executing such inscriptions.

August 8—Having suffered a good deal yesterday from the heat of the sun, we started this morning by a bright moonlight, at about half-past four A. M.

Entering the Pass of Fotoola, we ascended

* جو خُدا کریگا سو کویِ نہین کریگا

gradually for some five kos, and reached a considerable elevation, with a good deal of snow lying about on the mountains. A peak on the right was 19,000 feet above the sea level, and few of those in our immediate vicinity were under 17,000 feet. From the summit of this pass we descended about three kos to Lamieroo, without passing a single hut or village on the entire road. The only natives we encountered were a party of three from Ladak, on their way to Cashmere, with a couple of fine native dogs, as a present from the Thanadar to some of his visitors. The pedestrians one generally meets now are old ladies, carrying conical baskets filled with sulphur or saltpetre, in the direction of Cashmere, and so shy are they, that on beholding "the white face" they drop their loads as if shot, and scuttle away among the mountains, so that, if inclined, we could seize upon the Maharajah's munitions of war and carry them off without difficulty. On reaching the vicinity of Lamieroo, the inscribed stones became more frequent than ever. They were placed generally upon long broad walls, the tops of which sloped slightly outwards, like the roof of a house. Supplies of uncut stones were also in many instances collected together in their vicinity, as if for the benefit of any pedestrian who might feel inclined to carve out his future happiness by adding to the collection. Lamieroo, as its name would seem to imply, appears to have been a head-quarters of the Lamas and their religion. It contains a curious monastery, or Lamaserai, built upon the extreme top ledge of a precipice of concrete stone, and at its base (some hundred feet below) the habitations which constitute the village are also perched on pinnacles of rock, and scattered about, often in the most unlikely spots imaginable. Entering the bason formed by the valley in which this curious settlement is situated, one opens suddenly by an ascending turn upon the whole scene, and anything more startlingly picturesque it would be hard to conceive. As the view appears, the first objects presented are a host of little monument-like buildings, which line the path and are dotted about in groups of from three to twelve or fourteen together. They stand about seven feet high, and, as far as we could make out from the natives, are erected over the defunct Lamas and other saints of the Buddhist religion, after which they become sacred in the eyes of the living, and are referred to with scrapings and bowings and "Ûm mani panees" innumerable. In the monastery we found twenty Lamas at present domiciled—fat, comfortable-looking gentlemen they all were, dressed in orange-yellow garments, and not a bit cleaner than the rest of the natives, nor looking by any means more learned. Mounting the side of the hill, and passing under one of the red-ring pillared monuments, we entered the precincts of the monastery,

and threading some very steep and dark passages in the interior of the rock, were received by a deputation of Lamas, with the salutation of "Joo, Joo!"

We were then ushered with great ceremony into their temple, much to the awe and consternation of our guides, who apparently expected to see us as much overcome by the sanctity of the

LAMIEROO.

place as they themselves were. The temple we found a small square room with a gallery round it, from which were suspended dingy-looking Chinese banners, flowers, &c., and at one end were about twenty idols of various designs, seated in a row staring straight before them, and covered with offerings of Indian corn, yellŏw flowers, butter, &c. They were for the most part dressed in Chinese fashion, and in the dusky light had certainly a queer weird-looking appearance about them, which was quite enough to overawe our village guide; not being accustomed to such saintly society, he could hardly raise his eyes or speak above his breath, but stood with hands joined together and in a supplicating posture, enough to melt the heart of even the very ugliest of idols. The service (by particular desire) began by three of the most unctuous of the Lamas squatting down on some planked spaces before the divinities, and raising a not unmusical chaunt, accompanying themselves at the same time with a pair of cymbals, while two large double-sided tom-toms or drums gradually insinuated themselves into the melody. These were each fixed on one long leg and were beaten with a curved stick, muffled at the end. The performance of the cymbals was particularly good, and the changes of time they introduced formed the chief feature of the music, and was rather pleasing than otherwise. The service as it drew to a close, was joined by a duett upon two enormous brass instruments like speaking-trumpets grown out of all decent proportions; they were about five feet long, and were placed on the ground during the performance, and as two of the fattest of the Lamas operated and nearly suffocated themselves in their desperate exertions, the result was the most diabolical uproar that ever could have been produced since the first invention of music.

Not being able to trust the sepoy in such a delicate undertaking, I was unable to get any information from the Lamas on religious subjects and all signs and suggestive pointings, &c. were immediately and invariably answered by "Ûm mani panee," so that we left about as wise as we entered. The most interesting object in the place was a library of Thibetian books. It consisted of an upright frame divided into square compartments, each with a word cut deeply into the wood over it, and containing the volumes. These were merely long narrow sheets, collected between two boards, also carved on the outside with a name similar to the one on the shelf. The characters were beautifully formed, and I tried to purchase a small volume, if a thing about two feet long could be called so, but without effect. There were about thirty of these books in the place, ponderous tomes, carefully covered up, and little read, to judge by the quantity of dust collected on them. They read us, however, a small portion of one, in a drawling, sonorous tone, and with no very great facility.

These books, together with a number of rudely-printed papers, of the nature of tracts, one of which I carried away, containing some of the characters similar to that on the inscribed stones, appear to have been printed at Lassa,* the capital of Thibet Proper, and from there, the head-quarters of the religion in these parts, all the musical instruments and other paraphernalia belonging to the temples are also sent. One exception, however, I discovered; this was an empty brandy-bottle, bearing a magnificent coloured label, which certainly could not have been issued from the Grand Lama's religious stores. To the English eye, or rather nose, it had but little of the odour of sanctity about it; but here it evidently held a high position, and was prominently placed among the temporal possessions of "the Gods."

The women here, and those we met on the road during the last two marches, wore a curious head-dress, differing from anything of the kind we had before seen. It consisted of a broad band extending from the forehead to the waist behind, and studded thickly with large coarse turquoises. These generally decrease in size

* "Tibet may be considered the head-quarters of Buddhism in the present age, and immense volumes are still to be found in that country (faithful translations of the Sanskrit text), which refer to the manners, customs, opinions, knowledge, ignorance, superstition, hopes and fears of a great part of Asia, especially of India in former ages."—CSOMA DE KOROS, *Preface to Tibetan Grammar.*

from the forehead, where there is a larger turquoise than the others, down to the waist, and where the hair ends, it is joined into a long worsted tail terminating at the heels. Some of these bands must be of considerable value, but the proprietors, although otherwise in complete rags, will not part with them for any consideration. One lady whom I accosted on the subject, thought I was going to murder her, and took to her heels forthwith. In general, however, the fair sex here carefully hide both their charms and their turquoises behind the nearest rock or the most convenient cover that presents itself, and vanish like phantoms whenever they discern a white man in the distance.

The cooking department being delayed by the ascent, we got no breakfast to-day until one o'clock, unless a drink of milk and a biscuit on arrival could be called by courtesy a breakfast.

August 9.—Descended from Lamieroo through a precipitous pass for about three kos and a half, to Kulchee, a tidy little village of fifteen huts, situated in an oasis of apricot and walnut-trees, the first we had encountered since leaving Cashmere.

The people here seemed particularly simple and happy among their waving corn-fields and wild fruit-trees, and they were most anxious to supply us with apricots and milk, and whatever they could produce. The Gopa, or head-man of the village, could speak a little Hindostanee, besides being able to read and write his own language in two characters, and as he seemed unusually sharp and intelligent, I was very glad to have a chat with him while waiting for the commissariat to come up. The character most common on the inscribed stones, and one of

those now in actual use, he told me was Romeeque; the other, the square character on the

stones, is obsolete, and is called Lantza; * while a third character, which was the one he was most conversant with, but which did not appear upon any of the stones, he called Tyeeque.

His explanation of the stones was, that at the last day a certain recording angel, whom he called Khurjidal, would pass through the land, and inspecting these mounds of inscribed stones,

* These stones would appear to be peculiar to Thibet, although the sentence inscribed upon them has been occasionally discovered elsewhere. Mention of it is thus made in the Journal of the Asiatic Society of Bengal :—"On the main road from the Valley of Nipal to Tibet stands a diminutive stone, 'Chaitya.' Upon this is inscribed a variety of texts from the Buddha Scriptures, and amongst others the celebrated Mantra, or charmed sentence of Tibet. The system of letters called Lantzá in Tibet, and there considered foreign and Indian, though nowhere extant in the Plains of India, is the common vehicle of Sanscrit language among the Buddhists of Nipal Proper, by whom it is denominated Ranjá, in Devanagri रंजा

"Ranjá, therefore, and not, according to a barbarian metamorphosis, Lántzá, it should be called by us, and by way of further and clearer distinction, the Nipalese variety of Devánágrí. Obviously deducible as this form is from the Indian standard, it is interesting to observe it in practical collocation with the ordinary Thibetan form, and when it is considered that Lántzá or Ranjá is the common extant vehicle of those original Sanscrit works of which the Thibetan books are translations, the interest of an inscription traced on one slab in both characters cannot but be allowed to be considerable. The habit of promulgation of the doctrines of their faith by inscriptions patent on the face of religious edifices, stones, &c., is peculiar to the Buddhists of Thibet. The Mantrá is also quite unknown to the Buddhists of Ceylon and the Eastern peninsula, and forms the peculiar feature of Thibetan Buddhism."

would write down the names of all those who had contributed to the heap. What the inscription was he seemed unable clearly to explain, but believed it to refer in some manner to the Supreme Being. Whatever it was, all those who had contributed their share towards its dissemination, by adding stones to the mounds, were certain of future rewards, while those who had omitted to do so were as equally certain of punishment.*

This explanation of the difficulty caused me some qualms of conscience on account of the future prospects of the unfortunate writer whose

* This was the only explanation of the mounds of inscribed stones which I was able to obtain from a native source; and some foundation for the story may be traced in the legend—which will be found in Appendix B—upon which M. Klaproth has founded the only explanation of the mystic inscription, which I have been as yet able to discover.

By the Lamas themselves I never heard these mounds alluded to otherwise than by the words "Mani panee." Cunningham, however, who had ample opportunity of ascertaining their meaning and origin, terms them "Manís" (in another form of spelling, "Munees"), and thus describes them:—"The Maní—a word naturalized from the Sanscrit—is a stone dyke, from four to five feet high, and from six to twelve in breadth; length from ten or twenty feet to half a mile. The surface of the Maní is always covered with inscribed slabs; these are votive offerings from all classes of people for the attainment of some particular object. Does a childless man wish for a son, or a merchant about to travel hope for a safe return; each goes to a Lama and purchases a slate, which he deposits carefully on the village 'Maní,' and returns to his home in full confidence that his prayers will be heard."

particular stone I had appropriated; but for fear the Gopa himself might be the sufferer, I thought it better not to confide my emotions to him, but to leave the case in the hands of Khurjidal.

Regarding the state of the people here, he told me that each house paid a tax of seven rupees per annum to the Maharajah. This, for the entire village, would only give 105 rupees per annum towards the enrichment of the Treasury.

The Lamas, who have no ground of their own, appear to be a further burden on the population. They are supplied gratuitously with food, and appear to be somewhat similar to the Hindoo Fukeer, devoting themselves to religion and remaining unmarried. They, however, are not so violent in their opinions, and are more conversable, to say nothing of being decidedly cleaner.

We breakfasted under the spreading walnuts, among an audience composed of the entire village, who seemed much edified and amused by our novel manners and customs. Some of our English possessions took their fancy immensely. A cut-glass lantern and the label of a bottle of cherry-brandy in particular, seemed to them the very essence of the rare and curious, and they seemed never tired of admiring them. After breakfast we again took the road, and marched three kos to another little wooded settlement, called Nûrila, situated, like Kulchee, upon the Indus, or, as it is here called, the Attock. The noisy, dirty torrent, as it here appears, however, gives little promise of becoming, as it does in after life, one of the largest of the stately Indian rivers.

August 10.—From Nûrila we travelled along the Indus bank to Suspûl, a distance of seven kos or thereabouts, stopping for breakfast at a village whose entire population consisted of one woman! The river being shut in by high and rocky mountains, our path took several most abrupt turns and startling ascents and descents in its meanderings, and proved altogether the worst for coolies to travel that we had as yet encountered. The greater part of our march, too, was under a burning sun, whose rays the rocks on either side of us reflected in anything but an agreeable way, giving thereby a considerable addition of colour to our already well-bronzed countenances. Near Suspûl we had to take to the water, as a mass of overhanging rock jutted into the river and completely obstructed the path; and here one of our coolies, stumbling, dropped his load into the torrent. It was a particularly precious part of our expeditionary stores, containing, among other things, the small stock of brandy which was to last us back to Sirinugger. However, on inspecting the contents of the basket, the precious liquid was safe and sound, and the only damage was the conversion, *pro tem.* of our stock of best lump sugar into *moist.* Suspûl we found situated in a half-moon shaped break of fertility among the barren mountains. The snow was within half an hour's climb, while at the same time the sun shone with such power as to blister our faces, and even to affect the black part of the expedition, rendered somewhat tender, no doubt, by the unusual mixture of heat and cold to which they had already been exposed. We encamped here under a grove of apricot and apple-trees, which resulted in the production of an apple-dumpling for dinner.

August 11.—Leaving Suspûl, we ascended considerably to the village of Buzgo, another of the cloud-built little settlements so dear to the Lamas. The tenements were most picturesquely pitched upon the extreme tips of almost perpendicular rocks, and to many of them access seemed apparently impossible. Leaving this, we entered upon a desert of shifting sand and stones, in the midst of which there was an unusually long wall of the inscribed stones, one of which, although containing the same inscription, was of a different pattern from any I had hitherto discovered.*

The next oasis was Egnemo, formed, like all the others, by the existence of numerous little springs of crystal water, which enabled the waving corn to raise its golden head, and the apricot and the apple-tree to flourish in refreshing contrast to the general barrenness and sterility which reigned around.

After a grilling march, we enjoyed the de-

* This was in all probability intended to represent the form of the lotus. Vide Appendix B.

THIBETIAN MONUMENTS AND WALL OF INSCRIBED STONES.
ROAD TO EONEMO.

lights of a bathe under a waterfall of clear cold water, and got our breakfast by eleven o'clock.

To-day, some of our brigade of coolies begin to complain of sickness, which sounds alarming, not only to themselves, but to us, for none others are now procurable. This results from their making too free with unripe apricots, and drinking too many gallons of cold water on the road; also, however, from the fact of my having doctored the first patient who had presented himself, with a couple of pills and some tea—a piece of generosity which drove all the others nearly mad with jealousy and envy, and set them thinking how they also might be participators in similar luxuries. The pills, although in this instance selected promiscuously from a varied stock, were the great objects of desire, and such was their confidence in the virtuous properties of the remedy, that the character of the particular bolus that fell to their share was to them a matter of no consequence whatever. So great a rage is there for medicine among people who have never known the luxury of paying for it, that even the blind and deformed continually applied to us for it on the road.

August 12.—Halted to-day, and gave all hands a day of rest, which was rather required after our incessant marching. In the afternoon we explored the village, and enjoyed a magnificent sunset behind the ranges of distant snowy mountains. The crops here were more backward than those met hitherto, although the power of the sun was rather on the increase, than otherwise, as we advanced. Some of the fields were occupied by beans, peas, and wheat, all growing like a happy family together.

August 13.—Made an unusually early start, this morning, for our final march into Ladak. The first part of the journey was up a precipitous ascent, and over shifting gravel, which was very trying to our already well-worn boots; and it was a relief when, on arriving at the summit, we found a long and gradual descent before us, with an entirely new panorama of snow-clad mountains extending away towards Ladak.

In the distance, close to the river Indus, which here branched out into several small and separate streams, there was a high mound, topped with buildings, which we made for, under the full impression that it was our journey's end: however, on reaching it, and turning confidently round the corner, we found nothing but a deserted-looking building, surrounded by an immense number of the monuments which the natives call Permessur; while, stretched out at our feet, and forming, as it were, the bottom of a large basin among the mountains, was a dreary desert of glaring, burning sand. The place altogether looked like a city of the dead: not a soul appeared in sight, except one solitary old woman, who was slowly traversing the weary waste of sands, and all around was still and silent as the grave. In order to gain some intelligence of our whereabouts, I was obliged to give chase to this only inhabitant, and from her I discovered, that to reach Ladak—a green-looking speck which she pointed out in the far distance—we had to cross the desert sands, and still hold on our course for several miles. The sun was by this time high in the heavens, and we had already come a longish march, so that by the time I had traversed the arid plain under the blinding glare, and reached the green fields beyond, it was nearly twelve o'clock, and I had had nearly enough of the journey. It was, however, a couple of miles farther to the grove of trees, where, under very indifferent shade, travellers are in the habit of halting to pitch their camps; and on reaching this, I was glad to throw myself down on the grass, and, after a drink of milk, and the slight refreshment afforded by a leathery chupattie, to go to sleep on the grass, until the arrival of our servants and baggage should give us a prospect of breakfast. These made their appearance about two P.M., and all hands requiring a little rest from the toils of the road, we pitched our camp under the trees, and set ourselves to the enjoyment of a few days' halt in the city of Ladak.

PART V.

LADAK AND THE MONASTERY OF HEMIS.

The first event after being settled in our new quarters was the arrival of a sheep, presented to us by the Kardar, or chief dignitary of the town, as a mark of affection and distinction. This, according to the strict letter of the law, we should have refused to accept; twenty days marching, however, while it had sharpened our appetites, had rather diminished our stores. Sheep were not to be got every day, and an ill-looking animal which we had succeeded in purchasing at Egnemo, had been overcome by the heat of the weather and taken itself off on the road. Other supplies, also, were a good deal weakened by successive attacks; potatoes had been extinct many days, and the stock of ducks, which formed our main stay in case of future difficulties, was rapidly succumbing to the knife of the assassin. Under these circumstances we felt that we would be in no way justified in hurting the Kardar's feelings at the expense of our own, by refusing his present, and believing ourselves to be in this instance fit subjects for out-door relief, the new arrival was soon swinging about in the breeze, a welcome addition to our unfurnished larder.

Having thus ended the struggle between our duty and our feelings, we turned our attention to the exploration of the surrounding country.

The town of Ladak, although in a commercial point of view by no means a flourishing-looking settlement, was, as far as picturesqueness was concerned, everything that could be desired. It was built in the style so popular throughout the country—on pinnacles of rock, and such out of the way positions as seemed, of all others, the least adapted for building purposes—immediately outside the town, occupying a sort of bason among the surrounding mountains, was what might fairly be called a "city of the dead." It was of considerable extent, and was formed of groups of the numerous monumental buildings which I have described, and which in a country where the habitations of the living appear so

W. H. K Delt

Hanhart lith

RAJAH'S PALACE, LADAK.

few in proportion to those of the dead, form so curious and remarkable a feature. These tombs, although by no means of very modern date, bear traces, in many instances, of the more recently departed of the Buddhist population. Burnt fragments of bone, hair, &c., were scattered about in various directions, while, collected together in one corner, were the little mounds of mud with a rise at one extremity, where the sculptured turban ought to rest, which denoted the last resting-place of the Moslem faithful. Meeting with the Kardar's chupprassie, I entered into conversation with him about the manners and customs of the Thibetians, a subject on which he seemed to have very hazy ideas indeed, although not on that account at all the less inclined to impart them to one more ignorant than himself. His opinion of the inscribed stones was that they were all written by the Lamas, but he failed completely in explaining for what reason they were collected together. He was aware, however, of Khurjidal, who was to inspect them at the last day. The tomb-like erections, he said, were considered in the light of gods; the bones and ashes of departed Lamas having been pounded up together and deposited beneath them, together with such valuables as turquoises, Pushmeena, rupees, &c. This fact would perhaps account for their being so often in a ruined state—Gûlab Sing having, probably, taken a look at their foundations in search of such valuable pickings. The reason my informant gave me for the unwillingness of the people, however poor, to sell their superabundant ornaments, was that they regarded them as sacred, and held them as their own property during their lifetime only; on decease the jewels reverted to the possessions of the Church. The Lamas are provided, by the custom of dedicating in every family of two or more, one to that office; should there be a number of girls in a family, all those that do not marry become nuns, and adopt the male attire of red and yellow. The nuns, however, seem to be by no means kept in confinement; they work in the fields, and one of them enlisted with us as a coolie, and brought her load into camp before any of her male coadjutors. Among other curious information my friend told me, that the Thibetians by no means consider that each man is entitled to the luxury of a wife all to himself; but that a family of four or five brothers frequently have but one between them, and that the system is productive of no ill-feeling whatever among the different members.* He also

* Of this custom Turner remarks, alluding to Thibet Proper:— "Here we find a practice at once different from the modes of

pointed out a fact which I had not before noticed, viz., that the Thibetians invariably pass to the right hand of these piles of stones and other monuments, but for what reason he was unable to inform me.* Having finished his stock of information, which I received thankfully in default of better, he told me, with delightful coolness, that it was the proper thing for me to give him a bottle of brandy for the Kardar, and that it would be necessary to send also a corkscrew with the bottle, to enable him to get at it! The impudence of the request was almost worth the bottle, but brandy was too scarce and precious a commodity to justify us in pleasing the Kardar, so that all I could do was politely to decline sending the corkscrew or the bottle either. In the afternoon we explored the Bazaar, where we found abundance of dogs, dirt, and idlers, but little else. What little there was in the way of merchandise the proprietors seemed utterly indifferent about disposing of, and after visiting a

Europe, and opposite to those of Asia. That of one female associating her fate and fortune with all the brothers of a family, without any restriction of age or numbers. The choice of a wife is the privilege of the elder brother; and singular as it may seem, a Thibetan wife is as jealous of her connubial rites as ever the despot of an Indian Zenana is of the favours of his imprisoned fair."

* "As the inscription of course begins at opposite ends on each side, the Thibetans are careful in passing that they do not trace the words backwards."—TURNER.

few shops we went away in disgust. The people were a mixture of Cashmeeries, Chinese, Tartars, Bengalees, and Indians of all sorts and sects, and more idle, good-for-nothing looking scoundrels I never laid eyes on. One most amusing group of Mahomedan exquisites reminded one forcibly of *Punch's* Noah's ark costumes and Bond Street specimens of fashion. They were dressed in exaggerated turbans and long white. Chogas, or loose coats, which reached down to their heels; and, as arm in arm, with gentle swagger, they sauntered through the bazaar, they had, in addition to their heavy swellishness, an air of Eastern listlessness to which the most exquisite of their European prototypes could never hope to attain. On reaching our camp we found another traveller had added his little canvas to the scene; it was one of the Government Survey, whom the natives invariably designate by the comprehensive title of "the Compass Wallahs." Wallah is, in Hindostanee, as nearly as possible an equivalent to "fellow," and in explaining the character of this particular order of Wallah, the accent is always strong on the second syllable of the compáss. The Compáss Wallah in question we found quite a wild man of the mountains; his face, from changes of heat and cold and long exposure, was burnt and blistered into all sorts of colours, and, to make his appearance more generally striking, he wore as head-dress, a flyaway, puggery, or turban of blue cotton, of the most voluminous dimensions and wonderful construction imaginable. He gave us an amusing account of his operations among the clouds; how he always rode a cow! and was so much alone that he at times began to doubt the existence of other white men in creation besides himself; how he was *sea* sick at first, and unable to sleep at night from the great rarification of the atmosphere, &c. He joined us during dinner, just in time for a triumph of a plum pudding which our cook had unexpectedly produced, and his heart was so gladdened and expanded by either the suet, the raisins, or the brandy, that he chatted away until the dissipated mountain hour of eleven o'clock, when we sent him off to bed, much pleased with his entertainment, and again reassured, at least for a time, of the continued existence, not only of white men in the world, but of their plum puddings. Among other statistics he gave us the height of Ladak, as 11,000 feet, and that of the recently discovered monarch of the mountains, now set at rest as belonging to the Himalayan range, as being 29,003 feet above the level of the sea.*

* This is Mount "Everest," which has been called the King of

August 15.—Employed all the morning in endeavouring to procure supplies of tea, and after unearthing a queer-looking package containing seven pounds and a half, we differed about the price, the proprietor demanding twenty-four shillings, or about twice its local value.

August 16.—There being no tidings of the arrival of expected caravans, we marched for the monastery of Hemis, crossing the Indus immediately after leaving Ladak, and following it up towards its source. Outside the town we passed a mound of the inscribed stones, which must have been nearly a quarter of a mile in length, and probably contained as many as 30,000. The left bank of the river, which thus formed our path, was a continuation of detached huts, forming no regular villages, and affording very little shade or apparent prospect of shelter for man or beast. The right bank, however, was studded with picturesque-looking little villages, built generally on rocky summits, and surrounded by tombs and Mani panees, to an extent almost to rival the towns themselves in size and importance. About nine miles on the road we halted for breakfast, on the confines of a desert

the South. The King of the North, "Nunga Purbut," is 26,629 feet above the level of the sea.

of smooth stones, from which the heat ascended like vapour, and made our eye-balls ache again. There was no shade in sight, however, and milk was here forthcoming, so we made the best of a bad situation, and, after our repast, lost no time in getting again under weigh. After a hot tramp over a perfect desert, we reached the wooded little village of Chunga, where, as it was getting late, we called a halt and pitched our camp. All hands being tired by their march, we got our dinner at nine o'clock P.M.

August 17.—Started early for Hemis. From the formation of the mountains in which it is situated, the entrance to the village opens upon the traveller suddenly and as if by magic; and as we tramped this morning along the parched and sandy desert, welcome indeed was the unexpected vision of trees and rushing water which the sharp turn presented to our astonished gaze.

The entrance to the gorge in which the monastery is situated was, as usual, quite covered with Mani panees and walls of inscribed stones; one of the former was studded with human skulls, and otherwise ornamented, in a way that proved the vicinity of some stronghold of Lama talent, though not perhaps of the very highest order

The monastery we found situated in a beautifully-wooded valley, thickly planted, and having a dashing little torrent foaming through the centre.

It was built as usual, on the very face of the

rock, and towering above it was an airy fort, ensconced among a number of crows'-nest habitations, perched about apparently with more regard to effect than comfort.

While waiting for the kitchen to come up, we inspected the monastery, and were waited upon by half-a-dozen Lamas, who showed us through the various temples of the gods. Originally containing some two hundred Lamas, its numbers had now dwindled down, by their account, to fifteen or sixteen. We, however, saw actually more than that number ourselves while wandering through the building.

They owned to having treasure in the monastery to the amount of three lakhs of rupees (£30,000), but of this we saw small signs during our inspection.

Some of the divinities were, however, provided with vestments of cloth of gold, and were seated upon thrones, studded with would-be precious stones. Others were accommodated with large silver bowls, placed on pedestals, filled to the brim with "ghee," or rancid butter, and unless blest with inordinate appetites, these, from their enormous size, might fairly last them all till doomsday. We were altogether conducted through four temples, each inhabited by a number of Chinese figures, seated in state, with offerings of corn, flour, rice and ghee, &c. before them, and these were generally served in valuable cups of china, and precious metals. Hanging from the ceiling and the walls around were scrolls, decorated in the Chinese fashion, with figures of tightly-robed, narrow-eyed ladies and gentlemen, scattered about with the usual perspective results.

Some of these scrolls were decorated with scenes which it would take hours to decipher and appreciate. One, in particular, of the last day, was covered with innumerable little figures, and appeared well worthy of a close inspection.

The bad people might here be seen, falling into the hands of some of the most disrespectable looking monsters I have ever beheld; while the good were sitting up in a bunch, looking on at the dreadful scene, in a satisfied and undisturbed way, beautiful to behold.

The most curious things in the place, however, were the praying wheels, which I here saw for the first time. They were little wooden drums, covered round the sides with leather, and fitted vertically in niches in the walls.* A spindle running through the centre, enabled them to revolve at the slightest push. They were generally in rows of eight and ten, and well thumbed and worn they looked, but others of larger dimensions were placed by themselves, decorated with the words "Ûm mani panee," in the Lanza character, all round the barrel.

* Vide illustration, Hemis Monastery.

MONASTERY OF HEMIS.

In the vicinity of the monasteries were various small temples, probably chapels of ease, rudely decorated with grotesque figures, in red and yellow, and having queer-looking structures fastened on the top of them, generally a trident, with tufts of hair attached, or strips of coloured calico, horns of animals, and other rude devices.

In one place we came upon a praying-wheel, turned by water, but I was unable to ascertain whether the benefit accrued to the water, or to the possessor of the stream, or to the public generally. Sometimes the people carry portable wheels, and one old gentleman we met was provided with a huge brass one, with a wooden handle. It was suspended from his neck, in company with a collection of square leather charms, fastened by a string to his coat.

On my asking him what the structure meant, he immediately begun to set it in motion, and piously ejaculating "Ûm mani panee," passed on without another word, but in evident pity for my benighted spiritual condition.

Among other curious sights, we saw one of the Lamas sitting at a chapel door, having before him seven little brass pots. In each of these there was a letter of the words "Ûm mani panee," and the pots being filled with water, he was employed in strewing each with a few grains of corn from a heap at his side, keeping up at the same time a loud mournful chant, and swaying himself to and fro, in time with the music. To have inquired the meaning of this would only have again resulted in the comprehensive information contained in "Ûm mani panee," so we rested in our ignorance, and passed on, much to the relief of the chaunter. After going all through this curious monastery, we repaired to our tents, which had arrived in the interim, and which we found pitched pleasantly among the trees, within a few yards of the torrent. After a bathe and breakfast, we came unanimously to the conclusion that the water was so cold, and the air so cool and refreshing, we could not do better than halt for a couple of days, under the protection of the Church, before again taking the road on our homeward route.

August 18.—Out early for a day's stalk over the mountains, after deer, or anything there might be forthcoming. One of the coolies being a "shikaree," or what they call in Ireland a "sportsman," I took him with me, and with another to carry some breakfast, off we started at about five A.M. The ascent at first was so abrupt, that, although in pretty good walking condition by this time, I found myself halting very frequently to admire the prospect. Having attained the greatest height actually attainable, we spied quietly grazing, about half a mile off, some half dozen little animals, which my "sportsman" declared to be Ibex, and down we went again, best pace, with a view to making a circumbendibus, to get behind them. With a view to accomplish this, we had to pass across some very difficult ground, and at last came to a smooth face of rock, with nothing whatever about it to hold on by, and, moreover, an overhanging ledge, which fairly seemed to bar all further progress.

The coolie, however, whose every toe was as useful to him as a finger, managed to scramble up; and not to be outdone, I also attained some height, when, holding on fly-fashion, and clinging to the rock with my fingers and grass shoes, suddenly the pole which partly supported me slipped away, and my whole attention had to be directed to again reaching the ground in as soft and comfortable a manner as possible. In this I succeeded beyond my expectations, and, a second attempt being more successful, finally reached the top. On attaining our hardly-earned post of vantage, however, there was no sign of our friends, but, suddenly, on the mountain below us a herd of about five-and-twenty more appeared to our delighted view. They were standing gazing up at us in astonishment, and for some moments we remained fixed and motionless, hoping to be taken for the stones we were habited in imitation of. Then, crouching down and crawling along as if on velvet, down we went again, and after another long and trying stalk, over broken ground formed apparently of small slates placed edgeways, and crumbling rocks, whose slightest fall would have been destruction to our plans, we attained a rock about two hundred yards from the herd, and paused for breath once more. They were lying about sunning themselves, with an outlying sentinel posted here and there on either side of them on the look-out; and seeing an eligible spot some fifty yards nearer, we stole along to reach it. We were not, however, destined to take this unfair advantage of the enemy. Just as we had half crossed the distance, an ill-fated, abominable little fragment of rock suddenly broke off, and at its first bound away went the herd like lightning over the precipitous rocks, and with a little chirrupping noise like sparrows, were in a few seconds well out of range of bullets. As the natives express it, "they became wind," and we were left behind our rock, looking, after all our toils, to say the least of it, extremely foolish. A shot which I took at some 250 yards was more to relieve ourselves by making a noise than with any hopes of bringing down one of the light-heeled little creatures, for their bounding powers put all correctness of aim at that range out of the question.

The next part of the programme was breakfast, but alas! there were no signs in any direction of the bearer of our supplies, and I now recollected that the rock which had so puzzled us would be quite inaccessible to the coolie and his precious charge, without which he himself was useless. All we could do was to ascend a high peak of mountain, in hopes that the breakfast would ascend another, and that we could then exchange signals of distress and obtain relief. However, after reaching our look-out station, which took us some climbing, we could discern nothing around us bearing the slightest resemblance to a coolie, and our hopes began to descend below zero.

It was now about twelve o'clock, and taking advantage of the produce of the country, I made a light breakfast off two stalks of rhubarb, and tying a handkerchief to the top of my pole as a signal, lay down in the very minute portion of shade procurable under a midday sun, and indulged in the pleasures of imagination, conjured up by absent chicken legs and cold chupatties. After a long wait, I came to the conclusion that the two pieces of rhubarb were entirely insufficient to continue the day's work upon, so I reluctantly gave the order to retreat upon our camp, and turned from thoughts of breakfast to those of dinner. My grass shoes were by this time completely worn out by the pointed rocks and flinty ground we had traversed, and my spare ones were in the society of the cold chicken and the chupatties, so that I was soon walking in nothing but socks. Before long, this portion of my property was also run through, and I was finally obliged to borrow the sportsman's pointed slippers, in which I managed to get along over the ruggedest piece of creation I ever traversed, and reached our camp about three P.M. Tired, hungry, and burnt by the sun, a bathe in the rushing torrent and a visit to the kitchen were soon accomplished, and I then learnt that the coolie, being stopped by the rock, had come back at once, and, having been again immediately packed off by F. to search for us, had not been since heard of.

August 19.—Found the Q. M. G. to-day laid up with fever and influenza, and administered some quinine pills to him, besides ordering a steed to carry him on to Ladak to-morrow.

Explored the Lama's habitations and temples, and saw some very curious carvings and paintings on stones, some of them not altogether in the Church order of design.

Some of the ceilings were beautifully decorated, and must have cost a good deal of money in their day, but they were now rapidly falling into decay.

During the day we had a good opportunity of seeing the Lamas go through their private devotions. The operation appeared simple enough. Each as he entered the court and passed along the rows of wheels, by simply stretching out his arm set the whole of them in motion, at the same time repeating "Ûm mani panee" in a dolorous voice to himself. Coming then to the large wheel with painted characters, he gave it an extra energetic spin, which sufficed to keep it in motion for several minutes, and having thus expended his energies for the time being, he again disappeared as he had come. One of the smaller wheels I found in a state of neglect and dilapidation as to its outer case, and thinking it a good opportunity to discover something as to the meaning of the system in general and of "Ûm mani panee" in particular, I quietly abstracted the inner contents, in full assurance that it would never be missed; that the wheel itself would go round as merrily as ever, and that, as far as the prayers were concerned, there were still sufficient left behind, considering the reduced state of the monasteries, to satisfy the conscience even of the devoutest of Lamas.*

* The only information I here again received was "Ûm mani panee!" The wheel consisted of a roll of the thinnest paper, six inches in diameter, and five and a half in width, closely printed

As I passed out, however, a huge black dog, which was chained up in the yard, seemed, by the rabid manner in which he made feints at my legs, to be quite aware of what I had done, and he snapped and howled, and strained and tore at his chain as I went by, just as if he detected the holy bundle sticking out of my pocket, and thoroughly understood my consequent guilty appearance. The principal designs upon the stones here—some of which, in colour, were in wonderful preservation—appear to be cross-legged effigies of Buddha, seated in that state of entire abstraction from all passions and desires, which seem to be the end and object of Buddhists' aspirations.

A certain rotundity of form, however, and appearance of *comfortableness*, rather tend to suggest that the pleasures of the table at least

throughout with the eternally recurring words, which all appeared so ready to pronounce and none seemed able to explain. The roll was sixty yards long, and was composed of a succession of strips, one foot nine inches in length, and all joined together. The whole was inclosed in a coarse canvas cover, open at both ends, and marked with what was no doubt the official seal of the particular society for the diffusion of ignorance at Lassa, from which it had originally emanated. Each of the strips contained the mystic sentence, one hundred and seventy times, so that I was thus at once put into possession of all the valuable intelligence to be derived from "Um mani panee," repeated between seventeen and eighteen thousand times. Vide Appendix B.

have not quite been renounced among the other pomps and vanities of Buddhist life.

August 20.—Started for Ladak again, nominally at some desperately early hour of the morning, but in reality at about half-past five, the sun not shining upon our position until late, in consequence of our proximity to the mountains.

Mr. Rajoo being still indisposed, and, in his own belief, dying, we mounted him upon a hill horse, where he looked like a fly on a dromedary. Halted for breakfast half way, and had a hot wearisome march afterwards into Ladak, the sun being intensely powerful, and the greater part of the journey over a glaring desert of shifting sand and loose stones. So deep was this in some places, that it was with difficulty we could drag our steps along. The latter part seemed perfectly interminable, and not until four o'clock, burnt, tired, and parched with thirst, did we reach our old halting place. Since our departure, the Thanadar had changed his fancy as to brandy, and now requested a bottle of vinegar. This we promised in the event of his procuring us some tea, our stock being low, and none other procurable without government assistance. By this means we obtained a decorated bundle of pale-looking tea for thirteen rupees, or 1*l.* 6*s.* The bundle contained 7½ lbs., so that the price was heavy enough, considering our proximity to the land of tea.

My shoe-leather being in a doubtful state, I invested in a pair of the sheepskin Chino-Esquimaux ones of local manufacture, but soon found that the old saw of "nothing like leather" was quite a fallacy, when the leather savoured so strongly of mutton as that composing my new boots did. In the morning they were absent, and it was not until after much search that the mutilated remains of one foot was discovered, gnawed and sucked out of all semblance to Blucher, Wellington, or any other known order of shoe or boot, while the other appeared irretrievably to have gone to the dogs. Our lantern here was also carried off by some of the canine race, and left beautifully cleaned, but unbroken, not far from our tent door.

Finding that there was no news of caravans, or probability of their arriving, we determined upon striking our camp, and retiring again towards Cashmere, having attained the furthermost point which the limits of our leave allowed.

PART VI.

A RETREAT TO THE VALLEY.

August 21.—Left Ladak about four P.M. and halted for the night on the confines of the desert-plain at Pitok. On the road I succeeded —much to my astonishment—in getting a necklace of bits of amber, and a turquoise, from an old lady, whom I found at her cottage-door weaving goat's-hair cloth. She took two rupees for the family jewels, and, when the bargain was struck, seemed in a desperate fright at what she had done, looking about in every direction to see that no avaricious old Lama was near, nor any of her gossiping acquaintance, who would be likely to tell *the minister* of what she had done.

For the first time during our travels, the retainers turned a little rusty to-day. The scarcity of the tobacco supply and dislike to quit the amusements of city life were the chief causes, and the consequence was that the cook, who was sent off at two o'clock to have dinner ready for us on arrival, made his appearance about sunset and gave us dinner at nine P.M. The Q. M. G. and the Sipahee sauntered in afterwards at their leisure, having left the coolies and ourselves to pitch the camp how and where we liked. Smarting under these indignities, and knowing that the Sipahee was the head and front of the offending, I, in a weak moment, committed an assault upon that ferocious warrior. The consequence was that the representative of "The Army," feeling its dignity insulted in the face of the populace, immediately set to work upon the unfortunate natives, and assaulted even the gopa, or kotwal, of the village; and so severely was one of the coolies handled, that I was obliged to interfere in the cause of peace, and not without difficulty succeeded in stopping the stone I had thus so unwittingly set rolling.

This same Sipahee rejoiced in the name of Dilour Khan, which might be loosely translated the "Invincible One," and such we always called him. He was a fierce-looking soldier beyond measure to look at, and very terrible among the miserable Thibetians, making desperate onslaughts upon the unfortunate boors, to obtain supplies fit, as he said, for the Grandees, the Cherishers of the Poor, the Protection of the World, &c.

The style of head-dress generally worn among the natives facilitated his efforts immensely in these matters; for, throwing aloft his sword, and relinquishing his umbrella, he used to seize suddenly upon a pig-tail, and, handling it after the fashion of a bell-rope, proceed to insist upon the production of impossible mutton and other delicacies in a way that was almost always successful, even under circumstances apparently the most hopeless.

He had a sharp, detonating way, too, of delivering a volley of Thibetian, at the same time curling up his fierce-looking moustaches and whiskers, and gesticulating with both arms, which always had a great effect, the more so that the expletives were generally in Hindostanee, and not being understood, were all the more terrible to the unfortunate pig-tails on that account.

August 22.—Left for Egnemo, over our old ground, which, wanting the attraction of novelty, appeared to us rather longer than on first acquaintance. The sun, too, was more powerful than ever, and the deep soft sand more trying, so that we were glad enough to get under shelter at our journey's end. Here we found the apricot-trees, which were teeming with fruit when we passed, completely stripped and bare, and it was with difficulty we got a few from the houses for preserving purposes.

August 23.—Made an early start, and arrived at Suspûl after a pleasant march, a cool breeze from the mountains fanning our faces the entire way. Here we pitched upon a cool and shady camping-ground, close to a rushing torrent, where we were soon immersed in ice-cold water. While making a short cut back to breakfast up a precipitous face of concrete stone, I very nearly finished my wanderings in Thibet with an unpleasantly abrupt full stop. I had nearly reached the top, which was higher than I had imagined, when the treacherous lumps of stone to which I was clinging, came away in my hands, and, with a tremendous crash, down I came in a perfect storm of dirt, dust, and stones, very much to the fright and astonishment of F. and the mate, who were quietly finishing their toilet below. A broken bone in such a place as Egnemo would have been a serious misfortune, and it was therefore a matter of considerable satisfaction to find that, although half-stunned and doing but little credit in appearance to my recent washing, I had escaped with no worse injuries than torn hands and what the doctors would call abrasions of the side and elbow.

August 24.—Marched as usual, and reached Nûrila about noon. From the hilliness of the road and the laziness of the coolies combined, they did not arrive until two P.M., so that we breakfasted at three o'clock. To occupy the time, however, we took advantage of the products of the country, and set to work upon a quantity of apples, and having both thirst and hunger to assuage, I think we got through about sixteen each before the kitchen appeared. While bathing we were suddenly caught in a pouring shower of rain, which obliged us to snatch up our only garments and beat a hasty and not to say dignified retreat into a little den of a water-mill, where we crouched until it was over. After the rain had stopped, a curious fall of stones and rocks took place down the precipitous face of mountain which bounded the opposite side of the Indus to our camp. The noise and the commotion the stones made in their descent, reminded one exactly of volleys of grape, and to any traveller unfortunate enough to get in their way, the results would probably have been quite as disastrous.

Our larder having been low of late, we effected

the purchase of a sheep here, for which we paid two shillings.

August 25.—Left for Lamieroo. The khitmutgar, having reported himself sick to-day, we mounted him on a pony, the efficiency of that branch of the service being of vital importance to the future prospects of the expedition. Having discovered, by yesterday's experience, that nature abhors a vacuum, and no apples being forthcoming at Lamieroo, we halted for breakfast at the village of Kulchee.

Here I tried hard to purchase a curiously-contrived praying-wheel from an old Lama, but without success. My old acquaintance, the gopa, however, brought me one for sale, but it was in such a dilapidated state, and so highly valued as church property, that I let him keep his shaky religious curiosity at his own price. Leaving Kulchee, we crossed the Indus at a mud fort, and bid the roaring, dirty river a final good-bye. Near this the bhistie and khitmutgar, journeying together, lost the path, and found themselves well on the road to Iscardo before discovering their mistake. The road to-day, like all our return journeys, appeared twice the length it did on first acquaintance. The hills, too, were very severe on the coolies, and it was fortunate we halted for breakfast on the road.

At Lamieroo, we found a great change in the temperature; a strong cold breeze blowing, and a general winteriness prevailing, which affected our retainers considerably more than it did ourselves. The Q. M. G. in particular, not having entirely recovered his health, and being low in the article of tobacco, still believed himself to be dying, and was most unusually low-spirited and down in the mouth. As it threatened rain, we pitched our camp close to an old serai, in order to allow our servants to ensconce themselves under a roof, and to derive the full benefit of their wood fire, which they lost no time in kindling.

August 26.—Exactly a month to-day since leaving Sirinugger. The live stock begin to show signs of time on their constitutions; the four surviving ducks wandering about, with a melancholy sort of consciousness that the mysterious fate that has overtaken their late companions is also hanging over themselves, and appearing entirely changed in consequence from the joyous birds they used to be on first starting for their Thibetian travels. To-day being Sunday, we all enjoyed a rest; and the feeling on waking at dawn, and remembering that we were not to be rudely turned out of bed, was quite a delightful and novel sensation. The wind, too, was unusually chill, and as it made nothing of the trifling obstacle presented by the walls of our tent, we were some time before we finally emerged from among the bed-clothes. The people here we found employed in *pulling* their corn crops, and stacking them upon the roofs of their houses. At Suspûl, although much hotter than here, they had hardly begun to take in their crops, and at Ladak, the harvest was untouched when we left.

In the afternoon, while rambling about the crow's nests of Lamieroo, I discovered by chance a very curious temple in course of construction, and a number of Lamas and Zemindars superintending the proceedings. The principal decorative work was being carried on by a Chinese-looking, pigtailed artist, evidently not a local celebrity, who was embellishing the walls most profusely with scenes, portrayed in the purest style of pre-Raphaelite colouring. The figures in these had only been furnished with flesh-coloured spots where their faces were to be, and the foreign "pigtail" was employed, seated on a high platform, in furnishing them with features and casts of expression in accordance with the spirit of the scenes which they helped to compose. This he did certainly with very great skill, and the operation was a most interesting one to watch. The floor was covered with pigments, and materials of all kinds, and the little community, in the midst of the surrounding apparent solitude, were working away like a hive of bees. They appeared to have a hive-like dislike also of the approach of a stranger, and one old Lama, with a twisted mat of hair erected on the top of his head—a drone of the hive—took a particular dislike to me, and scowled savagely as I quietly examined the curious designs upon the walls.

The eternal "Ûm mani panee" formed a very large part of the decoration, being painted over the walls in every variety of coloured letters. In the inner part of the temple was a large coloured statue, with eight arms, and two-and-twenty heads.

The heads were placed in threes, looking every way, in the shape of a pyramid, a single head crowning the whole.* One of the hands held a bow, but the implements contained in the others were entirely Buddhist in character, and to me unknown.

Behind this figure was a star, with innumerable radiating arms from the centre, while from the points of the fingers were five other rows of

* The origin of this divinity is probably derived from the legend of Khoutoukhtou, which will be found in Appendix B.

hands, continuing the star-like circle. These were in half relief on the wall, the figure itself standing out some feet, as if to receive and appropriate the offerings of corn, flowers, oil, &c., which already began to be laid at its feet. Among the litter I remarked several tame partridges and "chickore" walking about, probably sacred to the newly installed divinities.

The whole scene was a very curious one, and not the less so from being entirely unexpected, and occurring in such an apparently deserted spot. One might have explored the place a dozen times without hitting upon the hive of workmen, and, even when discovered, the excellence of the designs and workmanship in so uncivilized a region, was in itself remarkable.

Some of the paintings were of rather startling a character to find occupying places in the order of church decoration, or indeed any other, but they were not perhaps more unsuitable than many I have seen in more avowedly civilized temples of worship.

August 27.—We found it very hard, in spite of our day of rest, to turn out early again this morning. The wind was sharp and cold, and the temperature altogether decidedly changed from that we had been having. The head of the cooking department being still sick, proceeded on a pony, and, having a certain air of the Sepoy about him, very grand and imposing he looked. The road being long and up hill, we breakfasted at a tomb in the pass of Fotoola, reaching Khurboo about three P.M.

In the evening, the comptroller of the household made his appearance upon the cook's pony, having from want of tobacco, and other causes, become done up on the road. The bhistie alone holds out, and seems, as far as servants go, the only hope of the expedition. To-day's march has again spoiled F.'s and my own lately amending complexions, the icy wind and the burning sun together completely blistering our faces. In the evening we enjoyed a lovely sunset, which tinted the magnificent range of mountains we had crossed with the most beautiful hues imaginable.

August 28.—Another bitterly cold morning. Got away well considering, and arrived at Waka in time for a late breakfast in the little native serai, where we had before halted. Mr. Rajoo and the cook came in with an air of great magnificence. They were each mounted, and each pony was provided with a well-grown foal, so that the two departments may be said to have performed their march with four horses.

August 29.—Descended the Waka Valley,

leaving Shergol to our left, and thereby saving about a kos and a half of already explored road.

Breakfasted under a shady grove of pollards, at the little village of Lotzûm, a cold refreshing bathe in a snow torrent enabling us to do full justice to our cook's very excellent performances in this line. That dignitary was upon his legs again to-day, and Rajoo convalescent once more. Arriving about three P.M. at our old ground at Pushkoom, we found the peaceful, quiet-looking little spot we had left, a scene of the greatest noise and bustle imaginable. We were now received in due form by the Kardar, and Thanadar of Kurgil, not to mention the Wuzeer, or Vizier of Pushkoom. This dignitary had formerly been its Rajah, but during Gûlab Singh's time was reduced to the post of Vizier, or Prime Minister to nobody in particular, with a salary of some thirty rupees per annum. Where our last camp was pitched, we found a circle of natives congregated, some standing, some sitting on their haunches, but all accompanying to the full extent of their voices—at the same time clapping time with their hands—the efforts of a band of six or seven artists on the pipe and tabor, who kept up a quavering strain of what they doubtless believed to be music. To the united melody thus produced, a string of a dozen or so of ladies, in their full war paint, were decorously going through the monotonous evolutions of a popular dance, waving their arms about, gesticulating, and at the same time lingering, as it were, over the ground, and comporting themselves in that staid, yet fitfully lively way, which seems to be the general style of Eastern dancing. They were attired most picturesquely, and evidently in their very fullest ball costume, so that we were fortunate in hitting upon such a good opportunity of seeing their gala manners and customs. They all wore caps of some kind, either of a small, close-fitting pattern, like a fez, or in the shape of a large, and very ultra Scotch cap, black, and very baggy; these were hung round with little silver ornaments, something in the shape of wine labels for decanters, but studded with turquoises; some of them, also, wore brooches, generally formed of three cornelians, or turquoises, in a row. The broad bands of turquoise, worn usually on the forehead, were for the time disrated from their post of honour, and were suspended instead from the nape of the neck, over a square piece of stiff cloth, embroidered with strings of red beads. Round the shoulders, and hanging low, in order to show off the turquoises, lumps of amber, and other family jewels, were the sheepskin cloaks, inseparable from Thibetian female costume; they were, however, of larger size than those of every day life, and were gorgeously decorated outside in red and blue, the *fur* merely appearing at the edges. Below this, everything merged in some mysterious way into the variegated sheepskin boots of the country, also decorated with red, blue, and yellow cloth patterns on the instep. These bore a very conspicuous position in the dance, as the ladies, contrary to the principles of modern art, were continually regarding and showing forth the aforesaid boots, as they glided about, and pattered the time to the well-marked music. The dance was altogether much more pleasing than the Indian nach, and the ladies, in spite of their savage jewellery, and rude manner, were much more womanly and respectable than their gauzy, be-ringed and bare-footed southern rivals.

After the dance was over, there was a general move to a large, open space of ground, where the male part of the community were to show off their prowess in the native games. To my astonishment, some fifty or sixty Thibetians here assembled, each provided with a veritable hockey stick, not on foot, however, but each man mounted on his own little mountain pony, and prepared to play a downright game of hockey on horseback. In the centre of the battle-field, between the two "sides," the pipes and tabors forming *the band* took their station, and each time the wooden ball of contention was struck off, set up a flourish to animate the players. The Thibetians, however, required no such artificial excitement, but set to work with an energy and spirit quite refreshing to behold, and the scene soon became most animated and amusing. The Thibetians, unlike Englishmen under similar circumstances, appeared to think the more clothes they had on the better, and in their long woollen coats and trowsers, and their huge sheepskin boots, they quite overshadowed the wiry little horses they bestrode. Besides having to carry all this weight, the ponies, most unfairly, came in also for all the *shinning*; but in spite of these disadvantages, they performed their parts to admiration, dashing about in the most reckless manner, at the instigation of their riders, and jostling and knocking against one another in a way that would have disgusted any other pony in the world. Conspicuous among the crowd of riders, was the thirty-rupee Prime Minister, who on a most diminutive little animal, charged about in a way he never could have condescended to do, had he had the misfortune to have still remained a Rajah. Each time that the ball was sent into the goal, the striker, picking it up dexterously, without dismounting, came again at full speed down the course, the band struck up, and throwing the ball into the air, he endeavoured to strike it as far as possible in the direction of the adverse party. Behind him, at best pace, came his own side, and a desperate collision appeared the inevitable result; however, not a single man was unhorsed during the entire struggle, nor were there any violent concussions, or accidents of any kind on either side.

The men rode very short, and their clumsy boots, stuck through the heavy stirrup-irons, gave them a ludicrous appearance, which was little indicative of the firm seat and active part they displayed in the games. After seeing the last of the hockey we pitched our camp under a grove of trees, and had an audience of the Kardar, with a view to obtaining information as to our new line of march, which here branches off from the old route. He, however, was unable to afford us much intelligence, and we were glad to get rid of him again, with a present of fifteen bullets, which were the objects he appeared, at the time, to covet most in the world.

To-day a charge was brought against our immaculate bhistie, by the Q. M. G., of secreting about half-a-pound of precious white sugar in his sheepskin bag. On being confronted with the Bench he confessed the crime, improving on it, like most natives, by declaring that it was for medicine for his little boy at home, who had sore eyes! The cook, being taken up with the festivities and the turquoises, gave us our dinner at an unusually fashionable hour.

August 30.—Started for a fresh line of exploration, not without some difficulty and opposition, in consequence of a desire on the part of the Sipahee and the servants to revisit Kurgil, with a view to the tobacco supplies supposed to exist there.

The consequence was that they obtained all sorts of information for us as to the badness of our proposed road, and the insuperable obstacles to be overcome from unbridged rivers, snow, &c. Persevering in our plans, however, we were rewarded by finding a great improvement in the scenery, and, from the novelty of the day's work, a corresponding benefit to the spirits of the entire expedition. Passing through a little village called Menzies, we halted for breakfast within view of the northern face of an entire new range of snow-capped mountains. Everything gave promise of fine scenery in advance, and about four P.M. we reached Thambis, a lovely piece of cultivation, surrounded on all sides by monster rocks, and overlooked by a peak of pure white virgin snow, and here we pitched our little camp. Entering the village suddenly from the rocky mountain-pass, the little place looked inexpressibly green and refreshing, and we were soon under the shade of a row of pleasant pollards, which lined the bank of a stream near which we halted. As at Pushkoom, the second crops were down, and the people employed in thrashing and grinding their corn. The new crop consisted principally of pulse of various kinds, radishes, and a few fields of tobacco, and nestled in pleasant nooks and corners there were occasional gardens of melons.

Here we got two fine sheep for one rupee ten annas, or 3*s.* 3*d.*, and one of them formed a sumptuous repast for the coolies and retainers, who held a most convivial banquet round their camp-fires in the evening. The primitive inhabitants seemed quite unaccustomed to the sight of strangers, and we found on this account, better and more plentiful supplies procurable, while the assembling of the entire village to behold the wonderful arrival, formed a pleasant excitement after the day's march.

To-day we had the choice of two roads, one on

either side of the torrent; that on the right bank was reported bad, and we accordingly decided upon the other, but an unexpected obstacle then presented itself in the shape of a bridge of rope of a very considerable length, crossing the torrent. It was formed of the twigs of trees, and being in an unpleasantly dilapidated condition, the passage was a matter of some difficulty if not danger. To save the direct strain a number of the villagers took up their position to distend the side ropes, and having to get over the outstretched legs of these officious aids, made the affair a very much more nervous proceeding than it would otherwise have been: The lowness of the side-ropes, and the oscillation of the ricketty structure rendered the feat altogether a rather more amusing performance to the looker on than to the actual performer, and I was not sorry to reach the opposite shore. On the arrival of the coolies, they all hung back, and regarded the machine with utter astonishment, and when one of them did essay the passage, his coat caught in one of the twigs, about half way across, and not having the use of his hands, he was completely caught as in a trap, and unable either to advance or retire. In endeavouring to turn, his load nearly upset him, and there he remained until extricated by one of the villagers.

A few of the coolies afterwards got across, and also the servants, with great trepidation, but the greater number, with the main body of the baggage, including, alas! all the cooking department, except one load, were afraid to essay the passage, and had to take to the bad road in despair. The fraction of the commissariat stores which did reach our side of the water turned out to be plates, knives, forks, and kettles, so that we had before us no prospect of breakfast until we arrived at a village some ten kos off, where a more respectable bridge was to re-unite us with our goods and chattels.

As promised, the path on our side was pretty good, and led us through several peaceful little villages, overhung by giant rocks, and dotted with enormous blocks of stone, which had descended to disturb the harmony of the scene during some convulsion or commotion in the interior economy of the mountains. Some of these were taken advantage of by the natives to serve as canvas for their designs, and were carved with effigies of four-armed divinities, and other *sacred* subjects. With the exception of these, we saw few traces of Buddhism about us here. Passing through one of the villages, I bought a medicine-book, or charm, from one of the natives. It was in Arabic, and was rolled and swathed like a mummy, and worn round his arm. He told me that he had inherited it from his father, and appeared by no means happy when it was gone.

Arriving at Sankoo, we found it a well-wooded thinly-inhabited valley, about a kos and a half in length. Here we had a new specimen of bridge architecture to pass. It was formed simply enough of two crooked trunks of trees, and, considering the torrent below, it required a considerable amount of confidence to enable one to traverse it successfully. From the scarcity of the population, I had great difficulty in finding anybody to procure me a drink of milk, and when I at last discovered a woman and two children, she was so thunderstruck that, catching up one of her offspring in her arms and shrieking to another to follow her, like a hen and chickens swooped at by a hawk, away they went as fast as their legs would carry them. As this was no satisfaction to me, however productive it might be of milk to the baby, I began to make signs of bringing down the family mansion that short distance required to raze it to the ground, and thus succeeded in calling forth from its interior a half-naked old gentleman out of his study to my assistance.

He, however, in an abject way informed me

that he had no milk himself, but would introduce me to a friend who had. I accordingly followed him, "at the point of the stick," until we reached another mud hovel, where we found the lady of the house sitting in her porch working, and a supercilious-looking gentleman reclining at her side.

Neither of them, however, seemed to pay the slightest attention to my wants, and savage with thirst, I charged the whole trio, saluting the gentleman at the same time with an application of my stick. Instead of his jumping up, however, as I expected, I found that the unfortunate man was kept in his recumbent position by rheumatism, or some such ailment, and that, in my ignorance of Thibetian, and want of milk and patience combined, I had committed an atrocious and unwarrantable assault upon an invalid. Meantime, however, the lady was off like a shot, and soon returned from the dairy bearing both milk and flour, wherewith to appease the ferocity of her visitor. Having nearly choked myself with the meal and brought myself round again with the milk, I gave the invalid full compensation and satisfaction as far as I was able, for my attack, and again took to the road in search of the bridge which was to re-unite us with our baggage and our breakfast.

Before reaching it, however, I was the unfortunate cause of the entire abandonment of some half-dozen houses, by merely halting to sit down for a few minutes under a tree in their vicinity. Whether the inhabitants—who appeared to be all women—thought that I was going to open trenches and beleaguer them or not I don't know, but, after a few minutes, I used to see one of them dart out from behind a mud wall and scuttle away like a rabbit; then another lady would steal out, carefully lock the door, and with a child on her back and a couple of olive branches in rear, crawl over the housetop and out at the back garden, there taking to her heels, and vanishing with her convoy suddenly from sight. This operation being repeated in other tenements, I found myself at last left in full and uninterrupted possession of the entire settlement I happened to be in the vicinity of, including the cocks, hens, firewood, dwelling-places, and messuages, &c. thereunto appertaining and belonging. When they re-occupied the evacuated premises I don't know, but Rajoo, I ascertained, wished them all no future happiness when, on coming up some time afterwards, he knocked at every door and looked down every sky-light and chimney in the village without being able to procure as much as a light to ignite the tobacco in his "hubble bubble." The coolies having found the path on the right bank of the torrent quite as bad as prognosticated, we got our breakfast shortly before sunset. From the proximity of a high rocky mountain, towards the westward of our camp, however, this was considerably earlier than might be imagined.

September 1.—Commenced our last month but one of leave, by a fine march of some sixteen miles from Sankoo to Tesroo, or Sooroo, at the foot of the grandest snowy range we had yet encountered. The path led us over a gigantic fall of rocks, evidently the deposits formed by successive and destructive avalanches.

In some parts the traces were quite fresh, the rocks being rent and uptorn in a wonderful way; and, in one place, we passed the ground where two villages had been entirely overwhelmed by an avalanche, the entire population of twenty-five having been killed in the ruins.

After walking about five or six kos, in the finest and freshest of morning air, we suddenly opened upon a noble mountain of pure unbroken snow, rearing its head proudly into the blue sky among a train of courtiers, not so noble, nor so purely, whitely, clad as itself, but still arrayed in robes of glistening snow. Here the path emerged from the side of the rugged mountain torrent, and about two kos over fine turfy grass brought us to within some three miles of Sooroo; and here we halted, under a grove of trees, for breakfast. After this, we had another rope bridge to pass, which was so little to the taste of the coolies, that they were glad to get the natives to carry over their loads for them. On crossing we found the Thanadar, a fine, old black-muzzled Cashmeeree, with his Moonshee, and a train of eight Sipahees waiting to receive us, and were conducted in due form to our camping ground. Here the breeze, as it whistled over our tent, savoured strongly of the snow, and reminded us of the vicinity of the chilly mountain Grandees we had seen on our road, and which still presided over us.

The natives even appeared to feel the cold, though in the winter months they are entirely snowed up, and ought to be pretty well inured to it by this time.

The entire valley is, in winter, totally submerged in snow, and a stranger might then pass over it without knowing there were villages beneath his feet. The bridges are annually swept away, and so suddenly does the hard weather make its appearance, that even now the inhabitants were in fear and trembling lest the snows should come down on them before their crops of wheat and barley were carried for the winter's use.

Numbers of fields of corn are still within a week or so of ripening, and, should they be lost, the chance of winter's subsistence would be small indeed.

The appearance of a Thibetian settlement here, as one looks down upon it from a height, is very much that of an ant-hill. The huts are built on the top of each other, and generally on mounds, and the people, like ants, are busily and laboriously employed in laying up their winter store, not only of grain, but also of fire-wood, and anything capable of serving in its place, to enable them to struggle through their dreary months of captivity.

Huge loads of corn and stacks are to be seen moving about, apparently spontaneously, disappearing through queer holes and corners of the earth, and again appearing on the house-tops, where they are stacked and stored. The bundles of fire-wood being placed with the branches outside, and neatly ranged, they give the peaceful settlement quite a bristling and warlike appearance, as if defended by *chevaux de frise*. The Zemindars here pay but two rupees a year to the Maharajah, but it seems a hard case that such hardly-subsisting people should have to pay anything whatever in such a sterile dreary territory as they possess.

To-day we came across one solitary mound of the inscribed stones, probably the last, as we now cross the mountains into Cashmerian territory again.

To the south of our camp, the road from Ladak through Zanskar joins the valley, and we half regretted not having risked the chances of that road; however, it was uncertain whether it was passable, and, as time was valuable, we had but little option in the matter.

September 2.—Being Sunday, we had a regular rest, explored the country, and made the acquaintance of the few Thibetians who inhabited the villages.

Everywhere there were signs of the invasion of Gûlab Singh, some twenty years ago. Houses in ruins, and forts reduced to dust and rubbish. To replace these latter, a new fort had been constructed by Rumbeer Singh, in what appears about the worst possible position in the entire valley to render it of any use whatever.

The people were busily employed in their fields, pulling and carrying corn, and treading it out with oxen. A team of six I saw, most uncomfortably performing this work. They were tied together by the noses, and so small a piece of ground had they to revolve upon, that the innermost animal had to go backward continually, while the centre ones were regularly jammed together by the outsiders. Two deformed natives were employed in driving this unhappy thrashing machine.

In the evening, the Thanadar's Moonshee came to beg a "razee nama," or "letter of satisfaction," which we gave him, together with a "bukshish," with which he seemed well pleased.

September 3.—Got up this morning with a peculiarly cold feel, and started with a fine piercing breeze in our teeth, blowing directly off the snows.

Our force was augmented to-day by three goats, as portable dairy, and a party of natives, with three days' supplies, also a guide, for our path lay over ground neither much frequented nor well known. To-day's has been the grandest scene of the panorama yet unfolded to us. From the last halt, no inconsiderable height in itself, we mounted continually towards the huge white masses of snow, which so lately towered above us in the distance. Passing the remains of mighty avalanches firmly fixed across the foaming torrent, we ascended the snow valley by the side of a perfect mountain of ice and snow, the accumulations of, possibly, as many years as the world has existed, which had formed itself immoveably between the mighty mountain's sides. The terrific force, with which the masses of snow had come down each season, to repair the ravages in the frozen monster's constitution caused by the melting away of his lower extremities, could be seen by the enormous blocks of stone which rested on its surface in all directions. In some places fantastic arches of snow were thus formed, with blocks of rock resting on their summits, and such a distance were these central accumulations of rocks, and snow, and ice, from the cradles in which they were reared, that it was impossible to conceive, without the occurrence of an earthquake, how they could ever have reached their present positions.

One begins now faintly to understand how it is that the enormous number of torrents dashing about are kept supplied with icy life. The vast quantities of snow wedged into solid masses, which must have existed since all time among these mighty mountains, would serve to feed rivers innumerable, and the supply, as long as rivers and mountains exist, would appear to be inexhaustible.

Our path, if path it could be called, was very bad in parts, and so difficult for the coolies that we were fortunate in getting our breakfast at two P.M., and, when we did get it, a snowstorm which came down upon us rather hurried our procedings in discussing it.

The entire afternoon it continued snowing, and the mountain-tops soon hid themselves and sulked away among the leaden mists. Our tent was pitched among a low sort of scrub, the only apology for fire-wood procurable, and here we soon had a fine carpet of fresh snow, which put the unfortunate coolies, and the servants, and the three goats and the four ducks, and, in fact, everybody but F. and myself, who now begin to feel thoroughly *at home*, to considerable discomfort and inconvenience.

About a hundred yards from us rises the central mountain of consolidated old snow; while the monarchs of the place, whose hospitality we have been enjoying, overtopped our diminutive little worn canvas dwelling with proud and gloomy magnificence, or hid themselves from us in their ermine mantles, with aristocratic frigidity.* Before us, the path continues towards the clouds, hemmed in, to all appearance, by a mighty glacier, which it would seem impossible to avoid in our to-morrow's route. To-day we again find the society

* The most remarkable of these were "Ser" and "Mer," otherwise called "Nanoo" and "Kanoo;" respectively 23,407 and 23,264 feet above the level of the sea.

of the little shrieking marmots, who seemed more than ever astonished at what could bring so strange and motley a group of creatures to disturb the universal quiet of their solitude. Of all our party the cook, perhaps, here fares the worst. The only things growing about us are a few plants of rhubarb and the miserable scrub, which he is obliged to use with all faith as firewood! this being thoroughly wet requires much coaxing to ignite, and what with the difficulties of his profession, the cold, the falling snow, and the increased appetites of the *Sahibs*, the unfortunate head of the cooking department becomes for the time the most intensely miserable being, black or white, upon the whole face of the globe.

September 4.—Awoke this morning to find the encampment, and its vicinity, covered with snow, and every prospect of a snow-stormy march before us. The coolies and servants were in a deplorable state of frozen discomfort, but all kept up their spirits by laughing at each other's woes. Just as the sun appeared above the mountains for a few minutes only, we got under weigh; the tent, however, took some time to disencumber of its load of frozen snow, and to pack, and all the baggage required excavating previous to becoming capable of removal.

The path up to the great glacier above us was

wild and barren, it lay over a little plain watered by branching streams, and covered over with ice and newly fallen snow. Crossing one of these streams, I flushed a solitary woodcock, the only inhabitant of the wild, and shortly afterwards, our guide, an uncouth bundle of sheep-skins, slipped over a frozen stone, and came down in the freezing water with a splash, which, at that hour of the morning, made one shudder all over involuntarily. The snow-shoes which F. and myself had donned, alone saved us several times from a similar, uncomfortable fate. Our path, properly speaking, should have led over the very centre of the glacier; but, in consequence of the numerous crevasses and the early appearance of the new snow, our guide steadily refused to take us over the pass by that route. To have taken it without a guide would have been simply impossible; so we diverged to one side, and, after a sharp ascent of two hours over the snow, reached a sort of upper basin among the very mountain-tops. Here the scene which opened on us was wild beyond description. We were now about 18,000 feet above the sea, and in every direction around us snow hemmed in our view. Under our feet was a plain of pure white snow; the mountain-tops were snowy *hillocks*, standing white against the leaden sky;

and fróm above the fleecy snow-flakes fell around us thickly as we trudged along. The ground was most treacherous, and required great care in traversing, and in one place, being ahead of the guide, the snow and ice suddenly gave way beneath me, and with a most unpleaşant sensation of uncertainty as to where I might be going, I found myself standing up to my waist in snow and to my knees in freezing water.

The guide, almost at the same moment, came to the same end, and it was not without much floundering and blundering that we both extricated ourselves from our difficulties. Shortly after this we crossed the highest point of the pass, and here the guide said his prayers to the presiding "peer," or divinity of the place, previous to asking for bukshish; after which he and the sepoy proceeded to smoke a pipe of peace and tranquillity together. The most trying part of our day's work we found to be waiting for breakfast, the coolies being much retarded both by the road and the state of the weather. We stopped at a sort of temporary abode, where some slight protection from rain and snow was obtained by the piling up of stones against an eligible rock, and here, after a long and dreary wait, we breakfasted in a little smoke-dried, draught-inviting den, the snow all the time coming down in a way not altogether adapted for the enjoyment of such *al fresco* entertainments. Descending from this, we came to a grassy slope at last, and so by a most precipitous path to the valley on the southern side of the mountains, down which a formidable torrent rolled along, dividing itself into a number of channels not very promising as to our prospects of reaching the opposite side. Here we saw an enormous flock of sheep grazing on the mountain-side, seeming, as they moved to and fro in search of pasture, like a floating cloud against the hill. There must have been several thousands, though accurate computation was out of the question. They made, however, all the other mountain-flocks we had met, appear as nothing in point of numbers.

Arriving at the many-branching river, I was for some time quite at a loss for a ford, until a native, seeing the dilemma I was in, crossed to my assistance. Finding me stripping to the work, he insisted on my mounting upon his back, and in an evil moment I consented. The consequence was that, after passing safely a couple of the streams, in the deepest spot of the whole torrent, he tottered and fell, and down we both came, he in the most ungraceful position in which man can fall, and I, luckily, upon my feet. The sensation, however, on suddenly finding the water rushing past, and one's feet slipping about among the clinking stones, was anything but pleasant, and it was with difficulty that I collected myself together and completed the uncomfortable passage. The tent being luckily pitched about a mile farther on, the loss of dignity in the eyes of the bystanders was the only evil result of the misfortune. Towards night it came on again to snow, and the coolies and retainers had another hard bivouac of it, while F. and I were obliged to keep all hands at the pumps, or, in other words, to fasten all available rags and wraps under our canvas, to keep out the soaking wet.

The cold was very great, and everything gave token of coming winter, and testified to what the Himalayas can do in the snow and ice line of business when their full time shall arrive.

September 5.—After a damp night's bivouac, we awoke to find "*a mixture as before*" falling—a mixture of rain, sleet, and snow—anything but promising for the comfort of our day's march. To avoid having to wait in the wet for breakfast, we sent on the kitchen and the cook, and, after some time, followed leisurely ourselves.

An overhanging ledge of rock afforded us some shelter for our meal, and, after warming and drying ourselves to some extent in this smoke-blackened and not very commodious little Himalayan hotel, we again pressed on. This was our third day away from either villages or regular shelter of any sort, and the retainers were naturally anxious to reach some settlement where they could, for a time at least, protect themselves from the rain and snow which still continued to fall. The consequence was, they pressed on some sixteen miles farther at a good pace, to reach a little wooden village at the head of the Wurdwan valley, and we saw nothing of them on the road. On reaching our halting-place, however, lo and behold, our unfortunate cook was absent, and nobody seemed to know anything whatever about him! The cooking things and the larder were all present, and dinner-hour was at hand; but, alas! the pots and kettles were without a lord, and the question of where was our dinner began to give way in point of interest to where was our cook. At the time F. and I left the "cave-hotel," the whole of the coolies, Rajoo, the three goats, and the two sheep, had all gone on ahead, as also the "Invincible One," the sepoy.

The bhistie and the missing cook had therefore only remained behind. The road, soon after leaving, entered a wooded gorge, and, as the valley narrowed, the torrent began to get considerably more rapid and boisterous, as it took to leaping down the giant rocks, which bound it in between their iron grasp and formed its only bed.

The path was wet and sloppy, and led in parts along the tops of rather dangerous precipices. Passing cautiously over these, and through

wooded paths lined with mosses and wild flowers, whose perfume scented the entire air, we came upon a curious bridge of well-packed snow, which spanned the torrent. A treacherous-looking specimen it was, and after taking its likeness in my pocket-book, I was passing it as a matter of course, when I suddenly heard a shout, and perceived F. and the mate at the other side of the torrent beckoning me to cross the snow. I accordingly, with no very good grace and some astonishment, essayed the passage. The snow I found hard as ice, and not liking the look of its treacherous convex sides, I held my course straight up the centre, and then descended with great care and deliberation along the junction of the snow and the mountain. So slippery was the passage, that without grass shoes I should have been sorry to have attempted it, and, as I halted to regard the curious structure from a distance, I could not help thinking what a likely spot it was for a traveller to lose his life without anybody being the wiser, and what a small chance he would have in the deep and rapid torrent below if he should happen to slip into its remorseless clutches. The path from this continued its perilous character, in one place traversing a precipitous face of rock only passable on all fours, beneath which a thick cover of long grass and weeds hung over the deep, treacherous-looking pools of the torrent. Having on a pair of grass shoes which had already done one day's work, I had broken down about half way, and was now nearly bare-footed. I consequently did not arrive till nearly the last of the party, and found the tent pitched and fires lit under a group of large trees, in the wooden village of about a dozen houses, called Sucknez. It was then getting dusk, and after waiting a reasonable time, we sent out a party from the village to make search for our missing man, while F. and I, lighting a fire almost in the tent door, proceeded to cook our own dinner.

The materials consisted of an unlimited supply of eggs and a box of sardines, hitherto neglected, and despised among the artistic productions of our lost professor. F. superintended the frying of the eggs, and produced a conglomeration of some eight of them, which we pronounced unusually delicious, while I laid the table and looked after the kettle, for we thought it better, under our bereaved circumstances, to knock tea and dinner into one meal. Although we had made a longish march, we managed, with the aid of the kettle and the brandy, to sit up by the light of a roaring pine fire until late, in the hopes of some news arriving of our searching party. None however came, and we went to bed *hoping* that the man had lost his way, and *fearing* that he had fallen either over the slippery snow-bridge or down one of the many precipices into the torrent.

September 6.—Morning came, but neither news of our cook nor of the party who went out in his search, and, after breakfast, donning a pair of grass shoes, and provided with some matches and a small bottle of cherry-brandy, I sallied out with the mate on a voyage of discovery. Outside the village I met the searching party, who had been out all through the bitter night, but had found no traces of the object of their search.

Sending a note to F. to dispatch all the coolies to search, I pressed on to the most dangerous precipice of our yesterday's route, and, descending to the torrent, searched about the grass and weeds at the bottom, but without finding any traces. About this place I met three lonely travellers, laden with meal, who had come along the entire path, but had seen no sign of a human creature anywhere. I now gave up our man as lost, but still held on, in a pouring mixture of sleet and snow, which added considerably to the gloom of the scene. Every now and then the old mate, who was in very low spirits, would raise a lugubrious wail at the top of his voice of "Ai Khansaman Jee! Ai Khansaman Jee?" "Oh, cook of my soul! oh, cook of my soul, where art thou?" at the same time apparently apostrophizing the deepest whirlpools of the torrent, while the roar of the waters effectually prevented his magnificent voice from reaching more than a dozen yards from the spot where he stood. Arriving at the snow-bridge, we examined it closely for signs of footmarks; it was, however, so hard that it baffled all our efforts.

At the other side I explored the path which I myself had followed in the first instance. It, however, only led to a small shelter among the rocks and trees, where the natives had evidently been in the habit of lighting their fires and halting for the night. After continuing the search to another snow-bridge above, we returned to our camp, and made the sepoy issue a notice that twenty rupees reward would be given for the recovery of our cook, dead or alive, and also that a reward would be given to any person who should bring us any reliable information about him. At the same time we sent the notice to the villages below, and spread it as much as possible; but though twenty rupees would be a small fortune to one of these people, they took but little interest in the matter, and looked upon the whole thing as "Kismut," or destiny. "If it was the will of God that the body should be found, it would be found, if not, where was the use of looking for it;" and so they took no steps whatever in the matter.

To add to the probabilities of the snow-bridge

having been the cause of our loss, it appeared that a short time before, a coolie carrying Pushmeena &c. had fallen there, and had never since been heard of; while another, who had also fallen into the torrent, was only discovered six days afterwards miles and miles below.

Having now despatched several searching parties, and received no tidings, we decided upon retreating to the next village down the valley, and halting there for a few days, in order to do all we could for our unfortunate man.

September 7.—Started on our march again in heavy sleet and rain, which, higher up the mountains, took the form of downright snow. The valley descended by a slight incline, through fir and other forest trees, and about four kos down, we reached another little wooden city, where, being wet through and through, we were glad to halt, and getting a good fire lit in one of the log-houses, we set to work to dry our clothes. The house was reached by a most primitive ladder, made of half the trunk of a tree, hollowed out into holes for the feet; and, as for the shelter afforded by the tenement, it certainly kept off the rain, but was not intended to keep out the wind, for the trees which composed the walls were so far apart, that we could see the face of nature between them, and, in spite of the open windows, which the architect had thought necessary to provide the building with, the breeze whistled through the chinks in a way that might be very pleasant in hot weather, but was not so cheery when snow and rain was the order of the day. The roofs were the most novel structures I had ever seen. They consisted merely of rudely split blocks of wood, some five or six feet long, through the upper ends of which stout pegs had been driven, and, thus suspended, these weighty wooden *tiles* overlapped each other, and formed a rude covering, which, unpromising as it was to outward appearance, answered its purpose sufficiently well, and was at least quite in keeping with the remainder of the wooden mansion. The people here were something like the Cashmeerees in appearance, and as we descend into civilization, fowls, and other hitherto foreign animals begin to show themselves once more. The entire substitution of wood for mud and stones effectually marks the difference between the Cashmerian and Thibetian sides of the snowy range we had just crossed. About eight kos from Sucknez we reached Bragnion, where we found the camp pitched in a most promising position, having a fine view of the valley below, and the distant ranges of mountains.

The torrent here spread itself into several channels, and the valley, widening to allow it fuller liberty to pursue its joyful existence, descended in a succession of wooded slopes, one beyond the other, while the eternal snows again bounded the view in the distance.

The small portions of comparatively level ground in sight were covered with crops of the richest colours. One in particular, which the people called "gunhar," was of the hue of beetroot, and grew upon its stalk in heavy, gorgeous masses, which added considerably to the richness of the landscape. The seed of this consists of myriads of little semi-transparent white grains, very like ant's eggs, and the taste is something similar to that of wheat. Above our camp, in a ravine of the hills, is the place where an officer had been killed by the fall of an avalanche, while out on a shooting expedition. His companion, a noted sportsman, was saved, by making a tremendous jump; but he himself, and three shikarees, were swept away, their bodies not being recovered for two months afterwards.

September 8.—After a cold night, during which I dreamt of our lost cook, we were awoke by a shout of "Jeeta hy!"—"He is living!" then, "Rusta bhool gya!"—"He lost his way!"

and gradually it dawned upon us that the man we had fancied floating down the torrent a mangled corpse was still actually in the land of the living.

It appeared that he had been discovered, sitting helplessly upon the mountain side, by a chance and solitary traveller from Thibet. He had lost his way at the snow-bridge, and, in trying to retrace his steps, completely got off the only track existing, and had consequently wandered about among the wood and cover as long as his strength enabled him.

The accounts of his movements amid the general excitement were rather conflicting, but this being the fourth day since his disappearance, and the weather having been very bad all that time, he must have had a very narrow escape of his life, from the combined effects of cold and hunger. By the man's account who found him, he was so weak, that he was unable to eat the chupàtties thrown across to him; and his rescuer accordingly leaving with him some meal, and means to make a fire, came on to Sucknez, and from thence sent out a party to carry him in. Sending a horse and some supplies for him, we looked forward with some interest to his own account of his most unsought-for adventures.

The villagers here, we found, were in the

habit of making regular expeditions among their crops at night, to keep off the bears who prowl about in search of food. Armed with torches, they keep up a tremendous shouting all through the dark hours, during the time their grain is ripening; and thinking to get a daylight view of the robbers, I started up the mountain with a native guide and a rifle. My "sportsman," however, in spite of many promises, failed in showing me anything more savage than a preserve of wild raspberry-trees, on which I regaled with much satisfaction.

A curious custom in the valley is that of hanging quantities of hay up among the branches of trees, and its object puzzled me immensely, till my guide informed me that in the winter the snow lies five and six yards in depth, and that the supplies of hay, which now look only meant for camel-leopards, are then easily reached by the flocks of sheep which abound in the valley. At present these were all collected among the mountains, to be out of the way of the harvest, and this accounts for the enormous herd we had seen while descending from the pass.

September 9.—Found the sun brightly shining again this morning, and everything looking fresh and beautiful after the rain. The man who had gone with supplies to the cook returned with news that he was ill from the effects of cold and fasting, and not able to come on to us. While at breakfast, my yesterday's guide brought us in a bowl of raspberries, which gave pleasant token of the change from the desolate country we had recently passed through, to the land of plenty we had reached. We also got about eleven seers (22 lbs.) of virgin honey, for which we paid three rupees. While trying it for breakfast, a dense swarm of the original proprietors came looking for their stores, and the noise they made buzzing about, made one fancy they contemplated walking off bodily with the jars. In the evening our long-lost cook again returned to the bosom of his family. The poor creature looked regularly worn out. From the combined effects of snow and fire he was quite lame; his turban, most of his clothes, and all his small possessions, had vanished while struggling through the thick cover, and he himself had subsisted for two nights and three days, unsheltered and alone, upon nothing but tobacco and snow! On losing his way, not thinking of crossing the snow-bridge, he struck right up the mountain side, in search, first of the path, and afterwards of some hut or shelter. He then gradually got into thick and almost impervious cover; not a habitation of any sort was within miles of him, and thus he wandered about for two days and nights. On the third day he descended again towards the torrent, and, falling and stumbling, reached a rock on its bank, and there seating himself, was, by the merest chance, seen by the passing traveller from the other side of the torrent. Making signs that he was starving, this man threw him some chupatties, and these, wonderful to relate, the cook put in his pocket without touching. Supposing him to be either too weak, or else, even while starving, too strict a Hindoo to eat cooked food, his rescuer then threw him across some meal in his turban, and went off for assistance. The poor creature was rather proud, I think, to find himself the centre of attraction, as well as of being valued at twenty rupees; and, as he falteringly related his sorrows and escape from death, the coolies and the rest of the forces gathered round him, listening with wide open mouths to the wonderful narrative of his adventures.

September 10.—Took another day's rest to give our unfortunate cook a little time to recover his energies. In the evening, the villagers produced us a couple of hives of honey, which we packed away in earthen jars for transport to the plains. The amount was 39½ seers, or 79 lbs. for which we paid ten rupees.

The unwillingness of the people to produce their honey the "Invincible One" accounted for by saying that they were afraid of *our* not paying them. On inquiry, however, the real cause turned out to be, that the Sepoy himself was in the habit of exacting a heavy tax on all purchases on our part, and fear of him, not us, was the true difficulty.

In the evening, we took a tour through the village, and *discoursed*, as well as we could, a native Zemindar, whom we found with his household around him, gathering in his crop of grain, which had been partially destroyed by the early snow. His land appeared to be about four acres in extent, and for this, he told us, he paid twelve rupees per annum to the Maharajah of Cashmere. He failed signally, however, in explaining how he produced that amount by his little farm. The produce of his land sufficed only to feed himself and his family, and the proceeds of the sale of wool, belonging to his twelve sheep, he estimated at only two rupees. Besides these, he possessed a few cows, and appeared as cheery and contented a landholder as I ever met, in spite of his losses by the snows, and his inability to make out, even by description, his ten rupees of ground-rent to the Maharajah.

The crops around consisted chiefly of bearded wheat (kanûk), barley (jow), anik, tronba, and gunhar, all otherwise nameless; and also a small quantity of tobacco, turnips, and radishes.

September 11.—Having with some difficulty procured a pony for the cook, we started again for Cashmere, and, after a very steep ascent, through woods of magnificent pine-trees, with every now-and-then a glorious peep of distant snow-peaks towering in the skies, we reached the summit of the peer, which separates the territory called Kushtwar from that of Cashmere. According to the "Invincible" authority, this territory belonged, some sixty years ago, to an independent Rajah, and, on his death without heirs or successors, it fell into the clutches of Gûlab Singh.*

* The true version of the story appears to be that Gûlab Singh had quarrelled with the Rajah of Cashmere, his rightful master, and entered into the service of the Rajah of Kushtwar. After about three years, hearing that Runjeet Singh was preparing an expedition against Cashmere, he went to him and offered his services. Being accepted, he was successful against his old enemy, and took possession of the country for Runjeet Singh; after which he wrote to the Rajah of Kushtwar, falsely telling him that the Maharajah was going to send a force against him also. The Rajah and his people prepared for resistance, and Gûlab Singh then forged a paper containing an invitation from the chief men in the army of Kushtwar to the Maharajah, encouraging him to come forward and invade the country.

This paper Gûlab then forwarded to the Rajah himself, with a note, in which he told him that it was folly to talk of resistance

The entire revenue, he stated, was 3,000 rupees. From the heights along our path, we could see the great glaciers of Dutchen, with its mountain peak of 25,000 feet, which we had been bound for when the misadventure of our cook interfered with our plans, and left us not sufficient time to carry out our explorations.

The summit of the pass we found evidently not long freed from the old snow, while the new supply lay about in masses all over the mountain.

Passing over a wild and marshy plain at the summit, we began to descend a lovely pine-clad valley once more into veritable Cashmere, and, about four P.M. encamped in a forest-clearing, which, in a very short space of time, was illuminated by no less than seven roaring camp-fires. Our own formed the centre, and was formed of a couple of entire pine-trunks, while the others were ranged about wherever a dry and prostrate tree presented a favourable basis for a conflagration. In the evening we enjoyed

when the chief men of his country were opposed to him. The Rajah, who had been in possession of Kushtwar for twenty-seven years, was completely deceived, and repaired, by invitation, with only a few followers to Gûlab's camp. Here he was kept for three months upon an allowance of 10*l.* a-day, which was afterwards reduced to 10*s.*, and Gûlab Singh in the meantime took possession of Kushtwar without opposition.

the warmth of our fires considerably, and discussed hot brandy and water seated on the very trees which formed our fuel. We were all the more inclined to appreciate our position, as we felt that we were nearly out of our cold latitudes, and rapidly descending to the land of dog days once again.

September 12.—Continued our march down the valley, through continued wooded grassy scenes, and attended by a not too noisy torrent. About a kos from our halting place, we began again to see the wooden houses, and came to a halt at the picturesque little village of Nowbogh, where there were two roads branching off to Islamabad.

Here we had a long wait for breakfast, the servants being overcome by the unaccustomed civilization and tobacco they met on the road. We accordingly set to work at our own kitchen fire, and breakfasted without further assistance off fried eggs, rice, and honey.

In the evening we found alas! that a fire at our tent door, as we had had hitherto, was rather too hot to be pleasant. We were here visited by the local prodigy, a rustic carpenter, who insisted upon making something for us with his rather primitive-looking turning lathe. His shop I found completely *al fresco*, between a couple of cows in the centre of a farm-yard, and here he set to work at a walnut cup, which he turned out creditably enough. The only thing against it was, that his lathe bored a hole right through the bottom of it, which spoiled the utensil a good deal for drinking out of. However, not at all taken aback, he plugged it up with a piece of stick, and at once requested the bukshish, which was the chief part of the performance. Like most of the Cashmeeries, he complained bitterly of the exactions of the Maharajah's government, and stated his own rent to amount to sixteen Huree Singh's rupees (£1) per annum. Not seeing how he could accumulate that sum, by even an entire year of work such as his, I took the liberty of disbelieving his assertion.

September 13.—Started for Kûkûnath. Our path lay over a finely-wooded hill, from which we had a full view of the Peer Punjal range, now divested considerably of the snows which lay upon it at the time we started for Thibet.

Gradually descending into the valley proper, we soon found ourselves once more among the waving rice-fields and apple-orchards, while the wooden tenements again gave way to mud and stone, and thatched erections. At a village called Soprû, we found some iron mines in working order, and passing Kundunath, a pretty little spot adorned with gardens of melons, pumpkins, sunflowers, &c., we shortly after reached Kûkûnath. Here we encamped close to a collection of bubbling crystal springs, which, bursting out of the hill side, and spreading into a dozen separate streams, took their course down to the innumerable fields of rice which they watered in their passage through the valley. To-day our little camp assumes quite a lively appearance again, three sheep and several fowls having been added to the farm-yard; these, together with three surviving ducks of the real original stock, and a wonderful white Thibetian cock, who owes his life entirely to his highly-cultivated vocal powers, strut about in front of the tent, and give an air of unwonted respectability to the scene. Two marches more take us to Islamabad, and it seems altogether about time that the present expedition should draw to a close. Supplies appear alarmingly low. Sugar out some days, brandy ditto, European boots worn out long ago, and both F. and myself living in grass shoes; clothes generally dilapidated, and decidedly dirty; servants very anxious for more tobacco and society, and everything, in fact, requiring rest and renovation after our seven weeks' wanderings.

September 14.—Reached the picturesque little

baraduree of Atchabull once more, after a pleasant march from Kûkûnath. Shortly after taking possession, a fresh arrival of Sahib's possessions and servants came in, the latter rather astonished to find the house occupied by such early birds. The owners turned out to be a colonel of the Bengal Artillery and a brother officer. These were almost our first acquaintances since starting, so that we were glad enough to fraternize and hear what was going on in the world. Two of our former boat's crew here also appeared, and gave us tidings of our rearguard and baggage. The latter had been ejected from its lodgings, and taken out for an airing on the river, having been visited by a flood caused by the melting of the snows shortly after our departure. The weather here began to be unpleasantly hot again; the disappearance of the snow from the mountains having removed the principal cause of the usual coolness in the valley.

Dined with the white men under the spreading sycamores, and enjoyed the luxuries of bread, beer, and sugar in our tea, to all of which we had now been long unaccustomed.

September 15.—A short march brought us to Islamabad, which we found unusually lively from the assembling of a host of pilgrims, who had come from far and wide for a religious fair at Mutton. The groups of different nations, and their manners and customs while bivouacking, were most picturesque, and served to amuse and interest us for the entire day.

September 16.—Started early by boat, in the fond expectation of reaching Sirinugger in the evening. Dusk, however, found us no farther than the ruins of Wentipore, and we only reached the capital at daylight in the morning. Finding our old quarters vacant, we were soon located once more under a roof; and, fifty days having elapsed since we had seen either letter or paper, we lost no time in applying to the postal authorities for our expected accumulations and arrears of correspondence. This resulted in the production of twenty-seven epistles and eleven papers, which we carried home triumphantly in our boat, and proceeded forthwith to devour in that ravenous fashion only known and appreciated by such as have ever undergone a similar literary fast.

PART VII.

LAST DAYS OF TRAVEL.

September 30.—For the last fifteen days we have been living once more the life of *otium cum dignitate* common to the travelling Englishman in Cashmere. Basking in the sun, taking the daily row upon the river, eating fruit, and buying trash in the city, have been our principal occupations and amusements.

About the 20th of the month an English general officer arrived, and was received with all honours, including a salute of heavy ordnance, which was happily unattended with loss of life or limb. A dance and grand review were also given in his honour; so that the arrival made quite a stir, and came fairly under the head of *an event* in the valley. At the review the Maharajah was decorated with unusual grandeur, and as he and his guest rode down the line together—the latter in a plain blue frock, and the other in all his cloth of gold and jewelled splendour—never were simplicity and display more strikingly placed in contrast.

The general's medals and crosses, however, appeared to have a greater interest and importance in the Maharajah's eyes than their intrinsic value could have commanded for them, and, during the marching past of "The Army," he kept continually poking his finger at them, and pointing them out to the courtiers who were gathered about his chair. The general, at the same time, was employed in explaining how many thousands the British Army consisted of, and how vastly superior it was to all other armies whatever, not even making an exception (as I thought he might fairly have done) in favour of the "Invincible Forces," then and there manfully throwing out their feet before him to the martial strains of "Home, sweet Home!" After the last of the army had marched past, the general, with an energy little appreciated by his friends in cloth of gold, jumped up, and, begging permission to manœuvre the troops himself, went off to throw the unfortunate colonel commanding into a state of extreme consternation, and to frighten the few English words of command he was possessed of, fairly out of his head.

In the early mornings my chief amusement had been to watch the colonel in question preparing both himself and his troops for the approaching spectacle, and very sensibly he went through the performance. He was arrayed on these occasions in the full dress of a green velvet dressing-gown, worn in the style affected by the *ferocious ruffian* in small theatres, and, in place of a bugler, was accompanied by a pipe-bearer. This aide followed him over the battle-field, wherever the exigencies of the service required, and supplied him with whiffs of the fragrant weed to compose his nerves at intervals during the action. Their united efforts, however, although slightly irregular in appearance, were attended with full success, for, with the help of ten rounds of ammunition, the troops, even when handed over to the tender mercies of the "Foreign General," got through their ordeal very creditably; and, as they shot nobody, and did nothing more irregular than losing their shoes upon the field, the event passed off smoothly and pleasantly, and to the satisfaction of all concerned.

Here we met an old Sikh acquaintance of the road, who informed me that he had taken service under the Maharajah. Next day he paid us a visit, by appointment, and expressed himself highly delighted with his entertainment; smoking and drinking, however, not being lawful in society to the Sikhs, we could do but little in the character of hosts, beyond letting him talk away to his heart's content, and with as little interruption as possible. He told us his entire life and history, in the worst of English, and we affected to understand the whole of the narration, which, perhaps, was as much as any host could have been called upon to do under the circumstances. The old gentleman's dress was extremely gorgeous, and contrasted rather strongly with our own woollen shooting-jackets and general exterior. He wore a turban of purest white, entwined in endless folds round a light green skull-cap; his waistcoat was of green velvet, embroidered, and richly bordered with gold. His pyjamas—striped silk of the brightest hue—fitted his little legs as tightly as needle and thread could make them, and his lady-like feet were encased in cotton socks and gold embroidered slippers. Over all this he wore a green and gold silk scarf of voluminous proportions, and of that comprehensive character which an Eastern scarf, and in Eastern hands, alone is capable of assuming. Round his wrists were massive gold bracelets, but of other trinkets he had few; and the enormous ear-rings, so usually worn by his race, were not among them. His long grey beard and almost white moustache were, perhaps, the only ornaments his fine old head required. The last time I had seen him, he was arrayed entirely in scarlet and gold, and he had, no doubt, a large reserve of dresses and jewellery; but, in spite of his tinsel and gilding, he appeared a perfect little Eastern gentleman, and the only one I had met as yet in our travels. After expressing a great desire to open a correspondence with us, which, considering the small number of topics we possessed in common, was rather a strange wish, the old gentleman and his retinue took their leave, and we had seen the last of Beer Sing Bahadûr and his glorious apparel.

October 1.—Busily employed to-day in packing away our possessions, and making final arrangements for again taking the road.

Paid a visit to Saifula Baba, the shawl merchant, whose dignity was considerably upset by a cold in his head, and bought a few specimens of his trade, though not sufficient to raise his spirits entirely above the influenza. The approaching winter, and the evacuation of the territory by the principal rupee-spending community, seemed a source of great unhappiness to the sun and silver-loving natives.

Their houses seem but badly adapted to keep out cold, and their efforts at heating them are frequently attended by the burning down of a whole nest of their wooden habitations

Their chief means of artificial warmth seems to be an earthenware jar covered with basket-work, which each native possesses and carries about with him wherever he goes.

This, which is called a Kangree, is filled with charcoal, and, as the Cashmeerians squat down upon the ground, they tuck it under their long clothes, where, until they again rise, it remains hidden from sight, and forms a hot-air chamber under their garments.* Among other artists I discovered a native painter, rather an uncommon trade in these parts, from whom I obtained some original designs, illustrating, with uncommon brilliancy, the very common ceremonies of Hindoo and Mahomedan Shadees, or marriage processions, and other manners and customs of native life.

After getting together everything we required for the road, and clearing out the whole of our possessions, much to the inconvenience of several large standing armies of fleas, we finally took our departure in two boats, manned by twelve boatmen, and started for Baramoula, on the road to Muree and the plains.

October 2.—After making but little progress during the night, we discovered in the morning that our boats were rather too large for the river, in its present weakly and reduced state. Every ten minutes we found ourselves aground upon the sand and mud, and the cooking boat behind us followed our example, while the river ahead showed no prospect whatever of deepen-

* The value which a Kashmirian sets upon his Kangrí may be known by the following distich :—

"Oh Kangrí! Oh Kangrí!
You are the gift of Houris and Fairies;
When I take you under my arm
You drive away fear from my heart."—VIGNE.

ing. The Manjees, under the circumstances, performed wonders in the nautical manœuvring line. Jumping overboard incessantly, they called upon Peer Dustgeer, their favourite patron saint, to aid them in their difficulties, and shrieked and screamed till the whole place resounded with their cries.

Sometimes the saints were stony-hearted, probably not being in a humour to be shouted at, and then the entire body of silky-skinned darkies would set to work, laughing and shouting, to clear away the bar of sand. Their paddles forming in this operation, very effective substitutes for spades and shovels, with much difficulty we reached the lake, and about nine o'clock arrived at Baramoula.

Here the river ceases to be navigable, and abandons itself for a short time to irregular and wanton habits, before finally sowing its wild mountain oats, and becoming the staid and sedate Jhelum of the Plains. Unlike some rivers, the Jhelum contains more water in the middle of summer than at other times. Its principal resources are the snows, and these mighty masses are so wrapped up in their own frigid magnificence that it requires a good deal of warm persuasion from the sun to melt their icy hearts to tears.

SEVENTH BRIDGE, SIRINUGGER.

October 3.—Took the road once more, and started for Muree. Our train was increased by a couple of volunteer native travellers, who were glad of our society in order that they might get clear of the Maharajah's dominions with as little questioning as possible. Our coolies numbered twenty-six, so that altogether our forces now reached to thirty-eight. After a fine march, we halted at Nowshera, where the dashing river afforded us an exciting swim before breakfast. Coming out of the water, however, I had the ill luck to slip upon a treacherous rock, and, falling heavily on my side, and so over into the rapid stream, had some difficulty in fishing myself out again, and was very near taking an unpleasantly short cut to the Plains. In the evening, when the cook came to inspect the larder for dinner, it was discovered, that, with an unusual want of presence of mind, a newly-killed sheep had been left by mistake in the boats for the benefit of the already over-paid boatmen. This was the third animal we had lost, from various causes, during our travels, and the mishap most seriously affected the success of our dinner arrangements for the day.

October 4.—Found great difficulty in getting up this morning after my fall, and still more in walking three miles, which I had to do before finding a pony. The view was beautiful the whole way; but we had been so gorged with scenery of all sorts and kinds, that rugged passes, shady dells, waterfalls, &c., however precious they may become in future recollection, were almost thrown away upon us for the time being. Breakfasted under the pine trees, near an ancient temple, and halted at Uree, where there was a baraduree for travellers. Except, however, to very dirty travellers indeed, it would be of little use. While descending a very steep part of the road, my saddle suddenly slipped over the pony's round little carcase on to his neck, and, *nolens volens,* I came to the ground, the pony remaining in a position very nearly perpendicular, with his tail towards the heavens and his head between my legs, in which predicament he luckily remained perfectly quiet, until the bhistie, coming up behind, set us both on our proper extremities once more.

October 5.—Started for Chukothee, and thinking, in an evil moment, to walk off the effects of my late mishap, I essayed the fifteen miles on foot.

Long before reaching half way, however, I began to look about for anything in the shape of a pony, that might appear in sight; but, none being forthcoming, I was obliged to finish as I had begun, and at last reached our destination, a snug little village, buried in fields of yellow rice upon the hill-side. On the way, I fell in with a fine old Mussulman Zemindar, trudging along on his return to Delhi, from paying a visit to Sirinugger.

Being an unusually talkative old gentleman, we fraternized by the way, and he told me that he had been to see the civil commissioner of his district, now acting as commissioner in the valley, to make his salaam, relative to a "jageer," or Government grant of certain villages to the amount of some three thousand rupees per annum, which he had succeeded in obtaining on account of his loyalty during the recent mutiny.

Of this three thousand rupees, it appeared that only one thousand would come into his own pocket, the remainder being payable as rent, &c. to Government.

His son had also a jageer of twelve thousand rupees, so that both he and his family were loyal and well to do in the world. His ideas of Cashmere were rather amusing. He appeared to think it a miserable spot enough, compared to his own land, and the only advantage he could hit upon, was, in my estimation, quite the reverse, viz: *that Sirinugger was very hot in the middle of summer.*

The rice he had a supreme contempt for. It was not to be compared with the Indian rice, and the Cashmeeries he pooh-poohed, as being no judges whatever of its qualities, and, in fact, not fit to eat rice at all. He seemed quite unable to understand my walking when I could ride; or, indeed, why I should leave such a charming country as India to be uncomfortable in Cashmere, without even having any jageer business to transact as an excuse.

Our coolies, being an unusually miserable crew, we got breakfast about two P.M. To-day our tent lamp finished its erratic life, according to the Dhobie's account, by self-destruction! That good for nothing piece of charcoal had, however, doubtless dashed the solid cut-glass globe, which formed the chief glory of the instrument, against a rock, while thinking of his hubble bubble, and his little blackamoors at home.

The lamp had got over all the difficulties of the road from Lahore to Ladak and back, and had been quite a peep-show to half the natives of Thibet, who were never tired of regarding their multiplied countenances in the numerous cut circles of the glass shade, so that we felt quite grieved at its melancholy loss. Our water bottle also to-day finished its existence, and the table came into camp a bundle of sticks; so that everything seemed to betoken the approaching dissolution of the expedition. The farm-yard consists of five ducks, all strangers, and a pet sheep, and the khiltas look haggard and dilapidated in the extreme. The musical cock, alone, of old friends still survives, but he appears in weak health, and his constitution is evidently undermined by the changes of climate it has undergone. We were here worried by a party of strolling mountebanks from the Punjab, who persisted in horrifying us by making two young girls and three boys, all apparently entirely destitute of bones, stand upon their heads, and go through similar performances on the grass. The girl actually pattered a measure with her feet upon the back of her head, and the proprietors seemed utterly unable to account for our apathetic disregard of so extremely talented and interesting a performance.

October 6.—Left for Hutteian, about fifteen miles off. Ponies being scarce, I had to walk part of the way; but the sepoy, pitching by chance upon our friends, the Punjabees, triumphantly carried off a stout little animal of theirs for my use. Before mounting, however, I was mobbed by the tumbling family, *en masse*, who went on their knees in their solicitations to be exempt from the seizure of their property. Finding me obdurate in retaining the pony at a fair valuation, with "the army" to bear me out, they proceeded to diplomatic measures to gain their end. First, a very small child, choosing a stony place in the path, suddenly stood upon her head, and proceeded to form black knots with her body. Finding that this only caused me to threaten her father with a stick, they produced a blind girl, who threw herself half naked at my feet and cried *by order*. The poor creature had lost her sight by the small-pox, and I had remarked her the day before patiently toiling over rocks and broken paths with one little child in her arms, and another half leading, half obstructing her, endeavouring to guide her footsteps down the rocks. She, however, got no immediate benefit from the pony of contention; so, giving her some money to console her in her forced misery, I still remained inexorable. After this, the encampment broke up, with all its pots and pans, cows and fowl, &c. and took to the road, leaving me in undisturbed possession of my new conveyance. The weather began to astonish us a little to-day, by a renewed accession of October heat. Still the climate was delightful. Morning and evenings always cool, and sometimes cold, and a bright cheery blue invariably over head, while a refreshing breeze made music through the pine trees, and waved the golden ears of rice. Encamped under a spreading sycamore, at the junction of two mountain streams. To-day a new order of bridge appeared, consisting merely of a single rope, the passengers being tugged across in a basket. From its appearance it was rather a matter of congratulation that we were not called upon to cross it.

October 7.—Being Sunday, we made a halt, and enjoyed a refreshing bathe in the stream, and a rest from the toils of the road.

October 8.—Left "Hutteian," and, winding along the valley, arrived, by a steep ascent, at Chukar, a little village boasting a fort and a small nest of Sepoys. It also owned a curiously *dirty*, and consequently *saintly* Fukeer, who we found sitting bolt upright, newly decorated with ashes, and with an extremely florid collection of bulls, demons, &c. painted about the den he occupied. On the road I again picked up the old Mussulman, who seemed delighted to chat, and gave me an account of the part he had played in the mutiny.

He appeared frequently to have warned his Commissioner that an outbreak was about to take place, but without his crediting the story; and when it actually did occur, the latter fled from his station at Lahore, and took shelter with a friendly Risaldar until the storm should blow over. From thence he sent for the old gentleman, my informant, and "Imam Buksh" forthwith mounted his camel and came with five and twenty armed followers to his assistance. While here, a party of rebels came searching for English, and Mr. Buksh narrated how he went forth to meet them, and proclaimed, that they might kill the Englishman if they would, but must first dispose not only of himself, but also of his five and twenty followers. Upon this they abused him, and asked him, "What sort of a Mussulman he called himself?" and denounced him as a "Feringee," or foreigner.

The rebels, however, finally went off, and the Commissioner and his family, by Imam Buksh's further assistance, succeeded in escaping all the dangers of the times. For this service it was that the old gentleman had just received his jageer of two villages, now some years after the occurrence of the events.

He appeared to think very little of the Maharajah's rule, and was of opinion that the people were miserably oppressed, paying, by his account, two thirds of the produce of their lands to the Government. This was in kind, but, where the revenue was taken in coin, a produce of about fourteen pounds of grain was subject to a tax of two rupees. On the subject of the cause of the mutiny in India, he said that greased cartridges certainly had nothing to do with it; for the rest, why, "It was the will of God, and so it happened." To induce him to argue on the *possibility* of the mutiny having been successful, I found to be out of the question. "It was the power of God which had prevented the rebels from gaining over us, and, in the name of the Holy Prophet and the twelve Imams, how then could it have been otherwise?" As to the probability, however, of there being another mutiny, he admitted that he thought there would be one, but that, as long as we maintained justice, no other power could hold the country against us. On my asking him if we did not maintain justice in the land, he said no, and adduced the fact that in every case brought before the courts an enormous amount of bribery goes on among the Rishtidars, and other understrappers, whereby the man with most money wins his cause. No Englishman, he thought, could take a bribe, but he seemed to be under the impression that those in authority were aware of the system being carried on by those beneath them. He admitted that he knew of one native who would not take a bribe! and dwelt largely on the subject, as if it were a wonderful fact, which I have no doubt it was.

In the evening we presented Mr. Imam Buksh with some of our sheep, which delighted his heart immensely, and he spent the entire evening in cooking and eating it, together with a perfect mountain of chupatties, which he manufactured with great care and deliberation.

October 9.—Left our camp very early, and had a sharp ascent up the mountains. A considerable descent again, brought us to the village of Mehra, where we pitched our tents, once more within sight of the territories of India.

October 10.—Marched into Dunna, our last halting-place in Cashmere. It is situated nearly at the summit of the frontier range of hills, and commanded a most extensive view of the mountains of Cashmere and Cabul, besides those on the Indian side.

October 11.—Took a last fond glance towards "the valley," and descended by a very steep and difficult path to the river Jhelum, which forms the boundary between the two territories. Here a couple of queerly-shaped, rudely-constructed boats, with two huge oars apiece, one astern and one at the side, formed the traveller's flying bridge. Into one of these the whole of our possessions and coolies, &c. were stowed, and we commenced the passage of the stream.

This we managed by, in the first instance, coasting up the bank for several hundred yards, and then striking boldly into the current; and it was amusing to see our well-crammed boat suddenly drawn into the rapid stream and whisked and whirled about like a straw, while a nice calculation on the part of the skipper, and a good deal of rowing and shouting on that of the sailors, enabled us to touch the opposite shore not very far below the point from which we had started. One last lingering look at Cashmerian ground, a step over the side, and we were once more standing upon the territories of Queen Victoria, and in the burning land of India—happily, however, still six days' journey from the Plains.

October 12.—Marched up the spur of the Muree Hill to Dewul, where we found a room in a mud fort converted into a halting-place for travellers, reached by a series of break-neck ladders, and looking very much like a cell in a prison, with its two chairs and clumsy wooden table. Here we found a little amusement in the arrival of the Chota Sahib, or " small gentleman,"—otherwise the Assistant Civil Commissioner of the district,—to review the fort and its dependencies. On the first tidings of his approach, the Thanadar immediately turned out the entire garrison, consisting of twelve military policemen, called "Burqundaz," or "Flashers of lightning!" These soon appeared in their full dress of crimson turbans and yellow tights, and, shouldering their "flint-locks," proceeded to perform a series of intricate evolutions, by way of practice for the rapidly-approaching inspection. When the great little man did arrive, there was, we thought, a good deal of irregularity among the troops, such as laughing in the ranks and treading on toes, &c. However, the only point the inspecting officer dwelt upon was the absence of uniformity in dress, caused by the deficiency of two pairs of yellow tights among the lightning flashers, otherwise he appeared perfectly satisfied, and all went off well. After his review he invited himself to our dinner-party, and honoured our repast with the further addition of a kid stew. He turned out to be one of the ex-Company's officers, a subaltern of eighteen years' service, *fifteen* of which had been spent away from his regiment on the staff. He was with his corps, however, when it mutinied, and escaped without much difficulty. The unfortunate colonel of the regiment, finding that none of his men would shoot him, had done so with his own hand. He gave it as his opinion that the cartridges *were* the cause of the mutiny; but allowed that his regiment was in a bad state of discipline some time before, and that all the native corps were *known* to be disaffected years before the event occurred, both by the officers present and those absent upon staff employ. Altogether, after the Chota Sahib had thoroughly discussed both the mutiny and the dinner, we were left under the impression that there was quite sufficient cause for the disaffection of the Bengal army without ever arriving at the vexed question of greased cartridges at all.

October 13.—Marched early into the Hill Station of Muree. Not being yet quite in walking trim, I had pressed a mule into the service, who carried me in good style as far as the entrance to the town. Here, however, he seemed suddenly to remember that we had each a character to support, and, stopping short, he utterly refused to budge another step. Not being willing even to be led, I finally abandoned him to his own devices, and walked on to the Commandant's bungalow, where I found my companion already hospitably received, and comfortably seated at breakfast, discussing kidneys and beefsteaks, and such like unwonted delicacies of the Muree season.

After getting somewhat over the novelty and discomfort of being again in a house with doors and glass windows, and other inconveniences, we sallied out to inspect the station.

Like its *confrères* of the Hills—Simla, Kussowlie, &c. Muree was a prettily-situated little settlement, with houses scattered about entirely according to the freaks and fancies of the owners, and with utter disregard of all system whatever. The Mall was a fine one, and its gaily-dressed frequenters, in jhampans and palkees, &c. were of the unmistakeable stamp of Anglo India in the Hills. Two or three of the ladies, however, were bold enough to walk, and looked none the worse for being divorced from their almost inseparable vehicles, and unattended by their motly crowd of red, and green, and variegated bearers.

October 14.—Spent a quiet day among the hospitalities of Muree, and became gradually accustomed to *city life.* Going to church seemed rather a strange process, and the building itself was but a bad exchange for the grander temples which we had frequented for so many Sundays.

October 15.—Laid our dak by doolie to Lahore, and, with our hospitable entertainer to guide us, started at five P. M. by a short cut, to meet our new conveyances.

Reaching the main road, we once more packed ourselves away in our boxes, and, the sun soon setting his last for us upon the Cashmere mountains, left us to make our way down to the miserable plains as fast as the flaring and spluttering light of a couple of pine torches would allow our bearers to patter along.

From this, until we reach Lahore, we are accompanied by an incessant shuffle shuffle of naked feet through the dusty road; jabbering and shouting of blacks, flickering of torches, bumping of patched and straining doolies against mounds of earth, glimpses of shining naked bodies, streaming with perspiration, as they flit about, and the whole enveloped in dense and suffocating clouds of dust, which penetrate everything and everywhere, and soon become, in fact, a part of one's living breathing existence; occasionally, outstripping our procession, a vision passes, like the glimmer of a white strip of linen, a stick, and a black and polished body, it rushes by like the wind, and disappears in the gloom of dust and night, and, in a second, her Majesty's mail has passed us on the road! As we near the plains this vision undergoes a slight change, and takes the form of an apparition of two wild horses tearing away with a red and almost bodyless cart; this also goes by like a flash, but gives more notice of its coming, and our torches, for a second, light up the figure of a wild huntsman, with red and streaming turban, who sits behind the steeds and blows a defiant blast at us as he also vanishes into the darkness. About seven miles from Muree, we halted for dinner, and made renewed acquaintance with that interesting object—the Indian roadside chicken.

October 16.—Arrived early at Rawul Pindee, and breakfasted at seven, apparently off gutta-percha and extract of sloe leaves. On again immediately, and reached Gugerkhan bungalow at seven P.M. hot, apoplectic, and saturated with dust.

The room smells thoroughly of the plains; an odour, as it were, of punkhas, mosquitoes, and mustiness, not to be found elsewhere, and entirely unexplainable to uninitiated sufferers.

The chicken, whose "fate had been accomplished," died as we entered the yard, and was on the table in the fashion of a warm *spread eagle* in fifteen minutes! After this delicacy is duly discussed, the doolies are emptied of dust, the bedding laid down, and jolt, jolt, creak,

creak, grunt, grunt, on we go again, until sleep good-naturedly comes to make us oblivious of all things. The kahars, or bearers, however, take a different view of life, and at every relief a crowd of sniggering darkies assemble, on both sides, with applications for bukshish. At first one hears, "Sahib, Sahib!" in a deprecating tone of voice, mindful of sudden wakings of former Sahibs, sticks, and consequent sore backs, then piu forte, "Sahib!" crescendo, "Sahib, Sahib!" and then at last, in a burst of harmony, "Sahib pûrana Baira kûtch bukshish mil jawe?" * and the miserable doolie traveller, who has been, probably, feigning sleep in sulky savageness for the last ten minutes, makes a sudden dive through the curtains with a stick, an exclamation is heard very like swearing, only in a foreign language, and the troop of applicants vanish like a shot, keeping up, however, a yelping of Sahibs, and Pûrana Bairas, and Bukshishs, until the new bearers get fairly under weigh, and have carried their loads beyond hearing. None but those who have been woke up in this manner from a comfortable state of unconsciousness, to the full realities of doolie travelling in Indian heat and dust, can form an idea of the trial it is to one's temper; and, from my own feelings, together with

* "Won't the old bearers get something, your honour?"

the sounds I hear from my companion's direction, I can testify as to the relief that the use of foreign expletives affords under the affliction.

October 17.—Arrived at Jhelum about eight A.M. to all intents and purposes dust inside and out. Flesh and blood can stand no more for the present, and we resolve to halt here for the day. The weather appears quite as hot as when we started, and the wind comes in, hot and dry, and makes one feel like a herring of the reddest; while an infernal punkha is creaking its monotonous tune, as it flaps to and fro in the next room, making one again realize to the full, "the pleasures of the plains." We begin, in fact, to discover that the thorns which were not forthcoming on the Cashmere roses are too surely to be found elsewhere.

October 18.—Reached Goojerat at cock-crow; thus completing a distinct circle of travel through Bimber, Sirinugger, Ladak, Kushtwar, Muree, and back to our present halting-place, from whence we had originally branched off.

October 19.—A dusty night's work brought us at two A.M. to Goojerwala. Here we found that there was no bungalow between us and Lahore, and, consequently, no chance of either a wash or breakfast should we go on; we therefore chose loss of time in preference to loss of breakfast, with the addition of a day under a broiling sun, and halted until the authorities should awake to feed us.

October 20.—Reached Lahore before sunrise, and got our letters and papers from the post once more. Afterwards we laid our dak for Cawnpore, and made all arrangements for a start in the evening.

October 21.—Arrived at Umritsur about three A.M., and remained in our coaches until sunrise, when we set off for a stroll through the city. This we found the cleanest, if not the only clean, town we had seen since landing in India. The streets were well drained and built, and were guarded by a force of yellow-legged, red-turbaned Punjabee policemen, who were provided, like their brother blue-bottles at home, with staves and rattles instead of the more usual insignia of sword and shield. The houses were almost all decorated, outside and in, with grotesque mythological and other paintings, such as Vishnu annihilating Rakshus, or demons of various kinds, or wonderful battle-pieces, wherein pale-faced, unhealthy-looking people, in tailed coats and cocked hats, might be seen performing prodigies of valour, assisted by bearded and invincible Sikh warriors of ferocious exterior. The shops were built with verandahs, and the piazza character of some of the streets, in conjunction with the unusual cleanliness, gave one a very agreeable impression of Umritsur and its municipal corporation, whoever that body may be. The inhabitants are principally Sikhs, fine-looking men generally, with long beards turned up at either side of their faces, and knotted with their hair under the voluminous folds of their turbans.

October 22.—Out at four A.M. to explore the great durbar, or head-quarters of the Sikh religion in the Punjab. Entering through a highly decorated archway in the kotwalee, or police-station, we came upon an enormous tank, with steps descending into the water on all sides, and planted around with large and shady trees. In the centre of this rose the temple of the Sikhs, a light-looking, richly-gilt edifice, the lower part of which was constructed of inlaid stones upon white marble. From this to one side of the tank, a broad causeway led, decorated with handsome railings, and lamps of gilt-work upon marble pedestals. Along this, crowds of people were passing to and fro, arrayed in every possible variety of costume and colour. Sikhs, Hindoos, Mussulmen—men, women, and children, crowded together like bees in a hive. Round the edges of the tank were handsome buildings, minarets, &c. with trees and gardens attached to them; and that, towards the causeway, was divided in two by a fine and richly-decorated archway, in the upper part of which a party of patriarchal old Sikhs were squatted on their haunches, discoursing the affairs of the nation. This whole scene opened upon our view at a glance. The sun had as yet scarcely appeared over the horizon, and the reflection of its light shone faintly upon the gold-work and ornaments of the central building, tipping it and the lofty minarets with rosy light, whilst the rest of the buildings remained shrouded in the morning haze. With the incessant bustle of the thronging, brightly-vestured crowd, and the accompaniment of the wild discordant tom-toming of a band of turbaned musicians, it formed a scene which almost persuaded one to put once more confidence in the brightly-coloured descriptions of the "Arabian Nights." While waiting for sun-rise, we ascended one of the minarets, from which we had a curious bird's-eye view of the tank and surrounding city at our feet, while the plains lay stretching away before us; the horizon level and unbroken, as if it bounded in the ocean. From this we had also a private view of the manners and customs of the natives. Just below us was an early morning scene in the life of a Sikh gentleman. He was sitting up in his "four-leg," on the open court of an upper story, which formed his bed-room, while his attendants were offering him his morning cup of coffee, and otherwise attending to his wants. In one corner, another Sikh gentleman, with one arm, was having a brass vessel of water poured over him, and a number of similar vessels stood upon a sort of rack, ready for the master of the house to have his bath.

Scattered about the foot of the bed, which had a grandly decorated canopy, was a deputation of white-robed Sikhs paying their morning visit, or having an audience upon some matter of business. These by degrees got up and went out, each making a profound salaam as he passed the bed. One of them only, the old man called back, and with him, as he sat upon the "four-leg," he had a long and confidential talk. This evidently was the medical adviser, and, judging by the dumb-show of the interview which ensued, the Sikh, as evidently, was the victim of a cold in his fine old nose, which he had doubtless caught from sleeping in the open air. After this we repaired to the kotwallee again, and, getting a pair of slippers in exchange for our boots, descended to the durbar and mingled with the crowd.

Although we were inadmissible in boots, no objection whatever appeared to be made to the entrance of Brahminee bulls; for we found a number of them walking about the mosaic pavement with as much confidence and impunity as if the place belonged to them.

In the building we found a collection of Sikh padres, or "gooroos," sitting behind a massive volume richly cased in cloth of gold and silver, while squatted around under a canopy, were the Sikh faithful, offering their presents of cowries, chupatties, balls of sweetmeats, and showers of yellow and white necklaces of flowers. The book was the original law of Gooroo Gurunth Sahib, which they had just finished reading, and, as we entered, they were commencing to cover it up again, which they did, with great pomp and ceremony, in a number of cloths of various patterns, after which they distributed the votive offerings among themselves and the people present, and held a sort of banquet over the sweets and flowers. In the midst of the proceedings, a very fine specimen of the race of Fukeer came in, and presenting an offering of the smallest, laid his head upon the ground before the book, and, without a word, took himself off again. He was girt round the loins with a yellowish-red cloth; his body, from head to foot, was covered with ashes. The hair of his head was matted together in strips, like the tail of an uncared cow, and reached to his waist. A shallow earthen pot was his hat, and over his shoulders hung two large gourds, suspended by a cord, while in his hand he carried a long staff, covered over with stuff of the same kind as that round his waist. Such was the figure which entered among the gaily-dressed multitude in the saintly durbar; and, although to the assembled people there appeared nothing whatever either strange or unusual in the arrival, to us, who were looking on, the contrast between the unclad dirty mendicant, and the pure white vestments of the Sikhs around, rendered it a most striking and remarkable apparition.

On entering, he had removed the earthen pot which formed his hat, and, one of the two gourds which were round his shoulders having fallen to the ground in the act, it was amusing to see him pause for a second, and anxiously examine whether any compound fracture had taken place in the precious article of his very limited dinner service. One extremity of the building we found was occupied for Hindoo worship; so that fraternity and equality, worthy of imitation, seems to be the order of the day among the religions of Umritsur. The interior was richly decorated with gilding and mirrors, &c., but was little worthy of remark in comparison with the richness of the exterior effect. Presenting a "bukshish" to the expectant padres who guarded the sacred book, we left them to their devotions, and betook ourselves once more to our bungalow.

October 23.—Travelling all night, we reached Jullunder at six A.M., and, after breakfast, again started for Loodianah, where we dined. We here again crossed the Sutlej, but, the water being low, boat navigation was dispensed with, and a shaky bridge, and about two miles of sandy river-bed, completed the passage.

At Loodianah we were stormed by a host of merchants, with pushmeena and other soft matters, who were rather disappointed at finding we had come from the birth-place of such like manufactures. Some of the local shawls, however, or "Rampore chudders," were beautifully fine and delicate, and seemed worthy of inspection.

October 24.—Reached Umballa at eight A.M., and started again shortly after. Our horses to-day were most miserable caricatures, and it was with difficulty we managed to progress at all. The last stage was accomplished at a walk; and what with this and the delay caused by a couple of sandy river-beds, we only reached Kurnaul at ten P.M. The miserable condition of the horses was accounted for by the enormously high price of grain and the absence of grass, in consequence of the want of rain. The general topic, in fact, is now the failure of the rains, and consequent apprehensions of a famine throughout the land. "Atar" is here eight seers the rupee, or in other words, flour sells at one shilling and ninepence a stone—an enormous price in these parts.

October 25.—Sunrise found us still half-way to Delhi, and we stopped to breakfast at the little bungalow of Ghureekulla. Here we found a fine old Khansaman, who gave us an account of the incidents of the Mutiny which came under his notice. He had received a flying party of two hundred men, women, and children, who arrived at dead of night, some on horses, some on foot, and all worn and haggard by their march from Delhi, from which they had escaped. These he took care of, and supplied with food until the following day, when they departed, without, by his own account, giving him anything, either as pay or reward. He afterwards assisted others also, and received about one hundred and twenty rupees, one way or another, for his services. At present he receives six rupees a month, with whatever he can pick up from travellers; not a very large amount in the out-of-the-way little jungle station of Ghureekulla.

October 26.—Passed through Delhi by moonlight, and reached the bungalow at one A.M. At gun-fire we emerged from our locomotives, and went to explore the king's palace. In spite of the late lesson on the subject of sepoys, we found the gates of the fort held entirely by native guards, and a very small body of Europeans located within the walls. After rambling through the place, and discovering that its only beauty lay at present in its exterior, we went to the Jama Musjid, a fine mosque of red granite, inlaid in parts with white marble. The cupolas, of great size, were entirely marble, and the minarets, also of marble, were closely inlaid. The place had been only recently handed over to the Moslems after its late seizure, and was not as yet used for worship. Ascending one of the minarets, we had a fine view of the city of the Great Mogul dynasty, with its minarets and ornamented streets; and in the distance we could discern the positions occupied by our besieging force, when the last of the kings was brought so rudely to the termination of his reign.

October 27.—Reached Koel, or Allyghur, at eight A.M. Started again at five, stopping on the way to inspect the Jama Musjid, and a very fine old tower, probably of Buddhist or Jain origin, which was covered over with ancient inscriptions. Just as the Muezzin was calling to evening prayer, we again resumed our monotonous order of travel, and branched off towards Agra to visit the famous Taj Mahul.

October 28.—Reached Agra at two A.M., and finding the bungalow full, had to go to the hotel. At sunrise we drove out to the Taj, and here, I think, for the first time, we were not disappointed in the difference between reality and description. The entrance to the gardens in which the Taj is situated was beautiful in itself, but one sight of the main building left no room for admiration of anything besides.

It is situated on the banks of the Jumna, with a fine view of the magnificent fort, with its mosque and minarets, and is entirely of pure white marble, inlaid with stones into shapes of flowers and arabesques, &c. At each corner rises a white marble minaret, like a pillar of snow, beautifully decorated and carved, but unsullied by a single line of any other colour whatever. The interior is profusely inlaid with minute stones of considerable value, and is lit by carved marble windows of the most beautiful design imaginable. In the centre, surrounding the tomb of Mûmtaz and her lord, is a marvellous white marble screen, in the form of a polygon, carved like perforated ivory, and also inlaid with minute stones of every shape and colour.* The queen, in whose honour the tomb was built, occupies the very centre of the enclosure, Shah Jehan's tomb being on one side of it, and larger in size, which rather spoils the symmetry of the space.

* According to M. Voysey, in his Asiatic Researches, " A single flower in the screen contains a hundred stones, each cut to the exact shape necessary, and highly polished; and, although everything is finished like an ornament for a drawing-room chimney-piece, the general effect produced is rather solemn and impressive than gaudy.

" In the minute beauties of execution, the flowers are by no means equal to those on tables and other small works in Pietra dura at Florence. It is the taste displayed in outline and application of this ornament, combined with the lightness and simplicity of the building, which gives it an advantage so prodigious over the gloomy portals of the chapel of the Medici. The graceful flow, the harmonious colours, combined with the mild lustre of the marble on which the ornamentation is displayed, form the peculiar charm of the building, and distinguish it from any other in the world. The materials are Lapis Lazuli, Jasper, Heliotrope or blood stone, Chalcedony, and other agates, Cornelian, Jade, &c."

Exactly underneath the tombs, in the main body of the building, one descends to a marble vault, where there are two others precisely similar in shape, but without any inscription or ornament whatever, and under these latter the mortal remains of the famous Shah Jehan and Mûmtaz repose in peace. Over the queen's tomb, in the very centre of the interior, a single ostrich egg was suspended by an almost invisible thread, probably to shadow forth something of the meaning of the "Resurgam" affixed to monuments elsewhere. On either side, without the mausoleum, are two buildings facing inwards, one of which is a mosque, built in red granite and white marble; and the whole are profusely ornamented with carvings in marble, which would take an age to examine thoroughly, and which produce an effect quite incapable of being adequately portrayed by either pen or pencil.

In one of these edifices, among the inlaid work and arabesques, and not far from the mortal remains of the departed King and Queen, we found a curious and interesting inscription, which seems to have been hitherto unmentioned by the many travellers who have visited the sacred spot. It was prominently placed and easily decipherable, being in unusually large letters, and in that character which might be called the "*Uneiform*," of which so many valuable specimens exist in all parts of the known globe.

It ran thus :—

IN MEMORY OF VALENTINE'S DAY.

The sentence appeared unfinished, and one or two words were probably required to complete the sense, but from similar existing records there could be no difficulty in filling in the missing syllables.

It was curious, however, to reflect what the feeling could have been that stayed the writer's hand, and prevented him from finishing his graceful tribute to the mighty dead.

Mûmtaz, from whose name the word "Taj" is derived (the letter "z" being incapable of being pronounced by many natives except as a "j"), was the daughter of the famous Noor Jehan's brother Asoph Khan. Shah Jehan followed his queen in A.D. 1665, and was laid in the building which he had himself originally designed in her honour alone.

With Noor Jehan and Jehangeer the case was reversed. The conqueror of the world ended his career in A.D. 1627, and the partner of all his Cashmerian wanderings, and many adventures, who wore no colour but white after his death, finally rejoined him in a tomb which she had raised to his memory at Lahore.

Having paid due homage to the beauty of the far-famed mausoleum, we went to the Fort, and, after visiting the Ram Bagh, the Ikmam Dowlah, and the various palaces built by Akbar Shah, once more took the road, and were soon again galloping through the dust, morning bringing us to the bungalow of Bewah. From this we again made for Ghoorsahagunge and Cawnpore, and by rail to Allahabad, there completing a circuit of travel extending to between two and three thousand miles :—

> " In heat and cold
> We'd roved o'er many a hill and many a dale,
> Through many a wood and many an open ground,
> In sunshine and in shade, in wet and fair,
> Thoughtful or blithe of heart as might befall :
> Our best companions, now the driving winds,
> And now the trotting brooks and whispering trees,
> And now the music of our own quick steps
> With many a short-lived thought that passed between
> And disappeared."

And now but one day more remains of our six months' leave. The 31st of October sees us again fairly in the hands of the authorities. Brothers in arms, who during our absence have been having "all work and no play," receive us with warm and disinterested welcome. The Q. M. G. is hauled away in triumph by a swarm of fellow blacklegs to glad the squaw-like partner of his sooty bosom. The last remnants of the expedition are fairly broken up, and already the days when we went gipsying have passed away "a long time ago."

ROUTE.

	Miles.
Allahabad	
Cawnpore	120
Ghoorsahagunge	72
Etawah	73
Kurga	72
Delhi	51
Kurnaul	73
Umballa	45
Kalka	40
Kussowlie	9
Simla	40
Hureepore	20
Kalka	29
Umballa	40
Thikanmajura	36
Jullundur	61
Umritsur	59
Lahore	35
Gûgerwalla	39
Goojerat	30
Bimber	27
Serai Saidabad	12
Nowshera	11
Chungas	11
Rajaori	12
Thanna	12
Burrumgulla	11
Poshana	6
Peer Punjal	9
Poshana	9
Aliabad	11
Heerpore	13
Shupayon	6
Ramoon	9
Sirinugger	14
Wûler Islamabad	} by water
Atchabull	6

	Miles.
Vernagh	11
Islamabad	15
Sirinugger Gunberbull	} by water
Kungur	11
Gûndisursing	12
Soonamurg	14
Foot of the Hills	9
Pandras	24
Dras	8
Tusgam	14
Chungun	12
Pushkoom	10
Waka	13
Khurboo	10
Lamieroo	12
Nûrila	16
Suspûl	14
Egnemo	10
Ladak	18
Chunga	18
Hemis	2
Ladak	20
Pitok	4
Egnemo	14
Suspûl	10
Nûrila	14
Lamieroo	16
Khurboo	12
Waka	10
Pushkoom	13
Thambis	14
Sankoo	16
Sooroo	12
Among the Mountains	11
Ditto	14
Sucknez	11
Bragnion	14

	Miles.
Peer	16
Nowbogh	9
Kûkûnath	10
Atchabull	8
Islamabad	6
Sirinugger Baramoula	} by water
Nowshera	8
Uree	15
Chukotheo	15
Hutteian	14
Chukar	9
Mehra	6
Dunna	6
Puttun	6
Dewul	9
Muree	11
Rawul Pindee	37
Gûgerkhan	30
Jhelum	37
Goojerat	31
Gûgerwalla	30
Lahore	39
Umritsur	35
Jullundur	59
Loodiana	32
Umballa	71
Kurnaul	45
Ghureekulla	36
Delhi	36
Allyghur	79
Agra	50
Bewah	82
Ghoorsahagunge	70
Cawnpore	72
Allahabad	120

Parts of the country not having been at the time correctly mapped, these distances are in some instances approximations only.

THE RELIGIONS

OF

CASHMERE AND THIBET.

THE RELIGIONS OF CASHMERE AND THIBET.

DURING all our wanderings, whether in India, Cashmere, or Thibet, the most striking feature throughout, was the outward display of religion and the prominent part which religious forms of worship take in the every-day life of the people.

X

Monuments and temples everywhere bear testimony to the universal belief in a Supreme Being; and Hindoo, Mussulman, and Buddhist alike, by numberless prayers and frequent offerings, confess their desire to propitiate His power and to cultivate His favour.

Every little village has its "Musjid" or "Shiwala," and everywhere, and at all hours, votaries of the different sects may be seen, in the fashion they have learnt from childhood, openly *remembering*, at least, their Creator.

The naked Hindoo, with loosened scalp lock and otherwise closely-shaven head, stands in running water, and with his face upturned to the sun apostrophises the Divine Essence, whose qualities and attributes he has alone been taught to recognise, through the numberless incarnations of his degenerate creed. Five times a day the Mussulman kneels in open adoration of his Maker, and, doffing his slippers, repeats, with forehead to the ground, the formula laid down for him by the only Prophet he has learnt to believe in. The Buddhist, too, mutters his "Ûm mani panee" at every turn, and keeps his praying wheel in endless motion, with entire confidence in its mystic virtues, and fullest faith in the efficacy of those forms which he has thus been taught to follow from his cradle.

Each worships after the fashion of his fathers before him, and each, by the dim illumination of his own particular light, fancies himself upon the true path, and is able plainly to perceive his neighbour groping in the outer darkness.

Seeing all this, and turning in imagination to other lands, it is curious to consider that the Church which possesses the only Lamp of Truth, and who by the help of its light pronounces all these zealous worshippers alike, to be but "Infidels and Turks," and says to all, in language not quite so polite as that of Touchstone, "Truly, shepherds, ye are in a parlous state," herself makes no such public demonstration of her faith. To an Eastern infidel travelling in the West, she would even appear, to outward eye, a tenfold greater infidel than her neighbours. Except on one day in seven, he would seldom find a place of public worship open to his gaze, while the Name which he himself has learned to reverence to such a degree that every scrap of paper that might chance to bear it, is sacred in his eyes, he might hear a thousand times, and perhaps not once in adoration; and while it commences every action of his own life he would there find it utterly excluded from its accustomed place. Even the form of parting salutation, which in almost all lands—Infidel and Heretical—greets him in the name of God, would, in Protestant England, fall upon his ear with no such signification. While the benighted Hindoo greets his parting neighbour to the present day with "Khûda Hafiz"—God the Preserver—the Englishman's "Good-bye," like well-worn coin, has changed so much by use, that now, no stranger could discern in it any trace whatever of the image with which it was originally stamped.

And although the comparison between the apparent creeds of East and West is truly that between a very large proportion of faithful professors of a false religion and, to outward eye, a similarly large proportion of unfaithful followers of the true religion, it is interesting to form some idea of the different systems which have existed for so many ages, and which, though proved alike by reason and revelation to be of human origin and unequal to the wants of human nature, have yet maintained their influence to the present day, and hold among their votaries still such zealous worshippers of an unknown God.

The oldest of all these religions appears to be that of the Hindoos. The Vedas, or Scriptures, date as far back as the Books of Moses, 1400 B.C.; and previously even to their then being committed to writing by the Sage Vyasa, they are believed to have been preserved for ages by tradition. The primary doctrine of the Vedas is the Unity of God. There is, they say, "but one Deity, the Supreme Spirit, the Lord of the Universe, whose work is the universe." "Let us adore the supremacy of that divine Sun, the Godhead, who illuminates all, who recreates all, from whom all proceed, to whom all must return, whom we invoke to direct our understandings aright in our progress towards His holy seat. What the sun and light are to this world, that are the Supreme Good and Truth to the intellectual and invisible universe; and as our corporeal eyes have a distinct perception of objects enlightened by the sun, thus our souls acquire certain knowledge by meditating on the light of truth which emanates from the Being of beings; that is the light by which alone our minds can be directed to the path of beatitude."

Every Brahmin must pray at morning and evening twilight in some unfrequented place, near pure water, and must bathe daily; he must also daily perform five sacraments, viz., studying the Vedas, making oblations to the manes of the departed, giving rice to living creatures, and receiving guests with honour. As to the doctrine of a future state, they believe in the transmigration of the soul, but that between the different stages of existence it enjoys, according to merit or demerit, years and years of happiness in some of the heavens, or suffers torments of similar duration in some of the hells. The most wicked, however, after being purged of their crimes by ages of suffering, and by repeated transmigrations, may ascend in the scale of being until they finally enter heaven and attain the highest reward of all good, which is incorporation with the Divine Essence.

Like more enlightened systems of religion, the Hindoo faith has degenerated from the purity originally inculcated. The Monotheism, though still existing, has been almost smothered by a system of innumerable incarnations; by means of which the attributes of an unseen Deity were to be brought to the understandings of the ignorant; and, as might be expected, the hidden symbol has been almost lost in the tangible reality. The later Scriptures, or Pûranas, are believed to have been compiled between the eighth and sixteenth centuries, A.D.; and though still upholding the existence of a Supreme Being, by whom all things are composed, they introduce a variety of incarnations and divinities almost innumerable. Of these, the three prin-

GUNESH.

cipal are, Brahma, Vishnu, and Siva, representing respectively the creating, preserving, and destroying principles; and their wives, Sereswutee, Lukshmee, and Dewee. These latter are the active powers which develop the principles represented by the triad. The divinity most commonly portrayed however, though not publicly worshipped, is Gunesh. Almost every dwelling has her effigy rudely painted over the entrance; and she is invoked at the beginning of all undertakings, and is the remover of all difficulties. Her peculiar appearance is accounted for by the fact of her having been killed at an early period of life by Siva, who cut off her head, and, afterwards relenting, replaced it with the first that happened to come to hand, which turned out to be an elephant's!

Gunesh was produced by the intense wishes of Dewee, and is now appealed to at the commencement of almost every act in Hindoo life.

The following invocation to this "household god" will give some idea of the position she holds in public estimation. It is taken from the "Prem Sagur," or Ocean of Love, a history of the life of Krishna, a son of Vishnu, who, with Siva and Dewee, or Mahadewee, monopolises almost the entire public respect and adoration :—

'Oh elephant-faced Deity, obviator of difficulties, of exalted fame resplendent,
Grant as a boon, pure language, wisdom, and felicity may be much promoted.
Thou on whose two celestial feet the world is gazing, worshipping both day and night,
O mother of the universe, grant unto me, remembering thee, true skill and utterance."

The "Ocean of Love" gives a full account of the various incarnations of Krishna, the favourite divinity of the Hindoos, and opens with the scene of his birth. Kans, his uncle, has placed guards, in order that the child may be killed at his first appearance, it having been predicted that Kans himself is to fall by the hands of Krishna. The Cashmerian artist—whose powers of colouring were his chief recommendation—has depicted the moment when Vasadeo and Devakee, the father and mother, viewing Krishna, with long-drawn sighs, both begin to say, "If, by some means, we could send away this child, then it would escape the guilty Kans." Vasadeo says, "Without destiny none can preserve him; the writing of Fate, that only will be accomplished."

Destiny being propitious, the guards fall asleep upon their posts, as shown in the accompanying design, and another child is substituted for Krishna. He is afterwards brought up as a

BIRTH OF KRISHNA.

herdsman, and spends his childhood among the milkmaids of Braj, upon whom he plays all sorts of tricks. "One day the divine Krishna played upon the flute, in the forest, when, hearing the sound of the instrument, all the young women of Braj arose in confusion, and hastened and assembled in one place. The dark-blue Krishna, with body of the hue of clouds, stood in the midst; and such was the beauty of the fair ones, as they sported, that they resembled golden creepers growing from beneath a blue mountain!"

The description of the state of the world, on Krishna's appearance, is given by the saintly Shukadeo to King Parikshah—"O King, at the time of the divine Krishna appearing, in the minds of all such joy arose, that not even the name of grief remained. With joy the woods and groves began to bear fruits and flowers, their verdure still increasing. The rivers, streams, and lakes were filled with water, and upon them birds of every kind were sporting; and, from city to city, from house to house, from village to village, rejoicings were celebrated. The Brahmins were performing sacrifice; the Regents of the ten divisions of the horizon rejoiced. Clouds were moving over the circuit of Braj. The deities, seated in their cars, rained down flowers; the holders of the magic pill, the celestial musicians, and heavenly bards, continually sounding drums, kettledrums, and pipes, were singing the praises of the divine virtues; and, in one direction, Urvasee, and all the celestial dancers, were dancing. In such a time, then, on Wednesday, the eighth day of the dark half of the month Bhadon, at midnight, while the moon was in the mansion of Rohanee, the divine Krishna was born, of the colour of clouds, moon-faced and lotus-eyed, with a girdle of yellow cloth passing round his loins, wearing a crown, and arrayed in a necklace of five jewels, produced from the elements of nature, and with ornaments set with gems, in a four-armed form, sustaining the shell, the quoit, the mace, and the lotus he presented himself."

Krishna afterwards espouses a fair lady, of the name of Rûkminee, and the marriage is thus poetically described. Rûkminee has written a letter, filled with love, and sent it by the hand of a Brahmin, to the Root of Joy, Krishna:—"The Brahmin having arrived at Dûarika, perceives that the town is in the midst of the ocean, and on the four sides of it there are great mountains and woods and groves, which add beauty to the scene. In these were various kinds of beasts and birds, and the limpid lakes were filled with pure water, and lotus flowers were blooming, upon which swarms upon swarms of black bees were humming. To the distance of many miles orchards, containing an endless variety of fruit and flowers, extended; along these enclosures betel gardens were flourishing. The gardeners, standing at the wells, were singing with sweet strains; and, working water-wheels and buckets, were irrigating the high and low grounds."

Beholding this beautiful scene, and being gladdened thereby, the Brahmin, still advancing, beholds that "on four sides of the city are very lofty ramparts, with four gateways, in which folding-doors, inlaid with gold, are fixed, and, inside the city, houses of five and six stories high, of silver and gold, adorned with jewels, so lofty as to converse with the sky, are glittering. Their minarets and pinnacles are gleaming like lightning, and banners and pennons of many colours are fluttering. The warm fragrance of perfumes was issuing from windows, air-holes, and lattices. At every door were placed pillars of the plantain-tree, with fresh shoots, and golden vessels. Garlands and wreathed flowers were festooned from house to house, and joyful music was sounding. From place to place, the recital of the Pûranas and discourse about Krishna was kept up. The eighteen classes were dwelling in ease and tranquillity."

On hearing the Brahmin's message, the warder says:—"'Great sir, be pleased to enter the palace; the divine Krishna reposes, in front of you, on a throne.' Krishna, descending, bows to him, and shows him much respect, and those attentions which a man would show to his friend. Having applied fragrant unguents, and caused him to be bathed and washed, he partakes of food, possessing the six flavours. Afterwards he gave him the betel leaf, made up with areca nut, spices, and chunam; and having perfumed his body with saffron and sandal wood oil, and arranged his dress, and put upon him a necklace of flowers, he conducted him into a palace adorned with jewels, and caused him to repose in a fair curtained bed, studded with gems." After sleeping profoundly, the Brahmin awakes, and relates his mission. Krishna goes to claim his bride, and orders his charioteer, Darak, to prepare his chariot. Darak quickly yokes four horses. Then the divine Krishna, having ascended, and seated the Brahmin, departs from Dûarika to Kundalpore. On coming forth from the city, behold! "on the right hand herds upon herds of deer are moving, and in front, a lion and lioness, carrying their prey, are advancing, roaring."

Having seen this auspicious event, the Brahmin, having mentally reflected, said, "Sire, from beholding, at this time, this good omen, it appears to my mind that, just as these are advancing, having accomplished their object, just so you will return, having effected yours." Arrived at Kundalpore, he finds preparations made for the marriage :—

"Swept were the streets, the crossings o'er-canopied, and with perfumes sprinkled and sandal oil;
Clusters were formed of flowers of white and of red, and interspersed with cocoa-nuts of gold.
The green foliage, fruits, and flowers, were in profusion, and from house to house flowering wreaths.
Banners and pennons and flowers, in golden tissues, were suspended, and well-fashioned vessels of gold;
And in every house reigned joy!"

"As for Rûkminee, with agitated frame, she gazed in every direction, as the moon is dimmed by the morn. Extreme anxiety showed in the heart of the fair one; she gazed, standing in a lofty balcony; her frame was agitated, her heart most sad; she drew deep sighs. While, through distress, tears rain from her eyes, she says, "Why has not Krishna arrived?" When the marriage-day dawns, she sends, by a Brahmin, to Krishna:

"Receptacle of favour,—When two hours of the day remain I shall go to perform worship in the temple of Dewee, to the east of the city." Her companions and attendants, arriving, first filled a square place in the courtyard with pearls, and spread a seat of gold set with pearls, on which they caused Rûkminee to sit, and anointed her with oil by the hands of seven married women whose husbands were alive. Afterwards, having rubbed her with fragrant paste, they adorned her with sixteen ornaments, and put on her twelve trinkets, and having arrayed her in a red boddice they seated her, fully adorned. Then the young Rûkminee, accompanied by all her handmaidens, went, with the sound of music, to perform her devotions. Screened by a curtain of silk, and surrounded by crowd upon crowd of companions, she appeared among the swarthy group who accompanied her, as beautiful, as amid dark blue clouds, the moon with its company of stars!"

Having arrived at the temple of Dewee, the royal maiden, having washed her hands and feet and sipped water, proceeded to offer sandal oil, unbroken grains of rice, flowers, incense, lamps, and consecrated food, and with earnest faith performed the worship of Dewee according to the prescribed ritual.

W. H. K. Del[t] Hexbart, lith.

TEMPLE DECORATION, HIMALAYAS.

"After which she fed women of the Brahmin caste with delectable food, and having attired them in fair garments, she drew a mark on their foreheads with a mixture of rice, alum, turmeric, and acid, and having caused to adhere some unbroken grains of rice, she received their benediction. Hearing from an attendant that Krishna has arrived, the Princess is filled with ecstatic delight, so that she cannot contain herself; and leaning on the arm of an attendant, in a graceful attitude, remains slightly smiling, in such a manner that no description can express her beauty. The guards become fascinated and remain immoveable. With trembling frame and coy of heart she finally departs with Krishna."

The domestic life and appearance of Krishna and Rûkminee is still further characteristically described in the imaginative pages of the "Ocean of Love:"—"Once on a time, in a palace of gold, studded with jewels, a gem-adorned bedstead, with curtains, was spread, on which a bedding white as foam, and adorned with flowers, with pillows for the cheek and for the head, continued to exhale perfumes. On all four sides of the bed vessels containing camphor, rose-water, saffron, sandal oil, and other ingredients, were placed; various kinds of marvellous pictures were delineated on the walls on all sides. In recesses, here and there, flowers, fruits, sweetmeats, and confections were placed, and all that could be required for enjoyment was at hand. Clothed in a petticoat and a full loose robe of dazzling splendour, embroidered with pearls, and a sparkling boddice, and a long refulgent wrapper, and wearing a glittering veil, covered with ornaments from head to foot; with red lines drawn across the forehead, having a nose-ring of the largest pearls, ornaments for the head, earrings, ornamental line at the parting of the hair, marks between the eyebrows, ornaments for the ears and forehead, a necklace composed of circular pieces of gold, a string of gold beads and coral, a breast ornament, a necklace of five strings and of seven, a pearl necklace, double and triple bracelets of nine gems, armlets, wristlets, and other kinds of fastenings for the arm; bangles, seals, seal rings, a girdle of bells, rings for the great toe, toe ornaments, anklets, and other ornaments of all kinds studded with jewels; the moon-faced, tulip-complexioned, gazelle-eyed, bird-voiced, elephant-gaited, slim-waisted, divine Rûkminee, and the cloud-coloured, lotus-eyed Krishna, ocean of beauty, splendour of the three worlds, root of joy, wearing a diadem like the crest of a peacock, and a necklace of forest flowers, a silken robe of yellow hue, and a scarf or the same, were reposing, when, all of sudden, the divine Krishna said to Rûkminee, 'Listen, fair one,'" &c.

Krishna afterwards takes 16,100 wives, and always at early dawn, one would wash his face, another would apply a fragrant paste to his body, another would prepare for him and give him to eat food of six flavours, another would make nice betel, with cloves, cardamums, mace, and nutmegs, for her beloved. "Each produced a daughter fair as Rûkminee; each ten sons, brave sons were they! 161,000 and all alike, such were the sons of Krishna!"

Such is part of the history of the favourite divinity of the benighted Hindoo as related in the flowery pages of the "Ocean of Love," and the history may be, more or less, read in the every-day scenes of Indian life which pass around one.

The description of Rûkminee, strange as it is, corresponds with many other fair portraits in the Hindee; witness that of "Oonmadinee," the daughter of "Rutundutt":—

"Her beauty was like a light in a dark house—her eyes were those of a deer, her curls like female snakes, her eyebrows like a bow, her nose like a parrot's, her teeth like a string of pearls, her lips like the red gourds, her neck like a pigeon's, her waist like a leopard's, her hands and feet like a soft lotus, her face like the moon, with the gait of a goose, and the voice of a cuckoo!"

More apparent even than in the earthly nature of the Hindoo's conception of the Divine attributes, the falsity and the human origin of his

Faith may be seen in the effect it produces wherever it is allowed to obtain undivided sway. Combining dirt, idleness, and religion together, the Hindoo Fukeer, attired in the minutest rag of raiment, at times in none at all, wanders from

place to place, and with long and matted hair, blood-shot haggard eyes, and scowling visage, fancies himself upon the path which leads direct to Paradise.

Attenuated to the last degree, he suffers all extremes of heat and cold, sleeps upon a bed of ashes, and sits moodily beneath the burning mid-day sun, lives on charity while scorning usually to ask for alms, and bears the reputation of a saint while reducing himself to the very level of the beasts that perish.

Something of the cheerful feelings which actuate these religious mendicants may be found in the following passage:—"He may be called a wise 'Jogee,' or 'Fukeer,' who has dried up the reservoir of hope with the fire of austere devotion, and who has subdued his mind, and kept the organs of sense in their proper place; and this is the condition of persons in this world, that their bodies undergo dissolution, their heads shake, and their teeth fall out. When men become old, they walk about with sticks, and it is thus that time passes away. Night succeeds day, and year succeeds month, and old age succeeds childhood, and we know not who we are ourselves, and who others are; one comes and another departs; and at last all living creatures must depart. And, behold! night passes away, and then day dawns; the moon goes down and the sun rises; thus does youth depart, and old age comes on, and thus Time pursues his course: but although man sees all these things, he does not become wise. There are bodies of many kinds, and minds of many kinds, and affections or fascinations of many kinds, and Brahma has created wickedness of many kinds; but a wise man, having escaped from these, and having subdued hope and avarice, and shaved his head, and taken a stick and water-pot in his hands, having subjugated the passion of love and anger, and become a 'Jogee,' who wanders and travels about with naked feet to places of pilgrimage, obtains final liberation. And, behold, this world is like a dream."

The derivation of the word "Fukeer," and an illustration of the disposition of the mendicant race, is given in a Persian tale, called the "Four Dervishes." The story was originally narrated to amuse a king of Delhi, who was sick, and was afterwards *done* into Hindostanee by a Mussulman author, who styles himself, "This wicked sinner, Meer Ammun of Delhi."

The speaker, a certain prince, who aspires to the title of "generous," has built a lofty house, with forty high and spacious doors, where, at all

W. H. K Delt. Hanhart lith.

ANCIENT JAIN TEMPLE.

times, from morning to evening, he gives rupees and gold mohurs* to the poor and necessitous, and whoever asks for anything he satisfies him. "One day a Fukeer came to the front door and begged. I gave him a gold mohur; again he came to a second door, and asked for two gold mohurs. I passed over the matter, and gave him two gold mohurs.

"In this manner he came to every door, and asked for an additional gold mohur each time, and I gave him according to his request. Having come to the fortieth door, and received forty gold mohurs, he came in again by the first door, and begged afresh.

"This appeared to me a very bad action on his part. I said to him, 'O avaricious man! what sort of mendicant art thou, who knowest not the three letters of "Fukur" (*poverty*), according to which a Fukeer should act?' The Fukeer said, 'Well, O liberal person, do you explain them to me.' I replied, 'The three letters are *f*, *k*, and *r*. From *f* comes "faka" (*fasting*); from *k*, "kinaüt" (*contentment*); and from *r* comes "reeazut" (*abstinence*). He is not a Fukeer in whom these qualities are not. Oh, avaricious creature! you have taken from forty doors, from one gold mohur to forty. Calculate,

* A coin of the value of thirty-two shillings.

therefore, how many you have received. And, in addition to this, your avarice has brought you again to the first door. Expend what you have received, and return and take whatever you ask for. A Fukeer should take thought for one day; on the second day there will be some fresh bestower of alms.' Having heard this speech of mine, he became angry and dissatisfied, and threw all he had received from me on the ground, and said, 'Enough, father; be not so warm; take all your presents back again. Do not again assume the name of "Liberal." You cannot lift the weights of liberality. When will you arrive at that day's journey?'

"When I heard this I was alarmed, and with many solicitations asked him to forgive my fault, and to take whatsoever he wished. He would not accept my gifts at all, and went away saying, 'If you were now to offer me your whole kingdom I would not receive it from you.'"

This studied indifference about a matter of more than a thousand pounds, though perhaps not often exercised upon so large a scale, is just that which these wandering fanatics display towards every offering they receive, and in every action of their useless lives. Whatever may be said against them, however, their profession of poverty and suffering is no mockery, as was that of the well-fed "monks of old," whose reasonings were something similar on religious points.

The Fukeer soliloquizes: "The condition of our being born is, that our griefs are many and our pleasures few, because this world is the root of misery. What happiness, therefore, has man? If any man should climb to the top of a tree, or sit down on the summit of a hill, or remain concealed in water, yet death does not allow him to escape. At the most, man's age is a hundred years, half of which passes away in night, half of the other half is expended in childhood and old age; the remainder is spent in altercation, separation from those we love, and affliction, and the soul is restless as a wave of the sea. No one who has come into the world has escaped from affliction. It is vain to fix one's affections on it, and therefore it is best to cultivate and practise religion." And so, as a remedy for the evil which he has discovered to exist upon the earth, and to work out a successful escape from it, he sits himself down in dust and ashes, and, mistaking the sign-post, adopts the path which leads him furthest from the point he wishes to arrive at.

As the Hindoo is the most ancient of religions, so the Buddhist is the one which is professed by the largest portion of the human race. It is the religion of Burmah, Ceylon, China, Siam, Thibet, and Russian Tartary, and is computed to claim as many as three hundred and sixty-nine millions among its votaries.* "Gautama," or "Sakya mounee," its founder, was born in Bengal about the seventh century before Christ. Yet India at present contains no modern temples of its worship, and no native of India, that I have ever met, knew anything of its founder, or was even acquainted with the term "Buddha," or "Buddhist." Its doctrines are the most curious of those that have ever been promulgated, and appear even now to be scarcely understood in all their ramifications. According to original Buddhism, there is no Creator, nor being that is self-existent and eternal. The great object is the attainment, in this life, of complete abstraction from all worldly affairs and passions, and the ultimate result, of entire annihilation. Like the Hindoo, the Buddhist believes in transmigration of souls, and until utter annihilation is reached, he is doomed to shift his earthly tenement, from form to form, according to the deeds done in the flesh. It is, therefore, the great object of all beings, who would be released from the sorrows of successive birth, to seek the destruction of the moral cause of continued existence, that is, the cleaving to

* Hardy's "Eastern Monachisms."

existing objects or evil desire. It is only possible to accomplish this end by attending to a prescribed course of discipline, and by fixing the mind upon the perfections of Buddha. Those who after successive births have entirely destroyed all evil desires are called "Rahuts," and after death the Rahut attains "Nirwana," or ceases to exist. The actual meaning of the word "Rahut," is "Tranquillity," and it appears to be the same word which is used on a small scale, to express the soothing qualities of that far-famed Eastern sweetmeat, the Rahut-lûkma, or "Morsels of tranquillity."

The Buddhas themselves are beings who appear after intervals of time inconceivably vast. Previous to their reception of the state, they pass through countless phases of being, at one time appearing in human form, at another as a frog, or fish, &c., in each of which states they acquire a greater degree of merit.

In the birth in which they become Buddha, they are always of woman born, and pass through infancy and youth like ordinary mortals, until at the prescribed age they abandon the world and retire to the wilderness, where they receive the supernatural powers with which the office is endowed. Their highest glory is that they receive the wisdom by which they can direct sentient beings to the path that leads to the desired cessation of existence.

The Buddhism of Thibet appears to be an innovation on the original system of religion. It was introduced into the country about the seventh century of our era; and although Sakya mounee, who is supposed by the Thibetians to have lived one thousand years before Christ, is still believed to be the founder of the present system, the Delai Lama, at Lassa, is regarded as an incarnation of Buddha, and is the supreme infallible head of the whole Thibetian religious community.

The original tenets, too, have been modified, and the modern Scriptures have been adapted to three different capacities of mankind—viz. the lowest, mean (or middle), and the highest. The principles thus declared are as follows:—

"1. Men of vulgar capacity must believe that there is a God, a future life, and that they shall therein reap the fruits of their works in this life.

"2. Those that are in a middle degree of intellectual and moral capacity, besides admitting the former position, must know that every compound thing is perishable, that there is no reality in things, that every imperfection is pain, and that deliverance from pain or bodily existence is final happiness.

"3. Those of the highest capacities, besides the above enumerated articles, must know that, from the body to the supreme soul, nothing is existing by itself, neither can it be said that it will continue always or cease absolutely, but that everything exists by a dependant or casual connexion."*

One cause of the extension of the religion of Buddha appears to be the broad basis upon which admission to the priesthood has been placed. No one can become a Brahmin except by birth, but the privileges of becoming a Lama are open to all who are willing to receive them upon the conditions implied in their acceptance. The principal duties to be attended to, by one about to become a priest, are thus laid down:—"He who, with a firm faith in the religion of Truth, believes in Buddha, shall rise before daylight, and, having cleaned his teeth, shall then sweep all the places appointed to be swept in the vicinity of the 'Vihara,' or monastery; after which he shall fetch the water that is required for use, filter it, and place it ready for drinking. When this is done, he shall retire to a solitary place, and for the space of three hours meditate on the obligations of his vow. The bell will then ring, and he must reflect that greater than

* Csoma de Koros.

the gift of 100 elephants, 100 horses, and 100 chariots, is the reward of him who takes one step towards the place where worship is offered. Thus reflecting, he shall approach the 'Dagoba,' where relics of holy men are placed, and perform that which is appointed; he shall offer flowers just as if Buddha were present in person, meditate on the nine virtues of Buddha with a fixed and determined mind, and seek forgiveness for his faults, just as if the sacred relics were endowed with life. He shall then meditate on the advantages to be derived from carrying the alms-bowl and putting on the yellow robe." The injunctions on the priesthood relative to their abstracting their thoughts and desires from all earthly matters whatever, are of the strictest nature. "The door of the eye is to be kept shut. When the outer gates of the city are left open, though the door of every separate house and store be shut, the enemy will enter the city and take possession; in like manner, though all the ordinances be kept, if the eye be permitted to wander, affection for worldly objects will be produced." A story is told of a priest named Chittagutta, who resided once in a cave, upon the walls of which the history of Buddha was painted "in the finest style of art."

The cave was visited by some priests, who

expressed their admiration of the paintings to Chittagutta, but the devotee replied that he had lived there sixty years and had never seen them, nor would he, except for their information, ever have become aware of their existence. There was near the door of his cave a spreading tree; but he only knew that it was there by the fall of its leaves or flowers; the tree itself he never saw, as he carefully observed the precept not to look upwards, or to a distance!

The priest of Buddha must possess but eight articles: three of these are matters of dress; the others, a girdle for the loins, an alms-bowl, a razor, a needle, and a water-strainer. The bowl receives the food presented in alms; the razor is for shaving the head; the needle keeps his yellow wardrobe in order; and the water-strainer is the most serviceable of all, for "if any priest shall knowingly drink water containing insects, he shall be ejected from the priesthood."

The Dagobas, or shrines of relics, which abound in such numbers in Thibet, have also been found in India and other countries. Some of them when opened have been found to contain what appears to be remains of a funeral pile, also vessels of stone or metal, and, occasionally, caskets of silver and gold, curiously wrought. "Some of these have been chased with a series of four figures, representing Buddha in the act of preaching; a mendicant is on his right, a lay follower on his left, and behind the latter a female disciple." This somewhat describes the appearance of the stone-carved figures at the monastery of Hemis.* These caskets have been set with rubies and chased with the leaves of the lotus. Besides these have also been found small pearls, gold buttons, rings, beads, pieces of clay and stone bearing impressions of figures, bits of bone, and teeth of animals, pieces of cloth, &c. The images are sometimes recumbent, at other times standing upright, with the hand uplifted in the act of giving instruction. Sometimes they have three heads and six or more arms.

In order to form clear and accurate ideas of the religion of Buddha, it would be necessary to study a vast number of volumes, some of them contradictory and of very doubtful authority, and the result would appear hardly to compensate for the trouble, so altered has modern Buddhism become from ancient, and into so many different systems has it been divided in the many different countries in which it is professed. Among its doctrines there is much that is virtuous and true. It preaches benevolence and goodwill towards men, but enjoins

* Vide page 202.

no active efforts to prove the sincerity of such goodwill. It requires its members to "confess their sins with a contrite heart, to ask forgiveness of them, and to repent truly, with a resolution not to commit such again. To rejoice in the moral merit and perfection of human beings, and to wish that they may attain beatitude; further, to pray and exhort others to turn the wheel of religion, that the world may be benefited thereby." Its general aim seems to be to overcome all emotions and preferences of the mind, and all that would disturb its repose and quiet. It seeks to destroy the human passions and not to regulate them; and with faith in Buddha only as its aid, it succeeds about as well as might have been anticipated.

Between these two religions of Brahma and Buddha, that of the "Jains" sprang up, apparently a heresy from both. It has nearly died out in India, though many ruins of its temples remain. The Jains agree with the Buddhists as to the transmigration of souls, and carry their respect for life to the still greater extent, that besides a strainer to remove all animalculæ from the water they imbibe, they carry a broom to sweep away the insects from their path. They differ from the Brahmins in repudiating their minor incarnations and gods, as the following translation will serve to show:—"A rajah, of the name of Gondshekur, had a minister, Abhûechund, who converted him to the Jain religion. He prohibited the worship of Vishnu, and all gifts of cows, land, and balls of flour and rice, and would not allow any one to carry away bones to the Ganges. One day the minister began to say, 'O great king, be pleased to listen to the judgments and explanations of religion: Whosoever takes another's life, that other takes his life in another world. The birth of a man after he has again come into the world does not escape from this sin; he is born again and again, and dies again and again. For this reason it is right for a man, who has been born in the world, to cultivate religion. Behold! Brahma, Vishnu, and Mahadeo, being under the influence of love, anger, and fascination, descend upon the earth in various ways; but a cow is superior to them all, for it is free from anger, enmity, intoxication, rage, avarice, and inordinate affection, and affords protection to the subject; and her sons also behave kindly to, and cherish the animals of the earth, and therefore all the gods and sages regard the cow with respect. For this reason, it is not right to regard the gods—in this world, respect the cow. It is virtuous to protect all animals, from the elephant to the ant, and from beasts and birds to man. In the world there is no act so impious as for men to increase their own flesh by eating the flesh of other creatures. They who do not sympathise in the griefs of animated beings, and who kill and eat other animals, do not live long on the earth, and are born lame, maimed, blind, dwarfs, and humpbacked, &c.; and it is a great sin to drink wine and eat flesh; wherefore to do so is improper. The minister, having thus explained his sentiments to the rajah, converted him to the Jain religion, so that he did whatever the minister said, and no longer paid any respect to Brahmins, Fukeers, Jogies, Dervishes, &c., and carried on his government according to this religion."

Next among the religions of the East, whose outward observances so forcibly attract attention, comes that of the Moslem—"The marvellous reformation wrought by Mahomet and the Koran in the manners, morals, and religious feelings of so many millions."

Mahomet, in truth, although "*The* False Prophet," would appear to have been a considerable benefactor to his species. The Arabs, at the time of his birth, were sunk in idolatry and the worship of the stars, while their morals were under no control either of law or religion. The Prophet's aim appears, in the first instance, to have been, to secure a system of orderly government, and at the same time to gain, for his own family, a dignity which should be exalted beyond all fear of competition — the dignity of lordship over the holy city of Mecca. This was then held under no higher tenure than the sufferance and caprice of the Arab tribes. To perpetuate this lordship by assuming an hereditary and inviolable pontificate was Mahomet's first idea, and at a banquet given to the whole of his kinsmen he revealed his scheme. They, however, rejected his appeal, and he then proclaimed himself as an apostle to all, and setting aside existing forms and traditions proceeded to a higher flight of ambition. For election by blood, he substituted election of God; and assuming a direct revelation from on high, he, by force of an ardent and ambitious will, carried out his project even at Mecca itself, where, to all who visited his shrine, he preached without distinction. From the powerful opposition brought against him, Mahomet was at last obliged to fly; but before doing so, and casting off the high position he held among his own tribe and kinsmen, he assembled his followers together on a mountain near Mecca, and there, without distinction of blood or calling, he enrolled them as equal followers in one community, and entered with them into a solemn and binding agreement. "That night Mahomet fled from Mecca to Medina, and then took its rise a pontificate, an empire, and an era." This hegira, or "flight," is believed to have occurred on the 19th June, A.D. 622,* but has been variously stated; it is, however, the era now in general use among no less than one hundred and sixty millions of people.

Although himself an undoubted impostor, and the Koran a manifest forgery, Mahomet would appear to deserve a larger share of appreciation, or at least of charitable judgment, than he usually receives.

"He was one richly furnished with natural endowments, showing liberality to the poor, courtesy to every one, fortitude in trial, and, above all, a high reverence for the name of God. He was a preacher of patience, charity, mercy, beneficence, gratitude, honouring of parents and superiors, and a frequent celebrator of Divine praise." The great doctrine of the Koran is the Unity of God, and in this creed Mahomet

* Muir's "Life of Mahomet."

himself seems to have been a sincere believer. "Its design was to unite the professors of the three different religions then followed in Arabia —who for the most part were without guides, the greater number being idolaters, and the rest Jews and Christians, mostly of erroneous and heterodox belief—in the knowledge and worship of one eternal and invisible God, and to bring them to obedience of Mahomet as the only prophet and ambassador of the truth." The "fatiha," or opening chapter of the Koran, is said to contain the essence of the whole, and forms part of the daily prayers of all zealous Mussulmans. It commences with the formula pronounced at the beginning of their reading on all occasions whenever an animal is slaughtered for food, and upon the undertaking of all important actions whatever:—

> "In the name of God, the merciful, the compassionate. Praise be to God, the Lord of the Creation, the all-merciful, the all-compassionate! Ruler of the day of reckoning!
>
> "Thee we worship, and Thee we invoke for help. Lead us in the straight path—the path of those upon whom thou hast been gracious, not of those that are the objects of wrath or that are in error."

The Moslem faithful pray five times in the twenty-four hours: in the morning before sunrise, at noon, before sunset, after sunset, and before the first watch of the night: and that these observances were not originally instituted merely that their prayers might be seen before men, would appear from the injunction which lays down that "what is principally to be regarded in the duty of prayer, is the inward disposition of the heart, which is its entire life and spirit, the most punctual observance being of no avail if performed without devotion, reverence, attention, and hope."

Prayer was held by Mahomet to be the "pillar of religion" and the "key of paradise," and in the performance of it, his disciples are enjoined to lay aside their ornaments and costly habits, and all that might savour of either pride or arrogance.

Its observance, however, at five stated times appears to be nowhere mentioned in the Koran, although the custom is now an essential part, and the most noticeable and characteristic feature of Mahomedanism.

Saints and sinners join equally in the form. A crime just committed, or one in immediate contemplation, in no way interferes with the "five-time prayers," and the neglect of them amounts to an abnegation of the Faith. The summons to prayer was originally only one sentence, "To public prayer." Mahomet, however, afterwards bethought himself that a more elaborate and striking call would be an improvement, and the present "Azzan," or call to prayer, was introduced.

While the matter was under discussion, Mahomet being unable to decide upon any suitable form, a certain Abdallah dreamed that he met a man arrayed in green raiment carrying a bell. Abdallah sought to buy it, thinking it would just suit the Prophet for assembling together the Faithful. The stranger, however, replied, "I will show you a better way than that; let a crier call aloud—

"Great is the Lord! great is the Lord!
I bear witness that there is no God but the Lord;
I bear witness that Mahomet is the Prophet of God!
Come unto prayer, come unto happiness—
God is great! God is great! There is no God but the Lord!"

Mahomet, learning the particulars of Abdallah's dream, believed it to have been a vision from on high, and sent his servant forthwith to execute the Divine command. Ascending to the top of a lofty house, this first of established Mûezzins, on the earliest appearance of light, startled all around from their slumbers with the newly-adopted call, adding to it, "Prayer is better than sleep! Prayer is better than sleep!" And ever since, at the customary five hours, have his successors thus summoned the people to their devotions.

Concerning the future state, the Mahomedan believes that all will be examined at the day of Judgment as to their words and actions in this life.

"Their time, as to how they spent it; their wealth, by what means they acquired it, and how they employed it; their bodies, wherein they exercised them; their knowledge and learning, what use they made of them," &c. "They enter Paradise, however, not by their own good works, but by the mercy of God. At that day each person will make his defence in the best manner he can, endeavouring to find excuses for his own conduct by casting blame on others; so much so, that disputes shall even arise between the Soul and Body. The Soul saying, "Lord, I was created without a hand to lay hold with, a foot to walk with, an eye to see with, or an understanding to apprehend with, until I came and entered the Body: therefore punish it, but deliver me." The Body, on the other side, will make this apology, "Lord, thou createdst me like a stock of wood, being neither able to hold with my hand, nor to walk with my feet, till this Soul, like a ray of light, entered into me, and my tongue began to speak, my eye to see, and my foot to walk: therefore punish it, but deliver me." Then shall the following parable be propounded: — "A certain king having a pleasant garden, in which were ripe fruits, set two persons to keep it, one of whom was blind, and the other lame—the former not being able to see the fruit, nor the latter to gather it. The lame man, however, seeing the fruit, persuaded the blind man to take him on his shoulders; and by that means he easily gathered the fruits, which they divided between them. The lord of the garden coming some time after, and inquiring after the fruit, each began to excuse himself; the blind man said he had no eyes to see it with, and the lame man that he had no feet to approach the trees. Then the king, ordering the lame man to be set on the blind, passed sentence on them both, and punished them together.

" In like manner shall be judged the Body and the Soul."

Such are some few of the religious tenets of

those among whom one's lot is cast while wandering in the East. Sunk for the most part in ignorance, and held as infidels for wanting faith in what they never heard, they nevertheless attract attention chiefly by their Faith, and by their zealous worship of the Being, whom, although in darkest ignorance as to His attributes and laws, their original creed would teach them to believe the one Eternal God.

Some idea of the number represented by these different sects may be derived from the following table:—

Asiatic Religions	Buddhists . .	369,000,000
	Hindoos . . .	231,000,000
	Mussulmen . .	160,000,000
Christians . . .	Roman Catholics	170,000,000
	Protestants . .	80,000,000
	Greek Church .	76,000,000
Jews		5,000,000
Other Religions		200,000,000*

And when we reflect how great is the proportion of those who sit in darkness, and that "even all who tread the earth are but a handful to the tribes that slumber in its bosom," it is but natural to consider what our own belief would

* M. Dietrici.

bid us hold as to the future destiny of so large a portion of the human family.

At the same time, the question, "Are there few that be saved?" not having been answered eighteen centuries ago, would appear to be one to which no definite reply was intended to be rendered, and which might well be left till now unanswered, by those who hold the religion of Faith, Hope, and Charity. When, however, the Church to which we belong boldly affirms, in words, which as the public profession of its faith, should be beyond all doubt or misconception by either friend or foe, that none *can* be saved but those who hold the Catholic Faith, as she would have them hold it, then, at least, we may fairly consider the matter so far as to doubt whether the answer thus forced upon us is one which, even on such high authority, we are bound to accept. Before, at least, concurring in a solution of the question which, thus virtually bringing it within the limits of a simple arithmetical calculation, would summarily dispose of so many millions of the human race, we may remember that some things have been taught as possible which men, and even saints, may deem impossible; and, before attempting to reduce "goodwill toward men" to human and determinable proportions, we may also remember that "good tidings of great joy" were promised to *all* people, and that they may possibly prove therefore to have in some way benefited even those who have never heard them with their mortal ears.

Meanwhile, in the matter of "Turks and Infidels," we may perhaps learn something even from an Infidel creed, and, borrowing a definition from the religion of Islam, may be allowed to hold with it, that

"Truly to despair of the goodness of God—this is '*Infidelity.*'"

سچ ہی • خدا کی مہربانی سے نا امید ہونا • یہ کفر ہی

APPENDIX.

APPENDIX A.

THE TEMPLES OF CASHMERE.

Extract from "An Essay on the Arian Order of Architecture, as exhibited in the Temples of Kashmír," by CAPT. A. CUNNINGHAM. *"Journal of the Asiatic Society," Vol. XVII.*

THE architectural remains of Kashmír are perhaps the most remarkable of the existing monuments of India, as they exhibit undoubted traces of the influence of Grecian art. The Hindú temple is generally a sort of architectural pasty, a huge collection of ornamental fritters, huddled together with or without keeping; while the "Jain" temple is usually a vast forest of pillars, made to look as unlike one another as possible, by some paltry differences in their petty details.

On the other hand, the Kashmirian fanes are distinguished by the graceful elegance of their outlines, by the massive boldness of their parts, and by the happy propriety of their decorations.

They cannot, indeed, vie with the severe simplicity of the Parthenon, but they possess great beauty—different, indeed, yet quite their own.

The characteristic features of the Kashmirian architecture are its lofty pyramidal roofs, its trefoiled doorways, covered by pyramidal pediments, and the great width of the intercolumniations.

Most of the Kashmirian temples are more or less injured, but more particularly those at Wantipúr, which are mere heaps of ruins. Speaking of these temples, Trebeck says: " It is scarcely possible to imagine that the state of " ruin to which they have been reduced has been the work " of time, or even of man, as their solidity is fully equal to " that of the most massive monuments of Egypt. Earth-" quakes must have been the cause of their overthrow." In my opinion, their *overthrow* is too complete to have been the result of an earthquake, which would have simply *prostrated* the buildings in large masses. But the whole of the superstructure of these temples is now lying in one confused heap of stones, totally disjointed from one another.

I believe, therefore, that I am fully justified in saying, from my own experience, that such a complete and *disruptive overturn* could only have been produced by gunpowder.

The destruction of the Kashmirian temples is universally attributed, both by history and by tradition, to the bigoted Sikander. (A. D. 1396.) He was reigning at the period of Timúr's invasion of India, with whom he exchanged friendly presents, and from whom, I suppose, he may have received a present of the *villanous saltpetre.*

As it would appear that the Turks had *metal* cannon at the siege of Constantinople in 1422, I think it no great stretch of probability to suppose that gunpowder itself had been carried into the East, even as far as Kashmír, at least ten or twenty years earlier—that is, about A. D. 1400 to 1420, or certainly during the reign of Sikander, who died in 1416.

Even if this be not admitted, I still adhere to my opinion, that the complete ruin of the Wantipúr temples could only have been effected by gunpowder; and I would, then, ascribe their overthrow to the bigoted "Aurungzíb."

"Ferishta" attributed to Sikander the demolition of all the Kashmirian temples save one, which was dedicated to Mahadeo, and which only escaped "in consequence of "its foundations being below the surface of the neighbour-"ing water."

In A.D. 1580, "Abul Fazl" mentions that some of the idolatrous temples were in "perfect preservation;" and Ferishta describes many of these temples as having been in existence in his own time, or about A.D. 1600.

As several are still standing, though more or less injured, it is certain that Sikander could not have destroyed them all. He most likely gave orders that they should be overturned; and I have no doubt that many of the principal temples were thrown down during his reign.

But, besides the ruthless hand of the destroyer, another agency, less immediate, but equally certain in its ultimate effects, must have been at work upon the large temples of Kashmír. The silent ravages of the destroyer, who carries away pillars and stones for the erection of other edifices, has been going on for centuries. Pillars, from which the architraves have been thus removed, have been thrown down by earthquakes, ready to be set up again for the decoration of the first Musjid that might be erected in the neighbourhood. Thus every Mahomedan building in Kashmír is constructed either entirely or in part of the ruins of Hindú temples.

TAKT I SULIMAN.

The oldest temple in Kashmír, both in appearance and according to tradition, is that upon the hill of "Takt i Sulíman," or Solomon's Throne. It stands 1,000 feet above the plain, and commands a view of the greater part of Kashmír.

The situation is a noble one, and must have been amongst the first throughout the whole valley which was selected as the position of a temple. Its erection is ascribed to Jaloka, the son of Asoka, who reigned about 220 B.C.

The plan of the temple is octagonal, each side being fifteen feet in length. It is approached by a flight of eighteen steps, eight feet in width, and inclosed between two sloping walls. Its height cannot now be ascertained, as the present roof is a modern plastered dome, which was probably built since the occupation of the country by the Síkhs. The walls are eight feet thick, which I consider one of the strongest proofs of the great antiquity of the building.

PÁNDRETHÁN.

This name means the old capital, or ancient chief town. The name has, however, been spelt by different travellers in many different ways. "Moorcroft" calls it Pándenthán, "Vigne" Pandrenton, and "Hugel" Pandriton.

The building of this temple is recorded between A.D. 913 and 921; and it is afterwards mentioned between the years 958 and 972, as having escaped destruction when the King Abhimanyú—Nero-like—set fire to his own capital.

As this is the only temple situated in the old capital, there can be very little, if any, doubt that it is the very same building which now exists. For as it is surrounded by water, it was, of course, quite safe amid the fire, which reduced the other buildings to mere masses of quicklime.

Baron Hugel calls the Pándrethán edifice a "Buddhist temple," and states that there are some well-preserved Buddhist figures in the interior. But he is doubly mistaken, for the temple was dedicated to Vishnú, and the figures in the inside have no connexion with Buddhism.

Trebeck swam into the interior, and could discover no figures of any kind; but as the whole ceiling was formerly hidden by a coating of plaster, his statement was, at that time, perfectly correct.

The object of erecting the temples in the midst of water must have been to place them more immediately under the protection of the Nágas, or human-bodied and snake-tailed gods, who were zealously worshipped for ages through Kashmír.

MÁRTTAND.

Of all the existing remains of Kashmirian grandeur, the most striking in size and situation is the noble ruin of Márttand.

This majestic temple stands at the northern end of the elevated table-land of "Matan," about three miles to the eastward of Islámabád.

This is undoubtedly the finest position in Kashmír. The temple itself is not now (1848) more than forty feet in height, but its solid walls and bold outlines towering over the fluted pillars of the surrounding colonnade give it a most imposing appearance.

There are no petty confused details; but all are distinct and massive, and most admirably suited to the general character of the building.

Many vain speculations have been hazarded regarding the date of the erection of this temple and the worship to which it was appropriated.

It is usually called the "House of the Pandús" by the Brahmins, and by the people "Matan."

The true appellation appears to be preserved in the latter, Matan being only a corruption of the Sanscrit Márttand मार्त्तण्ड, or the sun, to which the temple was dedicated.

The true date of the erection of this temple—the wonder of Kashmír—is a disputed point of chronology; but the period of its foundation can be determined within the limits of one century, or between A.D. 370 and 500.

The mass of building now known by the name of Matan, or Márttand, consists of one lofty central edifice, with a small detached wing on each side of the entrance, the whole standing on a large quadrangle surrounded by a colonnade of fluted pillars, with intervening trefoil-headed recesses. The central building is sixty-three feet in length, by thirty-six in width.

As the main building is at present entirely uncovered, the original form of the roof can only be determined by a reference to other temples, and to the general form and character of the various parts of the Márttand temple itself.

The angle of the roof in the Temple of Pándrethán, and in other instances, is obtained by making the sides of the pyramid which forms it parallel to the sides of the doorway pediment, and in restoring the Temples of Patrun and Márttand I have followed the same rule.

The height of the Pándrethán temple—of the cloistered recesses, porch pediments, and niches of Márttand itself—were all just double their respective widths. This agreement in the relative proportions of my restored roof of Márttand with those deduced from other examples, is a presumptive proof of the correctness of my restoration. The entrance-chamber and the wings I suppose to have been also covered by similar pyramidal roofs. There would thus have been four distinct pyramids, of which that over the inner chamber must have been the loftiest, the height of its pinnacle above the ground being about seventy-five feet.

The interior must have been as imposing as the exterior. On ascending the flight of steps—now covered by ruins—the votary of the sun entered a highly-decorated chamber, with a doorway on each side covered by a pediment, with a trefoil-headed niche containing a bust of the Hindú triad, and on the flanks of the main entrance, as well as on those of the side doorways, were pointed and trefoil niches, each of which held a statue of a Hindú divinity.

The interior decorations of the roof can only be conjecturally determined, as I was unable to discover any ornamented stones that could with certainty be assigned to it. Baron Hugel doubts that Márttand ever had a roof; but, as the walls of the temple are still standing, the numerous heaps of large stones that are scattered about on all sides can only have belonged to the roof.

I can almost fancy that the erection of this sun-temple was suggested by the magnificent sunny prospect which its position commands. It overlooks the finest view in Kashmír, and perhaps in the known world. Beneath it lies the paradise of the East, with its sacred streams and cedarn glens, its brown orchards and green fields, surrounded on all sides by vast snowy mountains, whose lofty peaks seem to smile upon the beautiful valley below. The vast extent of the scene makes it sublime; for this magnificent view of Kashmír is no petty peep into a half-mile glen, but the full display of a valley sixty miles in breadth and upwards of a hundred miles in length, the whole of which lies beneath "the ken of the wonderful Márttand."

The principal buildings that still exist in Kashmír are entirely composed of a blue limestone, which is capable of taking the highest polish—a property to which I mainly attribute the beautiful state of preservation in which some of them at present exist.

Even at first sight one is immediately struck by the strong resemblance which the Kashmirian colonnades bear to the classic peristyles of Greece. Even the temples themselves, with their porches and pediments, remind one more of Greece than of India; and it is difficult to believe that a style of architecture which differs so much from all Indian examples, and which has so much in common with those of Greece, could have been indebted to chance alone for this striking resemblance.

One great similarity between the Kashmirian architecture and that of the various Greek orders is its stereotyped style, which, during the long flourishing period of several centuries, remained unchanged. In this respect it is so widely different from the ever-varying forms and plastic vagaries of the Hindú architecture that it is impossible to conceive their evolution from a common origin.

I feel convinced myself that several of the Kashmirian forms, and many of the details, were borrowed from the temples of the Kabúlian Greeks, while the arrangements of the interior and the relative proportions of the different parts were of Hindú origin. Such, in fact, must necessarily have been the case with imitations by Indian workmen, which would naturally have been engrafted upon the indigenous architecture. The general arrangements would still remain Indian, while many of the details, and even some of the larger forms, might be of foreign origin.

As a whole, I think that the Kashmirian architecture, with its noble fluted pillars, its vast colonnades, its lofty pediments, and its elegant trefoiled arches, is fully entitled to be classed as a distinct style. I have therefore ventured to call it the Arian order—a name to which it has a double right; first, because it was the style of the Aryas, or Arians, of Kashmír; and, secondly, because its intercolumniations are always of four diameters—an interval which the Greeks called Araiostyle.

Extract from Vigne's "Travels in Kashmir."

The Hindú temple of Márttand is commonly called the House of the Pandús. Of the Pandús it is only necessary to say that they are the Cyclopes of the East. Every old building, of whose origin the poorer class of Hindús in general have no information, is believed to have been the work of the Pandús. As an isolated ruin, this deserves, on account of its solitary and massive grandeur, to be ranked not only as the first ruin of the kind in Kashmír, but as one of the noblest among the architectural relics of antiquity that are to be seen in any country. Its noble and exposed situation at the foot of the hills reminded me of that of the Escurial. It has no forest of cork-trees and evergreen-oaks before it, nor is it to be compared, in point of size, with that stupendous building; but it is visible from as great a distance. And the Spanish sierra cannot for a moment be placed in competition with the verdant magnificence of the mountain-scenery of Kashmír.

Few of the Kashmirian temples, if any, I should say, were Buddhist. Those in or upon the edge of the water were rather, I should suppose, referable to the worship of the Nágas, or snake-gods. The figures in all the temples are almost always in an erect position, and I have never been able to discover any inscription in those now remaining.

I had been struck with the great general resemblance which the temple bore to the recorded disposition of the Ark and its surrounding curtains, in imitation of which the Temple at Jerusalem was built; and it became for a moment a question whether the Kashmirian temples had not been built by Jewish architects, who had recommended them to be constructed on the same plan for the sake of convenience merely. It is, however, a curious fact, that in Abyssinia, the ancient Ethiopia, which was also called "Kush," the ancient Christian churches are not unlike those of Kashmír, and that they were originally built in imitation of the temple, by the Israelites who followed the Queen of Sheba, whose son took possession of the throne of Kush, where his descendants are at this moment Kings of Abyssinia.

Without being able to boast, either in extent or magnificence, of an approach to equality with the temple of the sun at Palmyra, or the ruins of the palace at Persepolis, Márttand is not without pretensions to a locality of scarcely inferior interest, and deserves to be ranked with them, as the leading specimen of a gigantic style of architecture that has decayed with the religion it was intended to cherish, and the prosperity of a country it could not but adorn.

In situation it is far superior to either. Palmyra is surrounded by an ocean of sand, and Persepolis overlooks a marsh; but the temple of the sun in Márttand is built upon a natural platform at the foot of some of the noblest mountains, and beneath its ken lies what is undoubtedly the finest and the most *prononcé* valley in the known world.

We are not looking upon the monuments of the dead. We step not aside to inspect a tomb, or pause to be saddened by an elegy. The noble pile in the foreground is rather an emblem of age than of mortality; and the interest with which we perambulate its ruins is not the less pleasurable because we do not know much that is certain of its antiquity, its founders, or its original use.

APPENDIX B.

THE MYSTIC SENTENCE OF THIBET.

Explication et origine de la formule bouddhique:—" Om mani padmè hoûm" par M. KLAPROTH. *"Nouveau Journal Asiatique."*

LES Tubétains et les Mongols ont perpétuellement cette prière dans la bouche. Les mots de cette inscription sont Sanscrits, et donnent un sens complet dans cette langue. En voici la transcription en devanagri :—

ओं मणि पद्मे हूं

"Om" est, chez les Hindous, le nom mystique de la divinité, par lequel toutes les prières commencent. Cette particule mystique équivaut à l'interjection, *oh!* prononcée avec emphase et avec une entière conviction religieuse. Mani signifie *le joyau*; Padma *le lotus*. Enfin Hoûm est une particule qui équivaut à notre "*Amen.*" Le sens de la phrase est très clair; "Om mani padmè hoûm" signifie "*Oh! le joyau dans le lotus, Amen.*" Malgré ce sens indubitable, les Bouddhistes du Tubet se sont évertués à chercher un sens mystique à chacune des six syllabes qui composent cette phrase. Ils ont rempli des livres entiers de ces explications imaginaires.

Cette formule est particulière aux Bouddhistes du Tubet.

Selon l'histoire de ce pays la formule Om mani padmè hoûm, y a été apportée de l'Inde vers la moitié du 7e siècle de notre ère.

La legende suivante traduite du Mongol contient des détails sur la conversion du Tubet par le dieu Padmá pani,* et sur l'origine des six syllabes sacrées, Om mani padmè hoûm. Ce dieu est appelé en Sanscrit "Avalokites' vara" ou "le maître qui contemple avec amour;" ce que les Tubétains ont rendu par "le tout-voyant aux mille mains et aux mille yeux:" Les Chinois on traduit le nom par "celui qui contemple les sons du monde."

"Autrefois, quand le '*glorieux-accompli*' (Sakya mouni ou Buddh) séjournait dans la forêt 'd'Odma,' il advint un jour, qu'étant entouré de ses nombreux disciples un rayon de lumière de cinq couleurs sortit tout-à-coup entre ses deux sourcils, forma un arc-en-ciel, et se dirigea du côté de l'Empire septentrional de neige (Thibet). Les regards du Bouddha suivaient ce rayon, et sa figure montra un sourire de joie inexprimable. Un de ses disciples lui demanda

* Padmà pâni, fils céleste du Bouddha divin du monde actuel, est, dans cette qualité, entré en fonction depuis la mort du Bouddha terrestre Sakya mouni, comme son remplaçant, chargé d'être après lui le protecteur constant, le gardien et le propagateur de la foi bouddhique renouvelée par Sakya. C'est pour cette raison qu'il ne se borne pas à une apparition unique comme les Bouddhas, mais qu'il se soumet presque sans interruption à une série de naissances qui dureront jusqu'à l'avénement de Maitreya, le futur Bouddha.

On croit aussi qu'il est incarné dans la personne du "Dalai Lama," et qu'il paraîtra en qualité de Bouddha, le millième de la période actuelle du monde.

Le Tibet est sa terra de prédilection; il est le père de ses habitants, et la formule célèbre. Om mani padmè hom, est un de ses bienfaits.—*Rélation des Royaumes Bouddhiques*, par Chy Fa Hian, traduit par M. Remusat.

de lui en expliquer la raison, et sur sa prière le glorieux-accompli lui dit:—

" 'Fils d'illustre origine! dans le pays qu'aucun Bouddha 'des trois âges n'a pu convertir, et qui est rempli d'une 'foule d'êtres malfaisans, la loi se lèvera comme le soleil 'et s'y répandra dans les temps futurs.' "

" 'L'apôtre de cet Empire de neige âpre et sauvage, sera 'le Khoutoukhtou' (Padmá páni).

" Après que 'Sakya mouni' eut prononcé ces paroles, un rayon de lumière, éclatant comme un lotus blanc, sortit de son cœur et illumina toutes les régions du monde et se plongea dans le cœur du *Bouddha infiniment resplendissant.* Alors un autre éclat de lumière sortit du Bouddha resplendissant et se plongea dans la mer des fleurs de *Padmá* (lotus), et y transmit cette pensée du Bouddha, qu'il s'en élèverait et qu'il en naitrait un Khoubilkhan* divin, destiné à la conversion de l'Empire de neige."

" Le Roi Dehdou qui était parvenu à participer à la béatitude de l'empire de Soukhawatee, voulant un jour offrir au Bouddha un sacrifice des fleurs, dépêcha quelques-uns des siens aux bords de la mer des *Padma* (Lotus), pour y cueillir de ces fleurs. Ses envoyés aperçurent dans la mer une très grande tige de Lotus au milieu de laquelle il y avait un bouton colossal entouré d'une foule de grandes feuilles, et jetant des rayons de lumière de différentes couleurs. Les envoyés en firent leur rapport au roi, qui, rempli d'étonnement, se rendit avec sa cour sur un grand radeau à la place de la mer où se trouvait cette tige merveilleuse."

" Y'étant arrivé, il présenta ses offrandes et prononça la bénédiction; le bouton s'ouvrit alors des quatre côtés, et

* Le mot Khoubilkhan, en Mongol, désigne l'incarnation d'une âme superieure.

au milieu apparut l'apôtre de l'empire de neige, né comme 'Khoubilkhan.' Il y était assis, les jambes croisées, avait un visage et quatre mains; les deux mains antérieures étaient jointes devant le cœur, la troisième de droite tenait un rosaire de cristal, et la quatrième à gauche une fleur de Lotus blanche, qui penchait vers l'oreille."

"Sur sa figure, dont l'éclat se répandait vers les dix régions du monde, se montrait un sourire qui pénétra dans tous les cœurs."

"Le roi et sa suite portèrent le 'Khoubilkhan' au palais, en poussant des cris de joie et entonnant des hymnes. Le roi se rendit devant le Bouddha éternel et lui demanda la permission d'adopter pour fils, le 'Khoubilkhan' né dans la mer de lotus. Mais sa demande ne fut pas agréé et il apprit, la véritable origine de ce 'Khoubilkhan.' Le Bouddha infiniment resplendissant posa alors sa main sur la tête de celui-ci et dit 'Fils d'illustre 'origine! Les êtres qui habitent l'âpre empire de la neige, 'qu'aucun Bouddha des temps passés n'a pu convertir, 'qu'aucun du temps futurs ne convertira, et qu'aucun du 'temps présent n'a converti, le seront par la force et la 'bénédiction de ton vœu. C'est excellant; c'est excellant! 'Khoutoukhtou!*'"

"'Aussitôt que les habitans de l'âpre empire de neige te 'verront et qu'ils entendront le son des six syllabes (Om 'mani padmè hoûm) ils seront délivrés des trois naissance 'de mauvaise nature, et trouveront la béatitude par la 'renaissance comme êtres d'une nature supérieure. Les 'esprits malfaisans de l'âpre empire de neige, ainsi que 'tous les êtres donnant des maladies ou la mort, aussitôt, 'Khoutoukhtou, qu'ils te verront et qu'ils entendront le

* Khoutoukhtou, en Mongol, signifie "*Un Saint Maître.*"

'son des six syllabes, ils quitteront la fureur et la méchanceté qui les anime, et deviendront compatissans.

"'Les tigres, les panthères, les loups, les ours et autres animaux féroces, aussitôt, O Khoutoukhtou! qu'ils te verront et entendront le son des six syllabes ils adouciront leurs hurlemens, et leur fureur sanguinaire se changera en douceur bienveillante. Khoutoukhtou! ta figure et le son des six syllabes rassaiseront les affamés et calmeront la soif des altérés; il tombera comme une pluie d'eau bénite, et elle remplira tous leurs desirs. Khoutoukhtou! tu es l'être gracieux destiné à annoncer la volonté du Bouddha à cet empire de neige.

"'Selon ton example, un grand nombre de Bouddhas s'y montreront, dans le temps futurs, et y répandront la foi.

"'Les six syllabes sont le sommaire de toute doctrine, et l'âpre empire de neige, sera rempli de cette doctrine par la force de ces six syllabes—

Om ma ni pad me houm.

"Après cette consécration, le Khoutoukhtou s'agenouilla devant le Bouddha, joignit les mains et prononça le vœu suivant: 'Puissé-je être en état de pouvoir faire parvenir à la béatitude les six espèces d'êtres vivans dans les trois royaumes! Puissé-je, avant tout, conduire sur le chemin du bonheur, les êtres vivans de l'empire de neige (Thibet).

"'Loin de moi le désir de retourner dans mon Empire de joie, avant d'avoir achevé l'œuvre si difficile de la conversion de ces êtres. Si une telle pensée, produite par le dégoût et la mauvaise humeur, s'empare de moi, que ma tête se fende en dix parties, et mon corps, comme cette fleur de lotus, en mille.'

"Après ces mots, il se rendit dans le royaume de l'enfer, prononça les six syllabes et détruisit les peines des enfers frois et chauds. De là il s'éleva au royaume des animaux, prononça les six syllabes et détruisit la peine que leur produit la chasse. Puis il se rendit dans l'empire des hommes, prononça les six syllabes et detruisit la peine de la naissance, de l'âge, des maladies et de la mort. Il s'éleva après à l'empire des génies du ciel, prononça les six syllabes et détruisit l'envie qui les tourmente pour se disputer et se combattre. Enfin, il aborda le grand Royaume de neige (le Tubet).

" Ici, il aperçut la mer d' 'Otang' comme un enfer terrible, et il vit que dêrêchef, plusieurs millions d'êtres y'étaient, bouillis, brûlés, et martyrisés.

" Le Khoutouktou se rendit au bord de la mer et dit : 'Oh! que tant de milliers d'êtres qui se trouvent dans 'cette mer, où ils souffrent des tourmens inexprimable 'par la chaleur, le froid, la faim, et la soif, puissent re- 'jeter loin d'eux leur enveloppe funeste et renaître dans 'mon paradis commes êtres supérieures. **Om mani 'padme houm!'**

" A peine le 'Khoutoukhtou' avait-il prononcé ces mots que les tourmens des damnés cessèrent ; leur esprit fut tranquillisé, et ils se virent transportés sur le chemin du Bouddha. Le Khoutoukhtou ayant ainsi rendu propres à la délivrance les six espèces des êtres vivans dans les trois royaumes du monde, se trouva fatigué, se reposa et tomba dans un état de contemplation intérieure."

" Apres quelques temps il vit qu'à peine la centième partie des habitans de l'empire de neige avaient été conduits sur le chemin de la délivrance. Son âme en fut si douloureusement affectée qu'il eut le désir de retourner dans son paradis. A peine l'avait-il conçu, qu'ensuite de ce vœu, sa tête se fendit en dix et son corps en mille pièces.

" Le Bouddha infiniment resplendissant lui apparût dans

le même moment, guérit la tête et le corps fendus du Khoutoukhtou, le prit par la main et lui dit : "Fils 'd' illustre origine ! Vois les suites inévitables de ton vœu ; 'mais parceque tu l'avais fait pour l'illustration de tous les 'Bouddhas, tu as été guéri sur-le-champ. Ne sois donc 'plus triste, car quoique ta tête se soit fendue en dix 'pièces, chacune aura, par ma bénédiction, une face parti-'culière, et au-dessus d'elles sera placé mon propre visage 'rayonnant. Ce onzième visage de *l'infiniment resplen-'dissant*, placé au-dessus de tes dix autres, te rendra 'l'objet de l'adoration.

" 'Quoique ton corps se soit fendu en mille morceaux, 'ils deviendront, par ma bénédiction, mille mains qui re-'présenteront les mille Bouddhas d'un âge complet du 'monde (en sanscrit Kalpa),* et qui te rendront l'objet le 'plus digne d'adoration.' "

Cette légende nous explique, non-seulement l'extrême importance que les Bouddhistes du Tubet attachent à la formule "Om mani padmè hoûm," mais elle nous démontre aussi que son véritable sens est celui que j'ai donné plus haut : Oh ! le joyau dans le lotus ; Amen ! Il est évident qu'elle se rapporte à "Avalokites' vara" ou "Padma pani" lui-même, qui naquit dans une fleur de lotus.†

* Le plus petit "Kalpa" est de seize millions huit cent mille ans, et le grand "Kalpa" est d'un milliard trois cents quarante-quatre millions d'années.

† Je ne l'ai encore trouvée cette phrase dans aucun ouvrage chinois ou japonais, et notre savant collègue M. Bournouf, m'a dit aussi qu'il ne l'a jamais rencontrée dans les livres palis, birmans et siamois.

ŬM MANI PANEE.

As will be seen by the foregoing extract from M. Klaproth's explanation, the mystic sentence, instead of being as I have represented it, is in reality, "**Om mani padme houm,**" or, in a form of spelling more English, if not more intelligible, "Om muni pudmay hoom," and the meaning, supposing its derivation from the Sanscrit to be beyond doubt, would, as therein translated, be, "Oh the jewel in the Lotus, Amen!" Almost every traveller who has mentioned the inscription in question appears to have followed M. Klaproth's pronunciation as above; but this, although the one actually given by the value of the Thibetian letters, is certainly not that in use by the people among whom it is chiefly, if not alone, to be found. This I can vouch for, as the words were so incessantly in the mouths of all to whom I applied for information, that I had ample opportunity of hearing and remembering their sound; and having written them on the spot in the Persian character, the pronunciation would not be open to the misapprehension or uncertainty to which, after the sounds themselves had been forgotten, the English form of spelling might have rendered them liable.*

A form, however, different from both these, is given by one who, with the exception perhaps of M. Huc, had better opportunities than most others for ascertaining the meaning of the words and hearing their actual pronunciation: this was Captain Turner, who was nominated by

* اُم مانِپانِي

Warren Hastings, in the year 1783, to undertake an embassy to the Court of Thibet, at Lassa.

He, however, makes no mention of the Sanscrit translation above given, and confesses his inability to obtain, even at the head-quarters of Thibetian Buddhism, a satisfactory explanation of the origin or import of the sentence. The following account, taken from Captain Turner's Report on his Mission, may be of interest, as it explains the circumstances under which an event so unusual as an embassy to the Court of Thibet was agreed to by the Grand Lama.

In 1772, a frontier warfare having broken out between the "Booteas," dependants of Thibet, and the English Government, in consequence of the aggression of the former, Teshoo Lama, at the time regent of Thibet and guardian of the Delai Lama, his superior in religious rank, united in his own person the political authority and the spiritual hierarchy of the country, subservient only to the Emperor of China. The Lama, interested for the safety of Bootan, sent a deputation to Calcutta, with a letter addressed to the governor, of which the following is a translation:—"The affairs of this quarter in every respect flourish. I am, night and day, employed in prayers for the increase of your happiness and prosperity. Having been informed, by travellers from your country, of your exalted fame and reputation, my heart, like the blossoms of spring, abounds with satisfaction, gladness, and joy.

"Praise be to God that the star of your fortune is in its ascension! Praise be to Him that happiness and ease are the surrounding attendants of myself and family! Neither to molest, nor persecute, is my aim. It is even the characteristic of our sect to deprive ourselves of the necessary refreshment of sleep, should an injury be done to a single individual; but in justice and humanity, I am informed, you far surpass us.

"May you ever adorn the seat of justice and power, that mankind may, in the shadow of your bosom, enjoy the blessings of peace and affluence."

The Lama then enters into the subject of the disturbances between his dependants and the British Government, and concludes:—"As to my part, I am but a Fukeer; and it is the custom of my sect, with the rosary in our hands, to pray for the welfare of all mankind, and especially for the peace and happiness of the inhabitants of this country; and I do now, with my head uncovered, intreat that you will cease from all hostilities in future. In this country the worship of the Almighty is the profession of all. We poor creatures are in nothing equal to you. Having, however, a few things in hand, I send them to you as tokens of remembrance, and hope for your acceptance of them."*

The Lama being in this unusually agreeable frame of mind, the British Government yielded without hesitation to his intercession.

The governor himself readily embraced the opportunity, which he thought the occurrence afforded, of extending the British influence to a quarter of the world but little known, and with which we possessed hardly any commercial connexion.

In 1774 a deputation was sent to carry back an answer to the Lama, and to offer him suitable presents. It was

* Amongst these were sheets of gilt leather, stamped with the black eagle of the Russian armorial; talents of gold and silver, bags of genuine musk, narrow cloths of woollen the manufacture of Thibet, and silks of China.

furnished also with a variety of articles of English manufacture, to be produced as specimens of the trade in which the subjects of the Lama might be invited to participate. The result was, that in 1779, when the Lama visited the Emperor of China at Pekin, desirous of improving his connexion with the Government of Bengal, he desired the British envoy to go round by sea to Canton, promising to join him at the capital. The Emperor's promise was at the same time obtained to permit the first openings of an intercourse between that country and Bengal, through the intermediate channel furnished by the Lama.

The death of both the Lama and the envoy, however, which happened nearly at the same time, destroyed the plans thus formed.

Soon after the receipt of the letters announcing the Lama's death, intelligence arrived of his reappearance in Thibet! His soul, according to the doctrines of their faith, had passed into and animated the body of an infant, who, on the discovery of his identity by such testimony as their religion prescribes, was proclaimed by the same title as his predecessor.

Warren Hastings then proposed a second deputation to Thibet, and Captain Turner was accordingly nominated on the 9th January, 1783.

His mention of the sculptured stones and inscription is as follows:—

"Another sort of monument is a long wall, on both faces of which near the top are inserted large tablets with the words 'Oom maunee paimee oom' carved in relief. This is the sacred sentence repeated upon the rosaries of the Lamas, and in general use in Tibet. Of the form of words to which ideas of peculiar sanctity are annexed by the inhabitants, I could never obtain a satisfactory explanation. It is frequently engraven on the rocks in large and deep characters, and sometimes I have seen it on the sides of hills; the letters, which are formed by means of stones fixed in the earth, are of so vast a magnitude as to be visible at a very considerable distance."

M. Huc's account of an explanation of the formula, which he received from the highest authority at Lassa, is as follows:—"Living beings are divided into six classes—angels, demons, men, quadrupeds, birds, and reptiles. These six classes of beings correspond to the syllables of the formula, 'Om mani padmè houm.' Living beings by continual transformations, and according to their merit or demerit, pass about in these six classes until they have attained the apex of perfection, when they are absorbed and lost in the grand essence of Buddha. Living beings have, according to the class to which they belong, particular means of sanctifying themselves, of rising to a superior class, of obtaining perfection, and of arriving in process of time at the period of their absorption. Men who repeat very frequently and devotedly 'Om mani padmè houm,' escape falling after death into the six classes of animate creatures, corresponding to the six syllables of the formula, and obtain the plenitude of being, by their absorption into the eternal and universal soul of Buddha."

One traveller only I have been able to find who mentions the sentence as I have done. M. Jacquemont writes, in his "Letters from Cashmere and Thibet," in 1830:—"I am returned from afar; I have often been very cold; I have had a hundred and eighteen very bad dinners: but I think myself amply recompensed for these trans-Himalayan miseries by the interesting observations and vast collections which I have been able to make in a country perfectly new. The Tartars are a very good sort of people. It is true that to please them I made myself a little heathen after their fashion, and joined without scruple in the national chorus, '**Houm mâni pani houm.**' "

Judging by the system of spelling he has adopted in other instances in his letters, this would be nearly—as regards the two main words—the same pronunciation as I have given. He however, in another part, follows it still more closely, and at the same time shows that he is aware of a translation which, although probably the true one, has no connexion whatever with the words as he himself actually represents them.

He says—" In Thibet they sing a good deal also—that is, one or two inhabitants per square league—but only a single song of three words—'**Oum mani pani**;' which means, in the learned language, 'Oh, diamond water-lily!' and leads the singers direct into Buddha's paradise.

" But, though composed of three Thibetian words, it is evidently of Indian origin, and I have proved it *botanically*. The lotus is a plant peculiar to the lukewarm and temperate waters of India and Egypt. There is not one of its genus, or even of its family, in Thibet."

The words, however, are not, as M. Jacquemont says, Thibetian, but Sanscrit; and, although one of the characters in which they are clothed is the current Thibetian, it would appear that neither their true pronunciation nor actual meaning is known to the people who thus make such frequent use of them.

The sentence itself is in the mouths of all. In the monastery of Hemis alone, probably as many as a hundred wheels are in continual motion, bearing it within their folds not less than 1,700,000 times. The very stones by the wayside present its well-known characters in countless numbers, and the hills repeat it, and yet to those into whose daily religious observances it thus so largely enters, it comes but as a vain and empty sound, without either sense or signification. The Lamas themselves, no doubt, believe that the doctrine contained in these marvellous words is immense, and the higher dignitaries of the Church may know their derivation; but, to the great majority, even the mystic meaning and dim legendary history which the true pronunciation and rightful origin of the words would bring to their minds, are unknown, and they are thus deprived of that large amount of comfort and consolation which they would otherwise derive from the glowing and all-powerful sentence —

"Oh, the jewel in the lotus, Amen!"

APPENDIX C.

A SKETCH OF THE HISTORY OF CASHMERE.

A Mahomedan writer, "Noor ul deen," who begins the history of Cashmere with the Creation, affirms that the valley was visited by Adam after the Fall; that the descendants of Seth reigned over the country for 1,110 years; and that, after the deluge, it became peopled by a tribe from Turkistan.

The Hindoo historians add, that, after the line of Seth became extinct, the Hindoos conquered the country, and ruled it until the period of the deluge; and that the Cashmerians were afterwards taught the worship of one God by "Moses;" but, relapsing into Hindoo idolatry, were punished by the local inundation of the province, and the conversion of the valley into a vast lake.

It would appear, from chronicles actually existing, that Cashmere has been a regular kingdom for a period far beyond the limits of history in general. From the year B.C. 2666 to A.D. 1024 it seems to have been governed (according to those authorities) by princes of Hindoo and Tartar dynasties, and their names, to the number of about a hundred, have been duly handed down to posterity.

Of the titles of these worthies, "Durlabhaverddhana" and "Bikrumajeet" will perhaps be sufficient as specimens. During these years, the religion seems at first to have been the worship of snakes, and afterwards Hindooism.

In the reign of Asoca, about the 4th century before Christ, Buddhism was introduced, and after remaining for some time, under Tartar princes, the religion of the country, was again succeeded by Hindooism.

The first Mahomedan king of Cashmere is believed to be "Shahmar," who came to the throne in A.D. 1341, and during the succeeding reigns Thibet appears to have been first subdued, and was annexed for a time to the kingdom.

The next monarch, who appears notably on the stage, was "Sikunder," who, influenced by a certain Syud Alee Humudanee and other religious fanatics recently arrived in the country, began to destroy the Hindoo temples and images by fire, and to force the people to abjure idolatry. Previous to this influx of zealots, the country was in a transition state as regards religion, and Mahomedanism then began to make some head in the valley.

After this period nothing of very great importance occurred in the kingdom of Cashmere until the year 1584, when the great Akbar summoned the then king "Yûsûf Shah" to present himself in person at the court of Lahore. Finding his orders not complied with, he despatched an army of 50,000 men to enforce obedience, and Yûsûf Shah, preferring apparently to die than fight, delivered himself up, and was sent to Lahore.

The imperial army was afterwards, however, repulsed in attempting to subdue the country, and it was not finally conquered for two years, when Akbar, overcoming all resistance, took possession of the province.

The purity of the emperor's motives in annexing the territory, and his opinion of his conquest, are amusingly shown in the following letter to his minister Abdûllah Khan:—

"On the mirror of your mind, which bears the stamp of Divine illumination, be it manifest and evident, that at the time when my imperial army happened to be in the territories of the Punjab, although I at first had no other views than to amuse myself with sports and hunting in this country, yet the conquest of the enchanting kingdom of Cashmere, which has never yet been subdued by monarchs of the age, which for natural strength and inaccessibility is unrivalled, and which, for beauty and pleasantness, is a proverb among the most sagacious beholders, became secretly an object of my wishes, *because* I received constantly accounts of the tyranny of the rulers of that region. Accordingly, in a very short time, my brave warriors annexed that kingdom to my dominions. Though the princes of that country were not remiss in their exertions, yet, as my intentions were established on the basis of equity, it was completely conquered.

"I myself also visited that happy spot, the possession of which is a fresh instance of the Divine favour, and offered up my praise and thanksgiving to the supreme Lord of all things. As I found myself delighted with the romantic bowers of Cashmere, the residence of pleasure, I made an excursion to the mountains of that country and Thibet, and beheld, with the eyes of astonishment, the wonders of the picture of Nature."

This visit was in A.D. 1588.

The emperor then appears to have entered the valley by the Peer Punjal Pass, and to have been received with every demonstration of joy by the people in whom he took such a fatherly interest. The loyalty of his children, however, was but short-lived, for about the year 1591 he again writes to Abdûllah :—

"I must acquaint your Highness, that just at this time certain persons, under the predominance of an unlucky destiny, raised an insurrection in Cashmere and breathed the air of rebellion and dissatisfaction at the bounty of Providence.

"As soon as the intelligence of this tumult arrived, regardless of deluges of rain, I hastened away by forced marches, but before the troops could get through the passes and enter into that kingdom, certain Omrahs, attached to my interests, who had been obliged by compulsion to join in that rash enterprise, availing themselves of an opportunity, brought me the head of the rebel commander.

"As my forces were near, I visited a second time that ever-verdant garden, and gratified my mind and senses with the beauties of that luxuriant spot."

With a view to keeping the capital in order, the Fort of Huree Purbut was built, about A.D. 1597, at a cost of over 1,000,000*l.*

Means were at the same time adopted of rendering the Cashmerians less warlike, and of breaking their independent spirit. To effect this, it is generally believed in Cashmere that the Emperor Akbar caused a change to be made in the dress of the people. Instead of the ancient, well-girdled tunic, adapted to activity and exercise, he introduced the effeminate long gown of the present day, a change which may have led to the introduction of the kangree, or pot of charcoal, now used in the valley.

During Akbar's reign much was done towards the

improvement of the province. The country was adorned with palaces and gardens, and various trees and shrubs were introduced and cultivated.

About the beginning of the seventeenth century, Akbar visited Cashmere for the third and last time, being succeeded, after a reign of fifty-two years, by his son Selim, or Jehangeer, A.D. 1605.

Jehangeer, during the early part of his reign, visited Cashmere many times, and the valley having been surveyed and brought to order by Akbar, nothing remained for his successor but to enjoy the delights of the country in company with his empress, the famous Noor Jehan. In 1621, and in 1624, he repeated his visit, when he built many summerhouses and palaces at Atchabull, Shalimar, &c., and in A.D. 1627 he visited the valley for the last time. He was succeeded in that year by Shah Jehan, who, in 1634, also visited his territories; and, besides improving the country by the introduction of fruit-trees, flowers, &c. from Cabul, he invaded Thibet, and taking the Fort of Ladak, annexed the country to Cashmere.

In 1645 he again visited the valley, and also in the following years, being accompanied by many poets and savants; among the former was a certain Hajee Mahomet Jan, a Persian, who composed a poem on the country; but the difficulties of the road appear to have impressed his mind rather more than the beauties of the scenery. He compares the sharpness of the passes to "the swords of the Feringees," and their tortuous ascents to "the curls of a blackamoor's hair!"

In 1657, Shah Jehan, being deposed by his son Aurungzib, was confined in the Fort of Agra for life; and in the year 1664 the new emperor also paid a visit to his Cashmerian dominions. Of this magnificent expedition,

M. Bernier, the monarch's state physician, gives an amusing and detailed description, purporting to be—

"A relation of a voyage made in the year 1664, when the Great Mogul, Aureng-Zebe, went with his army from Dehly to Lahor, from Lahor to Bember, and from thence to that small kingdom of Kachemere, or Cassimere, called by the Mogols the Paradise of the Indies, concerning which the author affirms that he hath a particular history of it, in the Persian tongue."

"The weighty occasion and cause of this voyage of the Emperor's, together with an account of the state and posture of his army, and some curious particulars observable in voyages of the Indies," are thus given by M. Bernier:—"Since that Aureng-Zebe began to find himself in better health, it hath been constantly reported that he would make a voyage to Kachemere, to be out of the way of the approaching summer heats, though the more intelligent sort of men would hardly be persuaded, that as long as he kept his father, Chah-Jean (Shah Jehan), prisoner in the Fort of Agra, he would think it safe to be at such a distance. Yet, notwithstanding, we have found that reason of State hath given place to that of health, or rather, to the intrigues of Rauchenara Begum, who was wild to breathe a more free air than that of the Seraglio, and to have her turn in showing herself to a gallant and magnificent army, as her sister had formerly done during the reign of Chah-Jean."

The Emperor appears to have made preparations on this occasion for a voyage of a year and a half.

He had with him, not only thirty-five thousand horse, or thereabouts, and ten thousand foot, but also "both his artilleries, the great or heavy, and the small or lighter."

For the carriage of the Emperor's baggage and stores,

no less than 30,000 coolies were required, although "for fear of starving that little kingdom of Kachemere," he only carried with him the least number of ladies and cavaliers he could manage, and as few elephants and mules as would suffice for the convenience of the former.

Crossing the Peer Punjal, some of the ladies of the Seraglio unfortunately paid the penalty of their too ardent desires to show themselves off to "a gallant and magnificent army," for "one of the elephants fell back upon him that was next, and he upon the next, and so on to the fifteenth, so that they did all tumble to the bottom of the precipice. It was the good fortune of those poor women, however, that there were but three or four of them killed; but the fifteen elephants remained upon the place." The historian rather ungallantly adds, "When these bulky masses do once fall under *those vast burdens* they never rise again, though the way be ever so fair."

On reaching the summit of the pass after this accident, the expedition appears to have encountered more misfortunes, for "there blew a wind so cold that all people shook and ran away, especially the silly Indians, who never had seen ice or snow, or felt such cold."

Aurungzib appears to have remained three months in the valley on this occasion.

After his death there is no mention of his successors having visited Cashmere, and the local governors became in consequence, in common with those of other provinces of the tottering Mogul throne, little short of independent rulers. Under the tender mercies of most of these, the unfortunate Cashmeeries appear to have fared but badly.

In 1745, however, a series of misfortunes from another source burst forth upon the inhabitants of the happy valley. A dreadful famine first broke out, during which it is said that slaves sold for four pice (three half-pence) each. The famine produced its natural result, a pestilence, which swept away many thousands of the people ; an eclipse also added to their terror, and storms of rain followed by floods carried away all the bridges.

In the year 1752, the country passed from the possession of the Mogul throne, and fell under the rule of the Dûranees, and during many years was convulsed by a series of wars and rebellions, and subject to numerous different governors. In A.D. 1801, Runjeet Singh began to come into notice, and, having consolidated the nation of the Sikhs, had, in the year 1813 become one of the recognised princes of India. In that year Futteh Shah entered into a treaty with him for a subsidiary force for the invasion of Cashmere. The price of this accommodation was fixed at 80,000*l.* yearly ; but, before the expiration of the second year, the Lion of the Punjab, on pretence of the non-fulfilment of the treaty, invaded the valley on his own account at the head of a considerable army. He was repulsed, however, and forced to retreat to Lahore with the loss of his entire baggage. In A.D. 1819, encouraged by recent successes against Moultan, Runjeet Singh collected an army "as numerous as ants and locusts," and invaded the valley a second time, and being successful, the country again fell under the sway of a Hindoo Sovereign.

It, however, remained for some time afterwards in a disturbed state ; and for signal services against the rebellious frontier chiefs, who were averse to Runjeet Singh's rule, Gûlab Singh (the late Maharajah) obtained possession of the territory of Jumoo, now included in the kingdom of Cashmere.

Runjeet Singh, dying in 1839, was succeeded by his son and grandson, successively, both of whom died shortly after their accession; and the state of anarchy and confusion which ensued among the Sikh Sirdars was terminated by Shere Singh being installed as Maharajah of Lahore.

Under his rule, in 1842, Gûlab Singh further brought himself into notice by reducing the kingdom of little Thibet with the army under Zorawur Singh, and on the termination of the Sikh Campaign of the Sutlej—Duleep Singh being established on the throne of Lahore—he was admitted, "in consideration of his good conduct," to the privileges of a separate treaty with the British Government.

The result of these privileges was, that he was shortly afterwards put in possession, for "a consideration," of the entire kingdom of Cashmere.

As indemnification for the expenses of the Sikh Campaign, the British Government had demanded from the Lahore State the sum of a crore and a half of rupees, or 1,500,000*l*. The whole of this amount, however, was not forthcoming, and it was agreed by Article 4 of the treaty of 9th March, 1846, with the Maharajah Duleep Singh, that all the hill-country between the rivers Indus and Beas, including the province of Cashmere, should be ceded to the Honourable East India Company, in perpetual sovereignty, as an equivalent for one million sterling.

Article 12 of the same treaty guaranteed to Gûlab Singh, in consequence of his services to the Lahore State, its recognition of his independence in such territories as might afterwards be agreed upon; and on the 16th March, 1846, the British Government, by special treaty, made over for ever, in independent possession to Maharajah Gûlab Singh and the heirs male of his body, the greater part of the territories previously mentioned in Article 4. In consideration of this transfer, the Maharajah was to pay to the British Government, within the year, the sum of seventy-five lakhs of rupees (750,000*l.*). To acknowledge the supremacy of that Government, and, in token of such supremacy, to present it annually the following tribute, viz.:—One horse, twelve perfect shawl goats of approved breed (six male and six female), and three pairs of Cashmere shawls.

Thus, "on the 16th day of March, in the year of our Lord 1846, corresponding with the 17th day of Rubbee-oolawul, 1262, Hijree, was *done* at Umritsur," the treaty of ten articles, by which Gûlab Singh was raised to the rank and dignity of an independent ruler.

For seventy-five lakhs of rupees the unfortunate Cashmeeries were handed over to the tender mercies of "the most thorough ruffian that ever was created—a villain from a kingdom down to a half-penny," and the "Paradise of the Indies," after remaining rather less than a week a British possession, was relinquished by England for ever.

THE END.

NEW BURLINGTON STREET: *July*, 1863.

MR. BENTLEY'S
RECENT PUBLICATIONS.

AT ODDS. A Novel. By the Authoress of "The Initials," "Quits." 2 vols. post 8vo. 21*s*.

ALEXANDER'S (COL. SIR JAMES) Incidents of the last Maori War. Post 8vo. with Two Illustrations, 10*s*. 6*d*.

AUSTEN'S (MISS) Novels. A Library Edition. 5 vols. Vol. I. Sense and Sensibility.—Vol. II. Emma.—Vol. III. Mansfield Park.—Vol. IV. Northanger Abbey and Persuasion.—Vol. V. Pride and Prejudice. Ten Illustrations, 16*s*.

ANDERSEN'S (HANS) Stories from the Sandhills of Jutland. Translated by Mrs. Bushby. Crown 8vo. 5*s*.

AUCKLAND'S (LORD) Diary and Correspondence. 4 vols. 8vo. With a Preface and Introduction by the Lord Bishop of Bath and Wells. With Two Portraits, 60*s*.

ANECDOTES of Animals. With Eight spirited Illustrations by Wolf. 5*s*. gilt edges.

BEDE'S (CUTHBERT) Tour in Tartan-Land. Post 8vo. 10*s*. 6*d*.

BROWNE'S (PROFESSOR) History of Roman Classical Literature. By R. W. Browne, M.A. Ph.D. Prebendary of St. Paul's and Professor of Classical Literature in King's College, London. 8vo. 12*s*.

BALDWIN'S (WM. CHARLES) African Hunting from Natal to the Zambesi, from 1852 to 1861. With Forty-eight Illustrations by Wolf and Zwecker, Map and Portrait. 8vo. 21*s*.

BENTLEY'S Popular Novels. Sell 2*s*. 6*d*. each; claret cloth, 3*s*. each.

1. RITA: an Autobiography.
3. The SEMI-DETACHED HOUSE.
4. The LADIES of BEVER HOLLOW.
5. VILLAGE BELLES.
6. EASTON. By The Hon. Lena Eden.
8. The SEASON TICKET.
9. The SEMI-ATTACHED COUPLE.
10. NELLY ARMSTRONG.

BENTLEY'S Popular Novels. Sell 3*s*. 6*d*. each; claret cloth, 4*s*. each.

2. ANTHONY TROLLOPE'S THREE CLERKS.
7. QUITS. By Author of "Initials."

BENTLEY'S Quarterly Review. 2 vols. 8vo. or 4 Parts, 6*s*.

BENTLEY, Tales from. 4 vols. 1*s.* 6*d.* each, sold separately; or in 2 vols. 6*s.*

BENTLEY BALLADS, from Bentley's Miscellany. Entirely new Edition, containing the gems of Prout, Maginn, Lover, Longfellow, Albert Smith, &c. &c. Crown 8vo. 5*s.*

BOSWELL, Letters of James, to the Rev. Wm. Temple. 8vo. 10*s.* 6*d.*

BRIGANTINE, The: a Sea Story. By James Pascoe. 2 vols. post 8vo. 21*s.*

BUCKLAND'S (FRANCIS) Curiosities of Natural History. 1st Series. Rats, Snakes, Serpents, Fishes, Frogs, Monkeys, &c. 6*s.*

——— 2nd Series. Fossils, Bears, Wolves, Cats, Eagles, Hedgehogs, the Rig, Eels, Herrings, Whales, Pigs, &c. 6*s.*

BURGOYNE. Military Opinions of General the Hon. Sir John Burgoyne, K.C.B. 8vo. 9*s.*

COLLINS'S (W. WILKIE) Rambles beyond Railways; or, Notes taken afoot in Cornwall; to which is added, a Visit to the Scilly Islands. Crown 8vo. 6*s.*

CAREY'S (LIEUT.-COL.) The War in New Zealand of 1860—1861. Post 8vo. 6*s.*

CUMMING'S (REV. DR.) The Millennial Rest; or, the World as it Will be. Crown 8vo. 7*s.* 6*d.* Third Thousand.

——— The Great Tribulation Coming on the Earth. Crown 8vo. 7*s.* 6*d.* Thirteenth Thousand.

——— Redemption Draweth Nigh; or, the Great Preparation. Sixth Thousand. Crown 8vo. 7*s.* 6*d.*

——— Readings on the Prophet Isaiah. Fcp. 8vo. 7*s.* 6*d.*

——— Answers to the Essays and Reviews. Fcp. 8vo. 4*s.*

CHANNINGS, The. By the Author of "East Lynne." 3 vols. 7*s.* 6*d.*

——— Popular Edition, with Two Illustrations. Crown 8vo. 6*s.*

CREASY (SIR EDWARD) The Fifteen Decisive Battles of the World—from Marathon to Waterloo. 8vo. Thirteenth Edition, 10*s.* 6*d.*

——— History of the Rise and Progress of the English Constitution. Sixth Edition, post 8vo. 7*s.* 6*d.*

——— History of the Ottoman Empire. 8vo. 10*s.* 6*d.*

CHATTERTON'S (LADY) Selections from the Writings of Plato. Fcp. 8vo. 4*s.*

CLIFFORD'S (EDMUND) Life of the Greatest of the Plantagenets; an Historical Sketch. 8vo. 12*s.*

CHAMIER'S (CAPT.) The Saucy Arethusa: a Naval Story. 2*s.*

DAVIS'S (DR.) Carthage and her Remains; being an Account of the Excavations and Researches on the Site of the Phœnician Metropolis in Africa. Conducted under the auspices of Her Majesty's Government, by Dr. N. Davis, F.R.G.S. &c. 8vo. Thirty Plates, 10*s.* 6*d.*

DELANY'S (MRS. MARY GRANVILLE) The Autobiography and Correspondence of Mary Granville (Mrs. Delany), with Interesting Reminiscences of King George the Third and Queen Charlotte. Edited by the Right Hon. Lady Llanover. 1st Series, 3 vols. Thirteen Portraits, 2*l.* 10*s.*

——— 2nd Series. 3 vols. Nine Portraits, and copious Index to whole work. 2*l.* 10*s.*

DEVEY (JOSEPH) Life of Joseph Locke, the Engineer. By Joseph Devey. 8vo. 14*s.* with a Portrait of Joseph Locke.

DUNLOP'S Adventures of the Meerut Volunteer Horse in the Indian Mutinies. 1 vol. with coloured plates, 3*s.*

DUNDONALD'S (EARL) Autobiography of a Seaman. Library Edition. 2 vols. 8vo. Portrait, 21*s.*

——— Popular Edition. Portrait, 5*s.*

DOBELL'S (SYDNEY) The Roman: a Dramatic Poem. Post 8vo. 5*s.*

DORAN'S (DR.) Lives of the Princes of Wales. 8vo. Portrait, 10*s.* 6*d.*

——— Queens of England of the House of Hanover. 2 vols. post 8vo. 16*s.*

DOUGLAS (REV. HERMAN) Jerusalem the Golden and the Way to it. With a Preface by the Author of "Mary Powell." Post 8vo. 6*s.*

EAST LYNNE: a Novel. By Mrs. Henry Wood. Crown 8vo. 6*s.* Two Illustrations.

EDWARDS' Andromache of Euripides; with Suggestions and Questions at the foot of each page; together with Copious Grammatical and Critical Notes; also with a Brief Introductory Account of the Greek Drama, Dialects, and Principal Tragic Metres. By the Rev. J. Edwards, M.A., and Rev. C. Hawkins, B.C.L. Used at Eton. A Greek Play prepared for Schools. 4*s.* 6*d.*

EVERYBODY'S Pudding Book; or, Tarts, Puddings, &c. in the Proper Season for all the Year Round. Fcp. 8vo. Third Edition, 2*s.* 6*d.*

EDEN'S (HON. MISS) Autobiography of a Navvy. 1*s.*

ELLIS'S (MRS.) The Mothers of Great Men. Handsomely bound for a Present Book. Crown 8vo. 5*s.*

——— Chapters on Wives. Crown 8vo. 5*s.*

ELLET'S (MRS.) Women Artists of all Ages and Countries. Post 8vo. Handsomely bound, 5*s.*

ELLIOTT'S (MRS. DALRYMPLE) Narrative of her Life during the Great French Revolution. With Three beautiful Portraits, 8vo. 5*s.*

FISHER (LIEUT.-COL.) Personal Narrative of Three Years' Service in China. By Lieut.-Col. Fisher. 8vo. with many Illustrations, 16*s.*

FRANCATELLI'S Modern Cook. 60 Illustrations and 1,600 Receipts. A Practical Guide to the Culinary Art in all its Branches. 8vo. 12*s.*

——— Cook's Guide and Butler's Assistant. 1,000 Recipes and 40 Illustrations. Crown 8vo. Thirteenth Thousand, 5*s.*

FRISWELL'S (HAIN) A Daughter of Eve: a Novel. 2 vols. post 8vo. 21*s.*

FORSTER'S (REV. CHARLES) Sinai Photographed; or, Inscriptions in the Rocks of the Wilderness by the Israelites who came out of Egypt, with Photographs, Glyphographs, and Lithographs. Folio, 4*l.* 4*s.*

——— Life of Dr. John Jebb, Bishop of Limerick. Post 8vo. 6*s.*

——— Sermons on the Life of St. Paul. 8vo. 10*s.* 6*d.*

GUIZOT'S (M.) Embassy to the Court of St. James in 1840; with Sketches of Lords Palmerston, Melbourne, Russell, Durham, Holland, Grey, the Duke of Wellington, Sir Robert Peel, &c. &c. Crown 8vo. 6*s.*

——— Personal Memoirs. Vols. I. II. III. IV. 8vo. 14*s.* each. Sold separately.

——— Church and Society in 1861. 2*s.* 6*d.*

——— Life of Oliver Cromwell. Crown 8vo. 6*s.* with a fine Portrait of Cromwell.

GUYOT'S (PROFESSOR) Lectures on Comparative Physical Geography in its Relation to the History of Mankind. Bentley's Edition, the only unabridged Edition. Post 8vo. 2*s.* 6*d.*

GRAHAM'S (COL.) History of the Art of War. Being a History of War from the Earliest Times. Post 8vo. 5*s.*

GREY'S (GEN.) Life and Opinions of Charles, second Earl Grey. 8vo. 7*s.* 6*d.*

GREY (EARL) An Essay on Parliamentary Reform. By Earl Grey. 8vo. 3*s.* 6*d.*

GLADSTONE'S (THE RIGHT HON. W. E.) Address to the University of Edinburgh. 8vo. 1*s.*

GUBBIN'S (MARTIN) History of the Mutinies in Oudh; with numerous Illustrations, Map, &c. 8vo. 10*s.* 6*d.*

HALLIBURTON'S (MRS.) Troubles. By the Author of "East Lynne" and "The Channings." 3 vols. 7*s.* 6*d.*

——— Popular Edition, in crown 8vo. with Two Illustrations, 6*s.*

HALL, Life of Dr. Marshall. By his Widow. 8vo. Portrait, 14*s.*

HOOK'S (DEAN) Lives of the Archbishops of Canterbury, from St. Augustine to Dr. Howley. Vol. I. 8vo. 15*s.*

——— Vol. II. 8vo. 18*s.*

HODGSON'S (CONSUL) Japan, and Residence at Nagasaki, in 1859–60. Post 8vo. Illustrations, 10*s.* 6*d.*

HAYES'S Arctic Boat Voyage in the Autumn of 1854. By Isaac T. Hayes. Edited, with an Introduction and Notes, by Dr. Norton Shaw. Crown 8vo. handsomely bound, 5*s.*

HILLIER'S King Charles the First in the Isle of Wight; with Original Letters from the King. Square post, 4*s.* 6*d.*

HERFORD'S (CAPT.) Stirring Times under Canvas. Post 8vo. Illustration, 10*s.* 6*d.*

HERVEY'S Hints to Christians on the Use of the Tongue. Post 8vo. 5*s.*

IRVING'S (PIERRE) Life of Washington Irving. Vols. I. and II. 7*s.* 6*d.* each; Vol. III. 10*s.* 6*d.* with fine Portrait of Irving.

INGOLDSBY (THE) Legends; or, Mirth and Marvels. Crown 8vo. 5*s.*

——— Bound in calf or morocco, 12*s.*

——— Another edition, in double post, on tinted paper, 7*s.* 6*d.* with the Illustration to the Dead Drummer.

——— Another edition, in 2 vols. 8vo. with the Illustrations of Cruikshank and John Leech. 21*s.*

JESSE'S (HENEAGE) Life of Richard III. and Memoirs of some of his Contemporaries. With an Historical Drama of the Battle of Bosworth. 8vo. 15*s.*

JESSOP (WM. R. H.) Flindersland and Sturtland; or, the Inside and Outside of Australia. 2 vols. post 8vo. 21*s.*

JAMESON'S (MRS.) Essays on Art and Literature. Crown, 2*s.* 6*d.*

——— Handsomely bound, 4*s.*

JAMES'S Naval History of Great Britain. 6 vols. 6*s.* each volume. With a Portrait to each volume.

JENKINS' (REV. C.) Life of Cardinal Julian, the Last Crusader; an Historical Sketch. 8vo. 6*s.*

KAVANAGH'S (JULIA) Madeline: a Tale of Auvergne. Fcp. 8vo. gilt edges, 4*s.*

KILVERT'S (REV. FRANCIS) Memoirs of the Life and Writings of the Right Rev. Richard Hurd, D.D. Lord Bishop of Worcester; with a Selection from his Correspondence and other Unpublished Papers. 8vo. 9*s.*

KNIGHT (CAPTAIN) Diary of a Pedestrian in Cashmere and Thibet. 8vo. With many fine Woodcuts and Lithographs.

LADY'S Dessert Book (The). By the Author of "Everybody's Pudding Book." Fcp. 8vo. 2*s.* 6*d.*

LAKE'S (GEN. ATWELL) Defence of Kars: a Military Work. With numerous fine Plans and Plates. 8vo. 9*s.*

LAMARTINE'S Remarkable Characters: Nelson, Bossuet, Milton, Oliver Cromwell, &c. &c. 1 vol. post 8vo. 5*s.*

LEE'S (DR.) Last Days of Alexander of Russia, and First Days of Nicholas. Small 8vo. 3*s.* 6*d.*

MOMMSEN'S History of Rome. Translated, with the Author's sanction and Additions, by the Rev. William P. Dickson; with a Preface by Dr. Leonard Schmitz. Vols. I. and II. Crown 8vo. 18*s.*

MARSDEN'S Dictionary of Christian Churches from the Earliest Ages of Christianity. 8vo. 900 pages, 12*s.*

MALET'S (REV. WYNDHAM) An Errand to the South in 1862. Fcp. 8vo. 6*s.* Illustration.

MARKHAM'S (GENERAL) Shooting in the Himalayas: a Journal of Sporting Adventures and Travel in Chinese Tartary, India, Thibet, Cashmere, &c. With Illustrations. 8vo. Lithographs, 21*s.*

MAGINN'S (DR.) Essays on some of Shakespeare's Characters: Sir John Falstaff, Jacques, Romeo, Bottom the Weaver, Lady Macbeth, Timon of Athens, Polonius, Iago, Hamlet. Crown 8vo. 5*s.*

MAXWELL'S (W. H.) Erin-go-Bragh: Stories of Irish Life. 2*s.*

MIGNET'S Life of Mary Queen of Scots. Two Portraits. Crown 8vo. 6*s.*

MITFORD'S (MARY RUSSELL) Selections from her Choice Poets and Prose Writers, and Memoirs of her Literary Life. Crown 8vo. Portrait, 6*s.*

MONTALEMBERT (COUNT) on the Polish Insurrection. 8vo. 1*s.* 6*d.*

——— Life of Lacordaire. 8vo. 10*s.* 6*d.*

MY GOOD-FOR-NOTHING BROTHER: a Novel. Post 8vo. 10*s.* 6*d.*

NOTES ON NOSES. By Eden Warwick. Fcp. 8vo. 2*s.* 6*d.*

OPPOSITE NEIGHBOURS: a Novel. 2 vols. post 8vo. 21*s.*

POPE'S Notes of a Residence in Algeria. Post 8vo. 7*s.* 6*d.*

PICHOT'S (AMEDÉE) Life and Labours of Sir Charles Bell, the celebrated Surgeon. Post 8vo. 5*s.*

POLEHAMPTON (HENRY), Life of (The Chaplain of Lucknow). Small 8vo. 5*s.*

——— (ARTHUR), Kangaroo-Land; or, Life in the Bush. Post 8vo. Vignettes, 7*s.* 6*d.*

RUSSELL'S (EARL) Life of Charles James Fox. Vols. I. and II. crown 8vo. 21*s*.

RAIKE'S (THOMAS) Private Correspondence with the Duke of Wellington and many Distinguished Politicians. 8vo. 8*s*.

ROSE'S (RIGHT HON. GEORGE) Diaries and Correspondence. 2 vols. 8vo. 10*s*. 6*d*.

RAISING THE VEIL. By John Pomeroy. 2 vols. post 8vo. 21*s*.

SIRENIA: Recollections of a Past Existence. Second Edition, post 8vo. 10*s*. 6*d*.

SPENCE'S (JAMES) The American Union; its Effect on National Character and Policy; with an Inquiry into Secession as a Constitutional Right and the Causes of Disruption. By James Spence. Fourth Edition, revised, 8vo. 10*s*. 6*d*.

——— On the Recognition of the Southern Confederation. By James Spence, Author of "The American Union." 8vo. 1*s*.

STEBBING'S (DR.) Lives of the Principal Italian Poets. Crown 8vo. 7*s*. 6*d*.

SALAD FOR THE SOCIAL. Contents: Bookcraft—Money—The Toilette—Pulpit Peculiarities—Mysteries of Medicine—The Humours of Law—Larcenies of Literature, &c. &c. Fcp. 8vo. antique binding, 5*s*.

SYLVANUS' Bye-Lanes and Downs of England; with Turf Scenes and Characters. With a Portrait of Lord George Bentinck. Fcp. 8vo. 2*s*. 6*d*.

SAY AND SEAL. By the Author of "Wide Wide World." 2*s*. 6*d*.; rose cloth, 3*s*. 6*d*.

SMITH'S (J. S.) Book for a Rainy Day; or, Recollections of the Events of the Years 1766—1833. Fcp. 8vo. 3*s*.

——— Rambles through the Streets of London; with Anecdotes of their more Celebrated Residents. Crown, 5*s*.

STORY OF ITALY (THE). By Author of "Mary Powell." Crown, 3*s*. 6*d*.

SULLIVAN (JOHN L. O.), Union, Disunion, and Reunion; a Letter to General Franklin Pierce, ex-President of the United States. By J. L. O'SULLIVAN, late Minister of the United States to Portugal. 8vo. 2*s*. 6*d*.

STAUNTON'S School and Family Geography. Crown, 3*s*. 6*d*.

SCOTT'S (LADY) Types and Antitypes of the Old and New Testament. Post 8vo. 5*s*.

THOMPSON'S (CAPTAIN MOWBRAY) Story of Cawnpore. Post 8vo. 7*s*. 6*d*.

TOWN AND FOREST: a Story of Hainault Forest. By the Author of "Mary Powell." 5*s*.

THROUGH ALGERIA. By the Author of "Life in Tuscany." Post 8vo. Illustrations, 10*s*. 6*d*.

TIMBS' (JOHN) Anecdote-Lives of Wits and Humourists. 2 vols. post 8vo. 12*s*.

——— Painters. Post 8vo. 6*s*.

——— Statesmen. Post 8vo. 6*s*.

TRUTH ANSWERS BEST; or, Jean and Nicolette. Fcp. 8vo. 1*s*. 6*d*.

TAYLER'S (REV. C. B.) Not of the World; or Lady Mary. Fcap. bound as a present, 4*s*.

TWO MONTHS IN THE CONFEDERATE STATES, including a Visit to New Orleans. By an English Merchant. Post 8vo. 8*s*. 6*d*.

TUGWELL (REV. G.) On the Mountain; being the Welsh Experiences of Abraham Black and Jonas White, Esqrs. Moralists, Photographers, Fishermen, and Botanists, &c. Crown, 7*s*. 6*d*.

VONVED THE DANE, the Rover of the Baltic. 2 vols. post 8vo. 6*s*.

WEBB'S (MRS.) Martyrs of Carthage: a Tale of the Times of Old. Bound as a present. 5*s*.

WHALLEY (REV. DR.): Life, Journals, and Correspondence of the Rev. Dr. Thomas Sedgwick Whalley. Including an interesting Correspondence with Mrs. Siddons, Mrs. Thrale-Piozzi, Mrs. Hannah More, Miss Seward, &c. &c. Edited by the Rev. Hill D. Wickham, Rector of Horsington, Somersetshire. 2 vols. 8vo. with Four fine Portraits, 30*s*.

WHATELY (ARCHBISHOP), Selections from the Writings of. Fcp. 8vo. 5*s*.

WILLS (WILLIAM JOHN): A Successful Exploration through the Interior of Australia, from Melbourne to the Gulf of Carpentaria. From the Journals and Letters of William John Wills. Edited by his Father, William Wills. 8vo. 15*s*.

WOOD'S (MRS. HENRY) Popular Stories. Handsome editions in crown 8vo. each with Two Illustrations.

I. East Lynne. 6*s*.
II. The Channings. 6*s*.
III. Mrs. Halliburton's Troubles. 6*s*.

WRAXALL'S (SIR F. LASCELLES) Remarkable Adventures and Unexplained Mysteries. 2 vols. post 8vo. 21*s*. Illustrated by Hablot K. Browne.

YONGE'S English-Latin Dictionary. Post 8vo. 9*s*. 6*d*.

——— Latin-English Dictionary. Post 8vo. 7*s*. 6*d*. Or the two together, strongly bound in roan, 15*s*.

——— New Virgil, with the Notes of Hawtrey, Key, and Munro. Post 8vo. 7*s*. 6*d*.

R. CLAY SON, AND TAYLOR, PRINTERS, BREAD STREET HILL.